Sweeping Out The Demons

Spiritual Warfare for the 21st Century

(What if Matthew 12:43–45 could change your life forever?)

Rob Hefner

Author of Evangelism and Church Planting and
A Manual for the Church in My House

WESTBOW
PRESS°
A DIVISION OF THOMAS NELSON
& ZONDERVAN

WestBow Press books may be ordered through booksellers or by contacting:

WestBow Press
A Division of Thomas Nelson & Zondervan
1663 Liberty Drive
Bloomington, IN 47403
www.westbowpress.com
1 (866) 928-1240

ISBN: 978-1-5127-4449-1 (sc)
ISBN: 978-1-5127-4451-4 (hc)
ISBN: 978-1-5127-4450-7 (e)

Library of Congress Control Number: 2016908891

Print information available on the last page.

WestBow Press rev. date: 05/27/2016

Contents

Dedicated to Phyllis, my partner in prayer, in life and in love. Thank you for sharing Christ with me so many years ago. Thank you for walking alongside me in Brazil. Thank you for encouraging me to continue fighting the good fight. Thank you for being my example of salt, light and true spiritual warfare.

Acknowledgments

God has guided me to so many awesome resources for knowledge and orientation during this writing journey. Some gave me seeds for a thought or essential concept. Others served to form large sections of the book. So please join me as I express my thanks to the persons that helped to make this book so much more powerful and effective for guiding you into this amazing journey of true spiritual warfare. I owe a debt of gratitude to my students in the Seminário Teológico Batista do Ceará (Brazil) and the many churches where I taught this book in its Portuguese version, *Varrendo O Mal: A Batalha Espiritual Pelo Século 21*. Their invaluable suggestions and contributions were the result of many candid interviews with persons from all walks of life. Their struggles and spiritual battles helped to deepen the content and effectiveness of this work.

In that vein, we all should be very thankful for my translator of the Portuguese version, Luciane (Lu) Krauser. Her tireless efforts, not only in translation but also her many redaction and editorial suggestions deserve our deepest thanks. During that same time frame, my wife Phyllis did numerous readings and corrections of the manuscript, as well as offering many valuable insights. Most likely, this book would not even be in front of you right now if not for her hours of tremendous encouragement as my prayer and accountability partner for over forty years.

Four men that deserve our deepest gratitude are Dr. Robert Lamb, Rev. Lynn Bullock, Mr. Jim Ellison and Rev. Eddie

Grigg. These wonderful friends and true servants of our Lord were such a great help in developing the text and adjusting the tone of the themes, as well as suggesting further corrections and improvements. Rev. Eddie Grigg was instrumental in tracking down a long lost resource for the basis of the concluding illustration in Day 9. It is loosely based upon *"Life Above the Snake Line"*, a sermon seed originally preached by Dr. Charles Koller and included in his book *Expository Preaching Without Notes*.

Many thanks go to Mount Pleasant Baptist Church, Mooresboro, NC for allowing me to teach *Sweeping Out the Demons* in the church format. They offered many great suggestions and exhortations to share with other groups. Finally, to you the reader, thank you in advance for considering this material seriously and prayerfully in your spiritual warfare.

Introduction:
Welcome, Fellow Soldier!

How much do you know about spiritual warfare? Spiritual warfare is one of those religious or "churchy" expressions about which many believers and non-believers like to discuss, debate and speculate with vague recollections about the who, what where and why of battling evil.

However, after many hours of interviews and informal discussions with folks on two continents, I came to the alarming conclusion that few of us really even know what genuine spiritual warfare really implies, let alone how to be a genuine soldier of the cross. Finding yourself on a battlefield doesn't mean you are a soldier...it only means that you are in need of some survival skills really soon! Otherwise, you will be attacked by the enemy regardless of whether you acknowledge him as real. Subsequently, you just may find yourself on an unexpected battlefield as I found myself some years ago, virtually defenseless and unprepared. I did not fully comprehend how spiritual warfare unwraps itself from the package of everyday life. I never realized how integral spiritual warfare is to preaching, teaching, evangelism, discipleship, stewardship and above all, victorious living through the power of God. I was underprepared for submitting to God in spiritual warfare, as my guide director, guard and protector from Satan's daily attempts to provoke great frustrations and interruptions to day-to-day living.

How are you handling the battlefield so far this week, this month or even the past year or so? If you have to think back and feel a little distressed over what you can recall, then this book just may help you to feel a bit more at ease and confident in the days to come.

Everyone has a life message that has served as a compass for everyday survival. This is mine. After nearly 30 years in Brazil on the mission field, I have tried to share this life message. My objective is to show you how it has served to help me to become a person obsessed with spiritual warfare. This book has been written so that you can do battle with Satan at the most basic levels of confrontation and assault. A key to understanding this process of becoming a true soldier of the cross is a rather obscure passage in Matthew that served to change the way I would fight the good fight.

Read Matthew 12:43–45 a time or two before you begin reading the book so that you can better understand what I mean by Sweeping out the demons. If you have any other translations or paraphrases available, take a little time to read the verses in order to deepen your understanding.

The Key Text for Sweeping Out The Demons:

But the unclean spirit, when he is gone out of the man, passeth through waterless places, seeking rest, and findeth it not. Then he saith, I will return into my house whence I came out; and when he is come, he findeth it empty, swept, and garnished, then goeth he, and taketh with himself seven other spirits more evil than himself, and they enter in and dwell there: and the last state of that man becometh worse than the first. Even so shall it be also unto this evil generation. (Matthew 12:43–45 KJV)

I'm sure that by now you are more than a little curious about the specific usage of the word "demons" as used in this study. For our purpose during our time together, what we will refer as demons are those persons, places or moments in life that Satan seeks to use against you to tempt, test, thwart, frustrate, or confuse. We can view our usage of the term as the devil's subtle suggestions or inferences for less than appropriate ways to respond to day-to-day crises.

In the passage Jesus was referring to demons as the actual fallen angels that followed Lucifer when cast out of Heaven (Isa. 14:12 and Luke 10:18). We will discuss this further as we journey together in the book, but for now, suffice it to say that when we talk about "sweeping out the demons" in this work, we are talking about the activity of evil by Satan and his downcast army to keep you from following God and experiencing what the Lord desires for you. Throughout the book, I hope you will get a handle on how Satan maneuvers and manipulates to accomplish this. Please begin to grasp that evil strategy from the get-go. By messing with your ways of thinking or your reasoning, he subtly and astutely tries to draw you away from trusting God and recognizing God's solution for everyday decisions with what Satan has attempted to distort as truth. His goal is zero influence from God in your day. His methods are as diverse as the world in which God has temporarily loosed him to roam, "as a roaring lion, walketh about, seeking whom he may devour". (1 Peter 5:8 KJV).

His ultimate victory is to delay or postpone his sure and certain demise a bit longer. In this study, you will be well acquainted with the process of *Sweeping, Filling and Keeping* as your ultimate weapon to bring God back to His command post in your life! Our objective will be winning over whatever evil has attempted, in order to invade your otherwise normal day. This battle objective will bring honor and glory to the Lord, causing the devil to feel that much closer to his destiny in the Pit. The book will help you to understand that the Devil attempts daily to do what he does best—to use half-truths to draw you away from walking with the

Lord through everyday bumps in the road of life. The collective description of Satan in Scripture is one who is arrogantly proud, fearfully threatened and bitterly resentful. Activity that you may have previously wrote off as bad luck, unfortunate circumstances or even as part of a really bad day, should be pinpointed as part of the desperation of a defeated enemy that is angrily scared and feeling the dread of his demise as never before.

Sweeping Out the Demons will help you to put Satan in his place. We must develop a scriptural understanding of evil, that doesn't underestimate his role in spiritual warfare. He is definitely astute and crafty. But, effectual fervent prayer and a compassionate examination of the Word remind us not to overestimate his role. We are God's children and His soldiers, so we know that just like Satan we are a part of creation! Reminding ourselves that the devil and his fallen angels are on a terminal, death row pathway to eternal destruction is a message that this book will help you to live by. Knowledge of Satan's short leash of freedom to do his dirty deeds reminds us why God has allowed evil and permitted many circumstances for which many question and lament. The weapons of Sweeping, Filling and Keeping will help you each time you encounter those events in life that make you shake your head and say, "Why, God, why this?" At that point, you will remember that Sovereign God is in control, that He DOES know best, and that He will lovingly teach you the why of the tragedy or calamity, and the apparent victory of some evil that has subtly crept into your life.

God is using this spiritual warfare to challenge true believers both to be and to do His will. Meanwhile, the devil is limited to be and to do only to the extent that God allows. He knows that he is defeated but he won't admit it because that brings him ever closer to the consummation of the ages and his sure demise. So if you ever wonder why evil is getting worse, not weaker, you need not wonder anymore! Evil is stepping up the "game" to keep on keeping on, like a squirrel on a treadmill that is powering the pump from which flows his water and food supply from a bin at the bottom of the cage. This book should be a great encourager for you to claim your commission as a soldier of the cross, so that you can be in on the victories over evil today, while victoriously living in anticipation of the marvelous victory to come! That commission is part of the Great Commission, which carries with it an eternal pension already invested in heaven!

Today you are embarking on a kind of spiritual journey that may take you farther than you really ever knew or dared to go in spiritual warfare. You'll be like the kid who took piano or the friend that learned how to pilot a plane or the co-worker that learned a foreign language. Just about the time the battle is hot and heavy in your daily stuff, you'll look back mentally and grin that you are the one who took the time to learn God's secret weapons for spiritual warfare in the fast paced, post Christian, post modern and post peace of mind twenty-first century. You will confidently trust God as an elite soldier in a war more fierce and ugly than all the wars combined.

Spiritual Warfare really *is* the war to end all wars, because when this one's over, my friend, it's *all* over as far as this world's concerned. Jesus will return in a glorious appearing and His followers will realize all that He promised about heavenly rewards. We will understand and experience the wonders of the Kingdom of God. And it will come as no surprise, shock or dismay for you, because you were ready!

But in the meantime, how do you handle the daily battles to be fought, in order to show Satan that we *know* that God has won already? Are you ready to show the Evil One *whose* you are and TO whom you are listening and with whom you are walking every hour? You can begin right now, by the way you allow God to do battle with the problems and frustrations that you will even face this very day.

Did you know that the soon to fall prince of this world has to hate your reading and prayerful study of this material? Here he has had Christians and non-Christians alike, floundering around, trying to be this, to do that, or to keep this law or that rule or that practice or those programs, when up steps (your name here). Here is where you begin the battle, a trusting soldier of Jesus, living the life, trusting in strife, basking in the light of the truth of the one with the Way! I pray this book will enable you to be that person!

This book will either remind you or convince you that Jesus followers must become soldiers of the cross. Your practical application of the principles of *Sweeping, Filling and Keeping* will become second nature to you as THE consistent way to allow God to free you and liberate you from the tension of overcoming evil with your good works or with your own strength and will power. God will be the first consultant and the supreme counselor you go to everyday to live in a manner that will win over evil tendencies time after time.

Are you aware that even the most normal, routine and mundane of situations in your day may be the ones that the devil will try to use in order to rob you of the practical applications of the fruit of the Spirit? In this study you will become well acquainted with those fruit: love, joy, peace, patience, kindness, gentleness, faithfulness and self-control.

Have you considered how much God is glorified and honored when you let go and let Him guide you to victory on a day when the toast burned and your stomach churned and the traffic spurned your frustration and stress levels off the charts? Jesus tried to teach the most religious and seemingly "holy" folk of his generation this lesson in Matthew 12:43–45, but they would not listen. They never knew what they had missed by not truly hearing what Jesus said that day...but you could listen and really hear as you read these pages!

My prayer is that after the last page you will truly understand how to fight spiritual battles as never before. This book is not a deep theological expedition, but rather a practical fact and faith finding tour to get your head cleared of Satan's junk! The desired outcome is you meeting your day head on with ALL of God: the Heavenly Father as Guide, Guard and Director, Christ as Master Tour Guide and Strategic General and the Holy Spirit as your Enabler, Life Professor and Equipper. You just have to trust Him and obey Him and follow His lead. It's hard to accept simple solutions in a complex world, is it not? Until you do let God be God of the entire journey, the devil will kick your tail more days than not. You will lie down at night wondering if the long day behind you was a waste of your limited days, full of unfinished business with God, complete with another list of worries and regrets. It is no small wonder why so many of us have insomnia, stressed to the hilt and so tired of it all...he Devil wants us all spiritually confused! It NEVER should have been this way after the day you decided to follow Jesus.

Above all, I pray that long after you have placed this study back on a shelf somewhere, that each day, after some intense spiritual warfare, as your head hits the pillow, that you will be able to conclude with the Psalmist, "I will both lay me down in peace, and sleep: for thou, LORD, only makest me dwell in safety." (Ps. 4:8 KJV)

DAY 1

The Game of Your Life!

"Welcome back to The Game of Your Life! This is Gabriel Angel with the play by play of today's contest between the Church of the Living God versus Satan Beelzebub and his Unholy Demons.

"It has been a rather exciting day with the church battling the forces of evil in spiritual warfare—I love this game! It is *fan*-tastic! These guys sure do know how to fight. Today we have witnessed the league championship, with the winner gaining first place in the control of your heart, soul, mind and strength. But in these closing moments it looks like Satan and the D's have just been outplayed and basically...oh how can I put it...*trounced*! Ever since the Old Testament season, these people of God have shown some impressive moves. Then last year during the New Testament season, the church led by Coach Jesus had just outclassed Satan and his band of fallen angels.

"Having not scored a single point, Satan and company continue a scrappy strategy of resistance and retaliation, focusing on surprise attacks and deception. But now with just ten seconds remaining it's the church of the Lord Jesus one million trillion, to Satan's Demons' disappointing zero. So yes, it looks like a shutout today and a grand celebration coming up for God's team, the church. Let's listen in as the home crowd counts this one down in their own inimitable style, "John **10**:10, 1Corinthians **9**:27, Romans **8**:28, Matthew **7**:7, Luke **6**:38, Romans **5**:8, John **4**:14, John **3**:16, 2Timothy **2**:15, 1John **1**:9"—and that's the game folks.

"But wait! There's a commotion down on the field. Satan and his team are continuing to set up for the next play. And there is the referee, informing Coach Beelzebub that it's over. What is Satan saying to the ref? Folks we are going down to Michael Archangel down on the field to learn more about what is going on.

"Michael, what is happening down there?"

"Gabriel, it looks like Coach Satan and his demon team are refusing to leave the field or admit defeat. And look! He's having some of the demon players block all exits so that no one can leave. Let's listen in on the conversation if I can get close enough."

"No, as Coach Satan prince of this world, I am telling you that it's not over until I say it's over! After all, I am Satan, God's best prospect for stardom until he fired me for being honest. I told Him that I am better than he is and deserve His job. Everyone knows that I should be God. But He did not agree—noooo! So here we are, after a long four thousand year season and He still just doesn't get it. I will battle until I win, and will do whatever it takes."

"Gabe, the referee is just staring at him in disbelief. Wait! By the bright blinding light from above the stadium, here comes Commissioner Yahweh to intercede. Let's hear what He has to say."

"I am the Lord thy God, the only *I AM,* the Creator of the universe and all that is within it, including you, Satan! As the great *I AM,* I am here to break some news to you. You were defeated since the beginning, and the final blow came at mid-season after my Son Jesus went all the way against you...to the cross He went, you fallen outcast angel of darkness! He finished you off three days later, rising from the dead to defeat you secret weapon, the fear of death. Why, you know as well as anyone what it says in my Word, over in Hebrews 2:14–15, now don't you?

"When He told all that He is the resurrection and the life, as John recorded in his gospel, in chapter eleven, verse twenty-five, you knew very well that the resurrection victory pretty well did you in, did you not? At His ascension, He commissioned an army of saints called my church. I then filled them with power through my own spirit a few days later.

"Oh, they have faltered through the years but always returned to me to honor and to glorify my name. That army has shown you her secret weapon today: effectual, fervent prayer and a loving knowledge and application of my rulebook for faith and practice—yes, Father of Lies, I am talking about my Word, the Holy Bible. They read it and study it. They meditate upon my Word, waiting for me to speak to them about it while they are reading. Some even memorize it, hiding it in their hearts, so that they can apply it to the game of life each day, just as they did so well today!

"So, *Fallen Angel of Darkness*, what do you have to say for yourself as you refuse to admit the victory that has occurred today by my followers as led by my Son Jesus and our powerful Holy Spirit?"

"Michael, what is Coach Satan saying to the commissioner?"

"Well, Gabe, I'm waiting to hear just like everyone in this stadium. I mean, how in the world will he answer such a complete and perfect response as Commissioner Yahweh issued just now? Let's listen in..."

"Esteemed former leader let me tell you something. As Satan Beelzebub, aka the Prince of Darkness—the Devil, I submit to you what some baseball player said years ago: **it ain't over 'til it's over!** In your so-called Word, there are conditions for the end, are there not? You have indicated that certain events will occur around the world before my time comes. Until that time, I will continue to do everything that you *think* that you are permitting me to do to test, tempt, thwart, frustrate, interfere and otherwise mess with the heads of Coach Jesus' players.

"Oh, maybe, just *maybe* you are stronger, Yahweh...I'm not saying you are, mind you. If in fact you are omnipotent, omnipresent and omniscient, even though I may not be, I will still roam around like a roaring lion to see just how many of your team members and potential prospects I can discourage, depress and defeat. I will use my team as well. When you unjustly kicked us off the team so many years before you created these players, I recruited my angels to be here to help me out with some pretty impressive tactics.

"For those who have not yet joined this so-called Team Jesus, I have and will be tormenting them and pulling their moral and ethical standards way down! You watch, Yahweh. And as for your Team Jesus, so-called church of the living God...well, you don't have that many great players or squads around these days, the way I see it. Weak churches with weak and uncommitted players are all over your team roster. They make my work easy. As for the others who seem so bent on battling with me, bring them on! Let the real season begin, Almighty One!

"From this twenty-first century all the way to the final conflict, this is no longer a game. This is war! I am calling on my demon soldiers to attack astutely and subtly any and every point of contact on the face of this planet. I will use their minds against them, suggesting evil whenever permitted. I will tempt them to give up when things get difficult. I will encourage them to give in to the world and the views of all those who don't call you Lord. I will influence the media to promote immorality and confuse right and wrong with half right and half-wrong choices—Remember the garden, God? You do remember Eve and Adam. That serpent disguise may not have fooled you at all but it did the trick for those two naive saps. Political regimes, false religions and possessed individuals you will come to call terrorists all will increase on this spiritual horizon! Yes, Father of Light, it looks as though I will lose, but with each battle I just may turn the tide and all that you have declared and as you say, predestined to come about...Well, we'll just see what I can do about that!"

"This is Michael Archangel again. Gabe, did you just hear all that Coach Beez had the audacity to say to the supreme leader of the universe?"

"Yep, Mike, I heard and so did all who are listening right now. This last part of the season is going to be known as *spiritual warfare*. It's not any ordinary game—and the stakes are the highest ever-eternal trophies, not just some temporal ones. We will watch with great excitement to see how the church of the Living God prepares for this final conflict. Mike, I don't have any doubt how it will all come out, but I am kind of concerned about how many casualties these battles will inflict. Satan means business. I just hope the church of the Living God will step up with our "A" game. I know we can; I've seen greatness all around, but I've also seen some weak links and some sloppy play the past century or so."

"Gabe, I could not agree more with what you are saying, but I would like to add that Satan must have some secret weapons and some surprise attacks up his sleeve to be that cocky and arrogant with our official of officials. You know, he has not yet revealed what he was referring to years ago, when we learned about the possibility of his off season draft of a so-called free agent known only as Antichrist...

"Our Christian Army has to raise the bar and do some serious preparation, or this thing could drag out for a lot longer than Commissioner Yahweh would desire before He sounds that trumpet! He wants the best for His team, and if they listen to His Word, I am going on record to say that the Glorious Appearing and Final Judgment All Stars as well as the MVPs will be named a lot sooner than we might expect."

"Mike, I have in the tower with me some of the coaching staff for the church of the Living God. Guys, welcome! Come on in and let's hear what your take is on what just came down on the field."

"Isaiah, you and Jeremiah have seen it all, haven't you?"

"Yes, Gabriel, we sure have. However, as my compadre Jeremiah here has heard from our Lord, we have not seen anything yet compared to the wars, rumors of wars, earthquakes and other natural disasters. How 'bout it, Jerry? Isn't it like you said as recorded in the Book (Jeremiah 12:1–5)?"

"Isaiah, that's a fact. The destruction of Jerusalem and the exile back in the year 586 before the Lord Jesus' incarnation time— well, that was horrible. But this world is a different playing field than back then. All of this technology and amazing developments since that Industrial Revolution of the last few centuries—Well, that's changed everything. People seem to lean on material things and pleasure far more than trusting in our Lord. Also, there was that Enlightenment period back in century nineteen, when many left the team to worship science and the arts — Why, some even went so far as to make all the amazing discoveries made by some of God's greatest minds as evidence that they no longer needed God!"

"Jeremiah, let's invite your defensive coach, King David in here to comment on what you have said..."

"Gabe, thanks for having us up here...it was very disturbing down there, seeing how Satan plans to end this season. I wrote a lot of psalms in my time, but none will help us prepare for this tough stretch coming up like Psalm 51. If you will recall, I spoke a lot about my own downfall and my terrible transgressions. We are going to have to hurl ourselves into that kind of repentance and ask Commissioner Yahweh to create in us clean hearts and renew our spirits—otherwise; this thing is going to get out of control. What do you think, Paul?"

"David, you know that you shouldn't have shaken my peach tree if you didn't want my peaches to fall!" Everyone chuckles, knowing Paul's propensity for verbosity.

"But seriously, I will try to be brief in my comments. I have to say that we are in position to win for sure, and win big, if we can examine what our strategy was for those Galatians, Ephesians, Philippians and Colossians. What a team they were! We can be even greater if we will study their playbooks and apply the same plays to our more intense final conflict. Besides, guys, we *have* to stand on God's promises. All of them are so very important. It's going to be the victory of the ages, but how well today's team will prepare and follow through? That remains to be seen."

"John, you have heard your counterparts share about all of this. When you received that vision we now call the Revelation, did you have any idea that after all these years that things would flesh out like they have?"

"Brother Gabriel, we all remember how sovereign God revealed that it would end, and we all believe that it will, praise God! However, I have to be honest, from our watching the game films these past two and a half millenniums, I had no idea that it would get this nasty and mean before the finals at Armageddon. I mean, how much farther could the church drift than during those Dark Ages? And what can we say about the Crusades? They were so painful to watch. I could go on, but my point is the team just has not been consistent in their play! They've frequently been like the roller coaster effect that Israel followed back before the exiles, even though they had all of our prophets' testimonies and teachings in hand! On top of all those ups and downs, the evil has become *exponential*, as I believe the mathematicians have come to call such growth! But guys, what God showed me back then, while on the Island of Patmos, is just around the corner, just as He promised.

"What is troubling me, however, is the battleground for these precious team members in this new millennium. We in heaven are all joining in the intercession of the saints, for their wisdom to obey God and follow Him through thick and thin, so that Satan will be found to be just as big a stinker as he always has been... Amen?"

"Yeah! I would like to thank all these giants in the faith for taking time to come up here so we could get just a small grasp of what is coming up in this final season. Spiritual warfare at its toughest will be witnessed in this millennium. I am sure that while we will see many casualties, we will see many more victories as the team prepares and gets out there on this planet, showing the world how to honor and glorify the Lord as never before. It ought to be exciting, and hey, we´ll be there for every single play, folks. This is Gabriel Angel for all the crew here at Christ Watch Network saying, so long for now."

OK. What you have just read was a modern day parable about the reason you are reading this book. The name for what you want to learn about as much as possible is *spiritual warfare*. It is what you and I must focus upon from now on. You begin talking about spiritual warfare and people will listen. People react in different ways to the topic. Many have a vague or erroneous understanding about spiritual warfare. Some want to ignore that spiritual warfare exists. Still others want to find some shortcut or easy alternative around it. But the truth is, we all must understand spiritual warfare. It is woven into the fabric of daily living, and we will confront the forces of evil this very day. Spiritual warfare, fought well, can change the very quality of your life.

Some think it is some kind of board game like *Dungeons and Dragons* or an interactive video game. But spiritual warfare is *no* game, I assure you, and you can bet your life on that! Now, you probably were already aware of that, if you have been a true follower of Jesus Christ for more than an hour! Just picking up this book shows your desire to learn as much as possible in how to engage the Enemy in spiritual warfare. Let´s identify spiritual warfare, and then decide how you can begin to be the best Christian soldier possible. In the time together, we will use as our strategy the practical application of Matthew 12:43–45, in order to learn how to **sweep out evil, fill the void with something better, and** *how to keep evil from returning*! Welcome to the basic training for a biblical, practical and comprehensive strategy for spiritual warfare that we will call **Sweeping Out The Demons**! Glad to have you among the troops! Whether a new recruit or veteran soldier of the cross, it is a privilege to learn and serve alongside of you!

Sweeping Moments for Today...

1) Now that you have read this modern day parable, go back and try to reconstruct the story to the best of your memory. For small groups, have various members of your group to participate.

2) Read the verses that were referenced in the "countdown" ending of the game. How does each one hold significance when related to spiritual warfare? For small groups, you might want to divide into groups of 2 or 3 to take a couple of these verses for each division.

3) Each character and symbol in this modern day parable helps us to understand some characteristics about spiritual warfare: Jot down your understanding of the role or symbolism for each character. For small groups you might use the same divisions as in exercise number two.

Gabriel, the announcer:
Michael down on the field:
The Score:
Coach Satan's response to the outcome:
Team Church of the Living God:

9

Team Devil and his Demons:
Coach Satan:
Coach Jesus:
Commissioner Yahweh:
Isaiah:
Jeremiah:
King David:
Paul:
John:

4) Have you ever had a time when you experienced intense temptation or testing? How did you handle it? Has it returned to do the same kind of dirty deed over and over, or did you find permanent victory? Why do you think things turned out as they did?

5) Why do we need to learn how to battle Satan if he is already a defeated foe?

6) What is your previous experience with spiritual warfare? Check all that apply to you. How has your spiritual warfare been affected by each factor that you checked? If in small group, discuss this with the group.

A. I have been in some studies and read books about spiritual warfare.

B. I have been personally involved in spiritual warfare for some time.

C. I am a new believer and don't know very much about spiritual warfare.

D. I think that the subject is not relevant for the twenty-first century, with all our knowledge and technology.

E. I don't think it is important. Besides, there is no such thing as a literal Devil or demons or such superstitious beliefs.

F. I think that only parachurch movements or backward folk would think of such things. The church is much more enlightened and sophisticated, aren't we? Besides, things are getting better and less evil, instead of worse and more evil, are they not?

DAY 2

Sweeping Out the Demons... what do you mean by that?

But the unclean spirit, when he is gone out of the man, passeth through waterless places, seeking rest, and findeth it not. Then he saith, I will return into my house whence I came out; and when he is come, he findeth it empty, swept, and garnished. Then goeth he, and taketh with himself seven other spirits more evil than himself, and they enter in and dwell there: and the last state of that man becometh worse than the first. Even so shall it be also unto this evil generation. (Matthew 12:43–45 KJV)

Do you ever wonder what it would be like if you had made a different choice or went a different way in how you responded to a missed opportunity? Were there regrets? Do you daydream and replay how it might have turned out if you had responded the "other" way? Do you long for a "do over"? As futile as it seems, every now and then we all have those flash backs where we wish we could somehow change how it came down and then just flash forward again! As I reflect on how it might have been, in each one of my missed opportunities in a ball game, a work decision, an investment or a relationship, I do confess there have been more than a few times when I thought, "What if?"

The Scripture you have just read was Jesus' attempt to warn some stubborn Pharisees that they were going down a pathway of legalism and close-mindedness to really loving the Lord. What if they had decided not only to live lawfully but also making a heart return to live the laws under the principle of loving obedience, or serving God with a godly love (Deut. 6:1-9)? Things would have been very different among the Jews of Jesus' day! The sweeping and cleaning described in Jesus' parable would have included a refurnishing of the man's "house" with godly items like love, joy, peace, patience, kindness, goodness, gentleness, self-control and faithfulness. Now that would have shown the "demon" and his buddies that the man's "house" or life was already full of better furnishings, and no longer available for evil to return. The state of the Pharisees who were stubbornly half-listening to Jesus would have been a sight to see...but hey, we all know they didn't go that way, don't we?

Now I am passing this on to you before you read further or do a small group discussion with this book. When you read about the sins, mistakes and errors in judgment that others have made, you need to *learn from them.* Whether the bungles or blunders were made by Biblical personalities, historical figures or persons you know and love (or even those you don't even like so much), always remember another very life changing counsel: just because they missed it or messed it up doesn't mean you have to make the same mistake! Instead, re-evaluate, restudy, rethink...review, reflect... and then respond in a manner that contradicts all the negative responses by those precious souls you watched as they made the wrong decisions. Learn from them and allow God to teach you how not only to *sweep* out the wrong, but in loving obedience to *fill* the empty space where the mistakes or errors were made and repented of, with something better, again generated out of loving obedience. Only then is it possible to maintain or to *keep out* the same errors as you grow in love for God through a powerful

13

relationship with Him in real prayer and a newfound love for applying His Word to your life as you read and meditate over His messages, which by this time have become quite personal. My friends, these principles that we will make more specific as you read on have the potential to enable you to recognize threats by evil, genuinely repent of them and allow your life to be so filled with "God-stuff" that God will be permitted to give you the quality of life that He has desired for you since...forever! Not only that, but He will be allowed to maintain those swept and filled areas of your life day, after day, after day!

Positive success stories abound in Scripture, literature and even once in awhile on CNN and FOX. They inspire as well as teach us. Anyone can see and learn from those...that's easy...that's so clear and positive. In studying the Word, we discover amazing examples like Abraham, Moses, David, Solomon, other kings of both Israel and Judah, Ezra and Nehemiah as well as many more. In the New Testament, we find even more intense examples of positive lessons that the Jesus followers gave us. You might notice the exclusion of one notable from the list...Joseph, the hero of the patriarchs who saved Egypt and his family from famine and starvation. His example of positive responses to negative situations is monumental and deserves your careful and prayerful reading of Genesis, chapter thirty-seven through chapter fifty. For our purposes, I would simply like to use Joseph's positive responses to God's tests to frame all of the examples where persons have followed God and gotten it right. We will call all of those lessons *"Joseph Lessons"*. A Bible study of all the Joseph type lessons in the Bible will inspire you and I hope you learn from those examples.

However, most of us miss or ignore some of the most powerful lessons in the Bible, in history or in our own lives. Those come from the other side of inspiration and success. I am talking about the negative lessons. I'm referring to that other list of life lessons, born out of wrong choices and rebellious decisions like the one those stubborn Pharisees made about Jesus' wise counsel in our key Scripture for this book, Matthew 12:43–45. We have already gleaned the three founding principles of that negative response. Not only those Pharisees, but believers today as well, could have responded with the *Sweeping Formula for Spiritual Warfare* in the twenty-first century. The first step is obvious from the story: *Sweeping repentance.* The second step complements and completes the first step: *Filling or Sowing* into the void left by reform and repentance with something far better. A third step to the formula is what makes the whole formula keep on keeping on: *Keeping out evil*, or enabling God to keep out that negative influence by maintaining a loving relationship with Him, grounded in an *effectual, fervent prayer life* that is guided and grounded **in** *a love for His Word.* The three points together were the desired response from the Pharisees, and is the best response for you and me!

Along with that example is a long list that we don't want to think about, so that we can read about, for example, Abraham's willingness to sacrifice Isaac and the godly obedience displayed by Abraham (and Isaac). No, instead of that one, please refer to that *other* list that reminds us of the same patriarch, years before, then called Abram, asking wife Sarai to say she was his sister to save his neck before a foreign ruler.

Oh yeah, *that list*...and it is long. It spans all of Scripture as well as the Joseph lessons. You know it well... The list is replete with those unwise, sinful choices that caused more problems instead of any solutions. Those examples abound, like with Moses striking a rock, or Samson giving in to lust and pride, or David...likewise giving in to lust and pride. What about Solomon...he ditched wisdom's riches for greed and pride? I suppose that example fits most of the kings of both Israel and Judah.

In the New Testament, we find more of those negative examples: like with Peter who first denied he would ever leave Jesus' side to his three-time denial of even knowing the Lord.

As for Pharisee Saul of Tarsus, his decisions to persecute those of the Way were pretty negative, right? Both then and now, such negative responses give Satan an inroad where he evokes negative results like guilt, discouragement, desperation and confusion.

In all of those examples, we all know that was not the end result, don´t we? Each learned from the negatives to follow God into a repentant reversal of the response, resulting in a resounding victory! That Bible study alone would give you a jolt of joy, as it did me as I saw my life influenced by those examples. One example I did not include in the list—Jonah. I did not include that one because for me he became the epitome of examples in how not to find and follow God. The correction of direction by Jonah was a prophecy of victory for God´s will over man´s rebellion, so I would like for you to remember all of the negative responses in Scripture, in history and in your own life to be clumped into one mental picture we will call *"Jonah Lessons"*.

We find these kinds of negatives in good, even great men throughout history. The lesson for us is learning to allow God to **sweep out** with our genuine repentance, **to fill up** the empty space where evil was once allowed to run and play...filling with great stuff like spiritual fruit from the Holy Spirit. Then, in order to maintain victory or **keep out evil**, negative decisions from returning to mess with your life repeatedly, you enter into a lifestyle of effectual, fervent prayer coupled with a love for Scripture. How different the negative examples would have turned out had they Swept, Filled and Kept out evil through God's presence and power!

Most responses on this *other* list are born out of the master of disaster called Satan, his demons and their attempts to influence your response, using astute and subtle tactics to confuse you, distort your reasoning, or distract you from God´s Word to you and your conversations with God. How intense is the desire by any human in Bible times right up to the twenty-first century, to avoid the guilt, dissatisfaction and displeasure that results from moral or ethical "detours"? *"Jonah Lessons"* are born out of evil influenced decisions, guided by half-truths, that cause people to take matters out of God's hands, deciding instead to pridefully conclude that "I can fix this myself—I don't need God to make this work."

Ironically, many biblical and historical figures have notables on both lists. We will learn how to identify those in Scripture, in history and in everyday living. Then, you can learn from them, and make life-changing adjustments from them that will include those positive life lessons as worthy refurnishing for your "house" or life in Jesus' Matthew 12:43–45 story counsel. That is how we will apply those three words highlighted a couple of pages back (**sweeping, filling** and **keeping**) to form the process we will call Sweeping Out the Demons.

By *"demons"* in this book, we are not referring to the demons themselves. Granted, there is demon possession in the world, as we have personally witnessed during our many years in Brazil. That is an intensive and horrendous journey traveled by billions of persons worldwide, only to be defeated by the army of God evangelizing the lost world. I believe that *Sweeping Out the Demons* will help many to be ready to allow God to accomplish this through them...through YOU, as you learn how the Devil and his band of Losers work to detour your life as a God-follower.

In this book, our focus is not on that activity in the lives of the lost, but rather upon the temporary, demon/evil activity in the lives of believers. These attacks by the Devil are designed to interfere, distract and even delay your continual growth-walk with God. Truly regenerated, born again, spirit-filled believers cannot be demon possessed, due to the abiding presence of the Holy Spirit. We believers are vulnerable only to the temporary attacks by Satan and his demon outcasts. He attempts these momentary assaults in order to keep you from perfect love and devotion for Almighty God. His evil army's ultimate objective is to maintain their evil presence in the world yet a bit longer, before being cast out into eternal oblivion and chaos, the lake of fire, eternal damnation. Just take a peek at Rev. 19:20, 20:10, 20:14 and 20:15 for a more thorough understanding about just how defeated your defeated enemy really is. He knows far better than you know of all the worst stuff God has promised for him... as described from Genesis 3:15 to Revelation 22:21! These and more evidences beyond the pages of God's Word remind Satan of his demise. The amazing victories by Christians throughout the ages herald and proclaim his dark end for the Prince of Darkness.

Sweeping Out the Demons, then, should refer you to the Prince of this World's astute and subtle battle in your life, designed to keep you from glorifying and honoring God. If you will read and study the principles I have gleaned from God's Word as well as examining my experiences in spiritual warfare, you should emerge as a Solder ready to battle victoriously day-to-day evil. We will work together to learn how to permit God to **sweep out** the evil or demon influences that are introduced into your life on a daily basis. We will work together to perfect the **filling of the void** left by the sweeping, replacing it with the most excellent attitudes and actions via fruit of the Holy Spirit and God's impenetrable armor. We will work together to perfect an enabling from God to guide you in **keeping out** that evil influence from now on, through a lifestyle of effectual fervent prayer, generated out of a love for the reading, studying, meditating, memorizing and practical application of His Word.

O.K...where can you find the models to examine for your first lesson in spiritual warfare? We will work together to learn how to learn from two lists, from God's Word and from human examples. You can use these lists to study and learn from Scripture and from all of human history, so you will not run out of either type of example, as long as you stay in the Word and become a student of human history. The first list has positive examples to follow, which we will call *Joseph type lessons*—a do as I say and do as I do kind of list. The second list chronicles those negative examples. It is a do not even go where I went list. These examples of how not to do it we will call *Jonah type lessons*. It is a longer, more frequent list, where we can learn from examples of disobedience and rebellion in order to do the exact opposite from the examples. Making positives out of Satan's desire to maintain negatives is the most intense form of spiritual warfare. This type of discerning Bible study and examination of lifestyles will serve you well as you train to be the best soldier of the cross possible! In this book, we will approach spiritual warfare from a bit of a different battle plan than you might have fought with previously. This is not to discount the hundreds of books already available to study about spiritual warfare...the ones I examined as I prepared for battle all helped me to grow, but in **Sweeping Out the Demons**, I want you to find keys that you can and must apply to your day-to-day temptations, tests and spiritual challenges. I hope that these keys or principles will become second nature.

Your ultimate victory goal is that your spiritual warfare will consistently keep the devil from successfully interfering with any of the three levels of relationships that you and I cherish: the relationship with God, our many relationships with others and yes, rightly relating with yourself as God would desire for you to see *you*.

Before doing real spiritual warfare, make sure that you are clear on the principles we have introduced in Day 2. They will serve you well as we continue to prepare for your real life battles with attitudes, actions and behaviors that you would just as soon never again permit to glare their ugly reflection in your daily living.

You might think of it this way. The so-called "*Joseph lessons*" are so named because they are examples of obedience like the inspiring model of Jacob/Israel's son from Genesis, chapters thirty-seven through chapter fifty. Do you remember how Joseph, Jacob's next to youngest son, inspires you with shining examples of consistent obedience and wisdom in times of testing? We all aspire to be like Joseph, do we not?

Nevertheless, more times than not you and I resonate more with *"Jonah type lessons"*. Jonah resisted and feared God's call for him to go to Nineveh in order to call them to repentance. He ran in the other direction from the challenge. He endangered a ship full of men with his foolish plan to escape from God's will. Even after the miraculous rescue by God via that big fish, he mumbled and grumbled about Nineveh not deserving pardon. In the *Book of Jonah*, you will find one prideful, disobedient and rebellious man. There you will discover several negative lessons that you can apply in your life, only with the exact opposite response from the ones Jonah made. Jonah type lessons exist throughout the Bible, and throughout history. We can copy Joseph lessons, but we must react to Jonah lessons by correcting and adjusting our response to contradict or reject the negative or incorrect response of that Bible personality, group of people or contemporary example.

With both types of lessons, you must answer these questions in order to apply the three key principles of Sweeping Out the Demons:

PRINCIPLE ONE - Sweeping: God is guiding you to sweeping repentance. That repentance is characterized by confession and contrition. In this principle you ask yourself:

What can I learn from this example?
How can I apply the positive lessons?

PRINCIPLE TWO - Filling: Filling the empty space left by sweeping out bad stuff, with genuine repentance—replacing that void with practical applications of God's instructions. Just ask yourself:

How can I react to the negative lessons?
What will be necessary to make positives out of the negative responses?

PRINCIPLE THREE: Keeping: Keeping out the negative responses from now on with the Word coupled with effectual fervent prayer. In order to maintain your sweeping and filling, ask God as you develop a hunger and thirst to read the Word and as you pray with true purpose and intensity. Such questions as these should come to mind in this principle:

What "sweepings" are most needed in my life today, Lord?
How is Satan trying to distract or detour me today?
What are you trying to teach me from your Word that will help me to be your soldier of the cross today, Lord?
What attribute of the fruit of the Spirit (Gal. 5:22–23) and what piece of the whole armor of God (Eph. 6:11–18) do I need most today, Lord?

Don't worry! At first Sweeping Out the Demons, sounds like a foreign language, but each "Day" or section of the book will help you to think, act and react to temptations, tests and trials. I have heard several preachers share a series similarly entitled "Dare to be a Daniel", in which I was challenged to be like other heroes who got it right the first time, like Joseph in Genesis, Joshua, Barnabas, or Timothy. In spiritual warfare, battling Satan needs another sermon series as well that we would have to call something like *"Don't you Dare to be a Jonah!"*, or *"Save yourself and Listen to God, Because it's Too Late for Me!"*

21

You can emerge as a Joseph from a Jonah world of temptations, tests, trials and potential traps by the devil. Remember, just because someone else fell into a trap does not mean that you must. Learn from the Josephs and the Jonahs that have preceded you, and adjust your responses accordingly! You can learn from those who have sinned, failed, fallen, or just plain messed it up. Who were (or are) they? What were the circumstances for their negative decisions? How can you learn *not* to make the same mistakes? As Peter so wonderfully advised us:

Be sober, be vigilant; because your adversary the devil, as a roaring lion, walketh about, seeking whom he may devour: Whom resist steadfast in the faith, knowing that the same afflictions are accomplished in your brethren that are in the world. (1 Peter 5:8, 9 KJV).

The practice of battling Satan against his attempts to lead us to follow bad choices and disobey God is **spiritual warfare**. Using examples from God's Word and my own experiences as a missionary in Brazil for nearly thirty years, we will make this journey together, training as soldiers in a war like no other. As you train, you will be a soldier prepared to understand every facet of Satan's evil strategy. This will help you to cooperate with our *Mighty Commander* in sweeping out the demons. Remember, when we use that phrase, for our purposes, we will be referring to demons as the result of Satan's evil influences in your life. Whether you acknowledge the existence or presence of Satan's fallen angel army (demons) or not, is an issue to be dealt with at another time. Right now, it is the desire of my heart that by the time you finish the book, you will change forever in how you deal with evil influences. That reality in itself will deliver a huge attack upon Satan and his influence!

The way I now fight evil influences in my life has changed forever by that simple story that Jesus told to some stubborn

Pharisees in Matthew 12:43–45. This is our key passage for all we will do in this book. I pray that you will never again look at Matthew 12:43–45 in the same way as before. After our through examination of our key passage, you will wonder why those Pharisees ignored such wise counsel, and why so many of us likewise have ignored that wise counsel throughout church history. Making the right response to that situation presented in Matthew 12:43–45 will make an amazing difference in how you deal with everyday temptations and evil influences in all areas of your life.

Would you agree that, in no way should we imitate how those Pharisees reacted to Jesus' teaching in Matthew 12:43–45? Instead, I can ask God to show me how to apply Jesus' lesson in my life to evict evil from my "house" forever (Jesus used the image of a house for the inner workings of this man's moral and ethical reactions to life. Sweeping Out the Demons is the result of learning how to permit God to guide you through this threefold process every time you are engaged by evil:

The first step is sweeping through genuine repentance.

The second step is filling by sowing where you repented, allowing God to sweep out evil. Thankfully, the repentance results in an empty or void space where evil was swept. God is permitted to fill the void with practical applications of spiritual fruit and other gems that God's Spirit will teach you as you pray and read carefully in His Word.

The third step is keeping out the evil influence from your life, never to return, by reaping the blessings of the spiritual fruit that has replaced the evil influence. That new influence is a prayer life that is effectual and fervent, coupled with a love for God's Word that develops into an intense desire for the Word to penetrate your heart.

In our time together, I will be sharing how I have battled with habits, bad behavior *and* inappropriate responses to life's frustrating moments. My testimony will show you how I have seen God gradually change my responses as I allowed Him to Sweep, Fill and Keep. This is my new normal for spiritual warfare in the twenty-first century. Even as I write, I am experiencing all types of "demons" designed to linger and hinder. But I am wholeheartedly commending to you how my practical application to this more biblical and more consistent response is helping me with the most stubborn and difficult of "sweepings". Some spiritual battles are more enduring than others are. That requires deeper focus upon my spiritual warfare in order to drive out existing and potential evil influences, dependencies, habits, and undesirable responses to life's most difficult moments. You or I cannot do this with any consistent or lasting success, but God can!

For years now, these three simple steps have enabled me to allow God to eliminate what I never could conquer on my own. As a flawed and rebellious sinner, saved by grace, I am so thankful that God has allowed me to experience more victories over relentless temptations and evil influences than I ever thought possible. Believe me; I tried so many of my own solutions, only to become my own worst enemy. The result involved many partial and temporary steps toward victory, but never sealing the deal or claiming the promise. Sweeping, Filling and Keeping has changed all that, praise God!

Spiritual warfare is essential to the Christian life in order to maintain a relentless offensive upon Satan and his demons with our spiritual victories. Inflicting that fear and torment caused by our spiritual warfare, he has to do whatever is necessary under his limited power to neutralize the presence and dominion of God. Our spiritual warfare further limits his ability to deceive you the believer, into settling for but a fraction of God's promises and power for overcoming daily temptations and tests.

Satan seeks to keep us slaves and blinded to the limitless power that is available through the Holy Spirit (Heb. 2:14–15). Pivotal to your success as a soldier is your obedience and submission to the **Supreme Commander**! Letting go and letting God be sovereign Lord in your life will permit Him to show you how to be the best possible soldier in the most challenging spiritual battles—like the ones you most likely already are facing every day. Spiritual warfare is all about letting go and letting God sweep, fill and keep out Satan's attempts to hang on to his very existence by hanging on to you with every dirty trick he can get you to fall for. His days are numbered and he knows it. Make no mistake, he will do all possible to make sure you know that as well, but for how long? The answer to that is for just as long as God allows him to test us. Spiritual warfare, then, is the highest form of showing honor and glory to God, as you experience victory over the one He has allowed to serve as the catalyst to maximum spiritual growth and intimacy. God is testing your metal, winnowing and purifying His church through how you respond to temptations, tests and evil attacks. So fight the good fight and just watch how much closer, and how much more devoted you are becoming to our Lord, the one who is fighting for you and who already has secured the victory!

My friend, we find ourselves at a time in history that bombards us with some of the worst and most evil influences, demonic challenges and diabolical deceptions yet faced by humanity. The same spiritual darkness and sin sickness that has existed since the fall of man has become exponentially darker, more astute and more subtle as Satan fearfully and desperately faces his already pronounced demise. He dreads the glorious appearing of Lord Jesus as much as we long for that day. The prince of darkness is fighting the light of the world with even greater fear and intensity. That means for you and me that all types of evil influences are seeking to devour us like a roaring lion (1 Peter 5:8). Evil is trampling the family values we hold to so dearly. Perversion and resistance to purity are on the rise as never before. Words and actions considered unthinkably wrong just ten years ago, are thrust upon us daily by all venues of media. The evil objective is to desensitize us toward eventual acceptance to a new norm... profanity, dishonesty, and sexual preferences are all seeking to push the envelope until they saturate into our everyday way of viewing society. The result is a more depraved, selfish and uncaring pattern for reacting and interacting with the rest of the world than ever before in human history. Satan's last stand depends upon your agreement with the secular worldview while gradually allowing the biblical worldview to fade into the background.

It is as though Satan has been somewhat successful in placing a mental or psychological *veil* over the ethical and moral vision of otherwise good people, so that even if they don't become the worst they can be, that they will not react or retaliate when those around them begin to live like Hades on earth. It's frightening and something we don't want to acknowledge. Nevertheless, acknowledge and react we must, before it's too late! In spiritual warfare, God helps us to determine how we must react to such subtle and astute attacks.

Your spiritual warfare must step up, man up, woman up and move up to the next level! You must pray effectually, fervently and honestly, how you can defend and propagate to a lost and dying world the way, the truth and the light of life.

SWEEPING OUT THE DEMONS -
Spiritual Warfare for the 21st Century
Get to know the key passage: Matthew 12:43-45

---

1 - SWEEPING THROUGH GENUINE REPENTANCE

Recognizing What Needs To Be Swept From My Attitudes And Actions...

Satan's Suggestions to provoke....

Inappropriate Responses to Crises And Bad Attitudes

Habits *Destructive Behaviors* *Tests*

Temptations *Subtle Suggestions*

After Sweeping Repentance, Recognize There Is A Void Where Evil Resided In Your "House"...Satan and his "demons" want to get back in after being kicked out....

2 - FILLING THE VOID WITH SOMETHING BETTER...

How? Through Effectual Fervent Prayer And Intensive Searching Of The Scriptures.

Fill The Void Left By Genuine Repentance With Practical Applications Of Spiritual Fruit.

Galatians 5:22, 23

HANG THE NO VACANCY SIGN FOR SATAN TO SEE CLEARLY!

Filling the void in your "house" With New Occupants:

The Practical Applications of Spiritual Fruit Evicts Evil from Returning... Remember the key verses:

(Matt. 12:43-45)

God's Armor (Eph. 6:10-18)

Assurance of God's Unfailing Promises As You Discover Them in His Word

3 - KEEPING OUT THE EVIL - MAINTAINING THE VICTORIES

When Satan Is Trying To Reoccupy Your "House"
After Eviction And Filling Are Complete.
(How to maintain when the Devil and his army are
trying to get back into your life with counter attacks.)
Maintaining With

Effectual Fervent Prayer

Intensive Searching of the Scriptures

The Powerful Weapon of your
Testimony Shared With Others.

Continual Reinforcements For Your Warfare Through
The Weapons of Your Local Church Body
(Worship, Witness, Discipleship, Service, Fellowship)

YOUR HEAVY ARTILLERY

EFFECTUAL FERVENT PRAYER +
AN INTENSIVE SEARCH OF AND A LOVE FOR
THE SCRIPTURES

Sweeping Moments for Today...

Whether you are in a small group or doing an individual reading, examine and discuss Graphics 1, 2 and 3.

1. Are you beginning to get a handle on sweeping through genuine repentance?
2. Are you clear on the significance of filling the void by sowing the appropriate fruit of the Spirit?
3. Do you understand and see the importance of keeping the evil from ever returning by reaping the blessings of a Spirit controlled lifestyle?
4. Prior to meeting with your small group, or as an individual seeker, work through the following devotional process, personalizing it to work for you.

Important: You'll never fully understand spiritual warfare unless you maintain a close personal time alone with God.

For me, one of the wonderful outcomes from Sweeping, Filling and Keeping was a renewed desire to spend time alone with God.

This book will mean so much more to you if you set aside a time each day to:

Know fully the God of the Word, by praying and digging deeper into the Word of God!

First, take your Bible and go somewhere private. A set time each day is best but not always practical, so each day choose a time and place when and where you know you can be alone and quiet for a few minutes—your rule of thumb can be: "whenever and wherever I can meet with God for some quality, undivided time with Him." Don't let anyone or anything rob you of these joyful moments!

Pray a brief prayer, asking God to guide these moments.

Open your Bible and allow a few minutes to read several verses or a chapter. Some places to start reading are the *Psalms*, the *Gospel of Mark* or *Ephesians*. Sometimes it is just a blessing just to open your Bible and read random selections of the Word. God can guide you to some great truths when you ask Him to show you where He would have you to read! The past few years I have been doing a daily rotation between reading a chapter from the Old Testament, the New Testament, Psalms, Proverbs, learning memory verses, and reading from a devotional/Bible study book — that's a six day rotation that I love to use.

You can use your upraised hand to remind you how to dig deeper in the word:

> **Use your thumb** to remind you **to read** the Word daily. Begin where you feel the most interest, and if possible, get yourself a Bible with devotional study notes. A systematic method for reading the Bible through may help you also.

> **Use your index (pointer) finger** to remind you to study the Bible.

> Sometimes Sunday school or discipleship class lessons help to get you on track studying the Bible. A word study or a theme you are interested in can help to spark inductive Bible study. Audio/video sermons or online Bible teachers can also ignite your desire to study the Word.

Use your middle finger to remind you **to meditate** on what God wants to show you from the reading. "Be still and know that I am God..." (Ps. 46:10a KJV). Ask God to speak to your heart and just listen and let your mind contemplate how wonderful He is...it is even cool to ask Him questions as you quietly meditate with Him. God is glorified when we just want to be still and know Him!

Use your ring finger to remind you **to memorize** special verses so you can call upon them anywhere. You might start by listing all of the verses you already know by heart. Then as you read or hear messages/lessons, mark verses that touch you as ones that you would like to hide in your heart for future spiritual warfare, comfort and strength. Old business cards or slips of paper with the verses written on one side, the verse references on the other

Use your little finger to remind you **to apply** what you learn from the Bible.

Conclude your time talking to God. Prayer *is* both talking to God and listening as God speaks to your heart. Once again, your upraised hand can help guide you as you spend time with the Lord:

Use your thumb to remind you to *praise God* for who He is and to show Him you love Him.

Use your index finger to remind you to *thank God* for what He has done, what He is doing and what He will do in your life.

Use your middle finger to remind you to *confess* any attitude or action that could interfere with your relationship with Him.

Use your ring finger to remind you to *pray for the needs of others.*

Use your little finger to remind you to *be quiet and listen to God.* Take a few moments to invite God to speak to your heart about anything He might want you to know.

Another Tip: **Try to finish your time alone with God by committing to memory, in your own words, The Key Message and Mission of this study:**

The Key Message and Mission of Sweeping Out the Demons

In Matthew 12:43–45, the Pharisees heard Jesus' counsel on spiritual blindness or religion without a loving relationship with God. They ignored and rejected what Jesus taught, but I do not have to respond as they did. Instead, I can pray and ask God how to respond positively to Jesus' teaching. In all situations of temptation, testing or disobedience, I can discover the "way of escape" (I Cor. 10:13) as I trust God to...

Sweep out the "demon" or evil influence through genuine repentance.

Fill the empty space in my life left by true repentance by sowing attitudes and actions consistent with the Fruit of the Spirit in Galatians 5:22, 23.

Keep the evil influence out of my life by reaping the blessings of spiritual fruit. Those blessings are the new attitudes and actions, which have replaced the evil influences, displacing them from ever returning into my life. This new normal is based upon a daily walk with God. The result is a completely new paradigm for daily decisions. As you pray, read His Word, and discover His desires for your heart, the very way you process your day will gradually change for the better!

Daily I will give glory to God as I see improvements in my relationship to Him, to others and with myself as my outlook and perspective changes through a more constant influence by the Holy Spirit upon everything I think, say and do.

I will refer to this Key Message and Mission often, so that Satan will not sidetrack me onto other issues and trivialities. He does not like focused individuals and he hates closers who confirm promises like Philippians 1:6:

Being confident of this very thing, that he which hath begun a good work in you will perform it until the day of Jesus Christ: (KJV).

I can't emphasize enough how these moments will help you. Time alone with God will keep you focused on what's *really* important. It is much easier for the devil to distract you if he can keep your attention divided and diverted from glorifying God in the way you Sweep, Fill to Sow and Keep Out to Reap!

DAY 3

Breaking News! We are at War!

"We interrupt your regularly scheduled program for this special report. Good evening, this is Roman Rhoades right in the middle of the town known as *Your Town and Country*, where we have just witnessed yet another blatant attack by Satan. It seems that the Devil has been prowling around like a— like a *lion, seeking whom he might devour*, to quote the inimitable Apostle Simon Peter. Satan's target this time was the **First Church of Your Town and Country!**

"He took advantage of the young and inexperienced pastor by influencing the people to argue over whether or not to paint the church. Well, they got into such a power hungry conflict over the issue that one prideful word led to another and the people decided to split the church. The young pastor has resigned, and two of the deacons are actually fist fighting!

"In a related report, our sources are reporting a marked increase in crime in this and other towns. Again, we believe that Satan and his demons, through society's increased tolerance in recent years to drug use, provoked this crime wave. His attacks upon the family unit have helped him to encourage many young people to turn to gangs for a sense of belonging and support. The resulting rise in violence and criminal activity has many scared to leave their homes after dark.

"We have just learned that new political leaders related to organized crime have succeeded in gaining widespread support to legalize gambling and recreational drugs, after the big victories by Satan some years back to get expanded acceptance for liquor by the drink and expansion of licenses for bars.

"The previous mayor, after a string of bizarre decisions related to his affair with singer Letter A, has run off with thousands of dollars from the town budget, making the transition almost unopposed for the evil group of new leaders backed by the syndicate Bad News.

"In other news, our Wallop Poll has determined that due to the bad economy, we have seen an alarming trend toward cynicism and pessimism among active Christians we polled, many of whom recently lost their jobs due to their factories moving their operations to other countries. This move came after behind the scenes negotiations included kickbacks, bribes and even government officials approving the exit of hundreds of manufacturing facilities to locations overseas. The decision to reward these companies with low import tariffs made no sense whatsoever, yet the government tried to make it look like a good deal for consumers. The greed to open those factories overseas at a fraction of the cost of stateside facilities seemed to go unnoticed.

"Sadly, and for no explainable reason we could determine, many of those unemployed have decided just to leave their families in order to pursue quick fortunes in the new gambling casinos that Satan convinced many areas nationwide to welcome in order to create more jobs. The downward spiraling economy and the bleak outlook for better days are to blame for several persons taking their own lives in the past month.

"Let's go live to our religious affairs reporter Agape Love, who is on the scene near First Church for some Breaking News. Agape, what is going on?"

"Roman, we have just learned that an alarming number of people have quit reading the Bible, citing it as an irrelevant and antiquated book. Many have decided instead to allow their church to use the Koran and other religious books as alternative guides for living. It was no secret that for several years now, many of the area ministers had begun to preach sermons based on culture and topics of interest instead of basing their messages in Scripture.

"The findings of the Wallop Poll about how of all this is affecting the home became quite evident in an alarming statistic that came out just today from City Hall. Findings indicate that one in three marriages of active church members ended in divorce during the last five years. Most of those seem to have left the church just prior to or during their marital crises.

"Roman, anyone who has ventured out lately knows that hunger and homelessness are at an all time high in YOUR TOWN AND COUNTRY, yet the remainder of members after the split of the First Church have decided to use their entire surplus budget for painting the building and for new uniforms for their basketball team.

"Roman, let me share a little background on First Church: Considered for years as one of the strongest churches in the entire region, the events of late in this congregation were just so unexpected and so out of character for them. It's like an evil influence just came over the church and gradually overtook many of them with pride, greed and an air of apathy and selfishness toward the community that for so many years had seen that fine church reach out to so many.

"Instead of their annual mission trip to the *Othercountry*, they voted just before the split to use the funds for the trip to get a brand new church bus. We learned last week that the same thing has happened in *Megacity, Small-Town*, largely because of the example of First Church and other well-known congregations. The Wallop Poll has seen a rippling effect from such compromise and weakness among USA churches. It seems that even Othercountry wants to follow suit. There is no doubt in this reporter's mind that the Devil is at the bottom of all this, influencing anyone he can to turn away from God and listen to his half-truths and deceptions.

"Roman, after all these desperate attempts by Satan, I am pleased to report that finally—*finally*, many of the denominations, have decided to meet in order to pray and fast, study the Scriptures together and determine if anything can be done about these acts of aggression by the *Enemy*, before if it is too late. They have been in meetings closed to the press all this past week, and we are awaiting word from them in an announced press conference at any moment.

"That is where we are at this point, Roman. The church of the third millennium has just concluded that unprecedented emergency session and we have been informed that they are about to make a statement about the meetings. We have been told that the statement will be made by the Pastor, Dr. W. W. Jay Dee— oh, wait, here he comes to the microphone. Let's hear what he has to say."

"Good evening. I am Pastor W. W. Jay Dee. I am representing a meeting just held, which included all the leaders of the major denominations of evangelical Christianity. What an exhausting but exhilarating week we have just experienced! After three days of arguments, bickering and griping, one dear brother suggested that Satan just might be at the bottom of all of our poor fellowship and self-serving attitudes. Many agreed and what followed was a day of prayer and fasting, testimonies and Bible studies in small groups, followed by a time in which hundreds confessed sins of pride, arrogance, greed and secret sins known only to the Lord. Many asked for forgiveness for wrong attitudes and actions that they had permitted to dominate their lives over many years. Still others just confessed how far their lives had drifted from God. We laughed, we cried and we rejoiced in what was nothing short of a genuine revival among us.

"What began as an hour to celebrate the end of Satan's bonds turned into three more days of God's people falling on their faces and repenting...I mean *truly* repenting of sin and *genuinely* seeking God's face. It was unreal, but was the sweetest and most precious time of worship I have ever known.

"When we came back together, we were overjoyed to see that God was in control of the group again, and we all finally agreed that the worldwide church has no other alternative but to make a *Declaration of War* against the vicious, malicious and unprovoked attacks by Satan.

"This meeting comes after years of attempting to ignore the reality of the Devil and his demons as they constantly influenced elements in church life and work to distract, disrupt and discourage, an already confused and drifting church from our *Great Commission*, given by our Lord to go, preach, teach, disciple and baptize. It comes on the heels of well over a hundred years of ignoring our *Great Commandment* from Jesus Himself, to love God with all of our hearts, souls, minds and strength, while loving our neighbors as we do ourselves.

"We concluded that the damage is serious and the church is very sick in many places, even dying in other places, but in dire need of revival in nearly all corners of the globe. As a result, we feel the church's impact is far weaker than at any point in recent history. It was a unanimous conclusion that only the divine intervention of our Lord will rescue God's people from an even worse decline in the years to come.

"Therefore, we concur that the church has no alternative but to go all out in Spiritual Warfare against the forces of evil. This comes after several centuries in which the church endured many difficulties caused by our inadequate responses to world events. Now, when I speak of the church, I mean all denominations, from all the theological horizons of evangelical Christianity—which I might add, was no small miracle!

"We concluded that the widespread decline in the church's impact on lostness and spiritual growth was the result of internal strife. That strife caused many divisions in the local churches. Many testified to the successful attempts by Satan to bring moral and ethical decline to a critical burn point in which we find ourselves today.

"Terrorists in the guise of religious groups, as well as a host of false religions both outside and inside the parameters of Christianity threaten to destroy the true church, indicting us as hypocritical, uncaring and disobedient to the mandates of our Scriptures. Even as we speak, there are those who propose a syncretistic theological adjustment in the form of a new version of Christianity, which embraces the belief systems of many religious movements such as Islam, Hinduism and Buddhism. In the guise of this new heresy, those who are promoting this argue that such a religion would bring us all together under some relativistic higher being that they would call *Godallah*.

"Of course, we know too well, who is at the bottom of these as well as many other influences designed to operate and flourish. Battling the biblical viewpoint, Satan worked in the background for years, convincing the minds of so many Christian leaders to listen to the world, the flesh and yes, the Devil. He purposed to move them to the pleasant sounding liberal compromises in how see and relate to the Bible, to Christian ethics, core values and subsequent theological positions.

"Fine leaders, whom we value as some of the great minds of 20th Century Christianity, unwittingly moved in the guise of sophistication and academic pursuits, toward unbiblical positions about many social ills and moral choices. This all occurred as our theological institutions had moved toward positions that treated Scripture as more of an academic document than the living Word. In a century and a half, Satan had subtly moved the church away from the heart reaction to the Word and its powerful capacity to draw us toward God instead toward the world. Much of what we were hearing in seminaries and even in pulpits brought alarming contradictions to how the Bible should operate in our minds and hearts, as Hebrews 4:12 reminds us:

"For the word of God is quick, and powerful, and sharper than any two-edged sword, piercing even to the dividing asunder of soul and spirit, and of the joints and marrow, and is a discerner of the thoughts and intents of the heart." (KJV)

"In our prayerful discussions, we agreed that Satan tricked us into bringing many of the church's downfalls upon ourselves. A large part of the nineteenth and the twentieth century saw biblical studies moving us toward scholarly, intellectual pursuits of Scripture as it relates to history, philosophy and world events.... studying about the Word of God to the exclusion of allowing that Word from God to impact their hearts and lives. However, praise be to God, He has finally been permitted to move in the hearts of some believers in order for them to see how this academic or clinical dissection of God's Word has stripped believers of spiritual power. Many are beginning to see that power only comes from allowing God's Spirit to influence the study of His Word. Another words, we see the exegesis and careful scholarly examination of Scripture as essential, but only as it leads the reader to really seek His face in genuine repentance through effectual, fervent prayer. We conclude that the Devil made a crushing blow in this regard over the past one hundred and fifty years, to which we must launch an even more powerful and aggressive counterattack!

"We cite those seemingly noble academic pursuits with the Bible viewed as any other book, vehemently contesting the view that the Bible merely *contains* truth instead of *being truth*. We declare that those well-intentioned efforts went from theological classrooms to the leadership in local churches where those seminary students ended up. Unfortunately, their having been influenced by those erroneous assertions just naturally influenced lay people who trusted these leaders to guide them in their churches. We further indict Satan for being subtly and astutely behind this frontline attack.

"We declare our full awareness and condemnation of his worldwide assault upon morals and ethics via news media, entertainment and the commercial exploitation of human nature, further weakening the church's influence. Now we can see how astutely and subtly the Devil influenced average church members to have a casual view of Scripture and a weakened influence upon a lost and dying world. Now we can see the deception of a largely secular worldview as a response to the needs of that world. Now we see that negative influence upon worship, evangelism, discipleship and stewardship.

"It is clear to us that because of Satan's negative influences, many churches began to decline in the quality of worship and quantity of worshippers. Decisions in major denominations soon began to reflect the trends of the secular worldview instead of the biblical worldview. What we are seeing today in many parts of the world is a weak church guided by the world's sin-sickened and politically correct responses instead of an empowered church as a source of salt and light for that sin-sickened world.

"In the meantime, Satan has unleashed an evil assault upon the world while the church has blindly followed his lies, by deceiving us in what we truly need to be happy, healthy and prosperous. His laughter is almost audible in the actual results of his worldview influences like: exponentially rising crime rates. Another result is the astonishingly passive acceptance by society to drug abuse. Who can ignore the rise of openly acknowledged promiscuity, abortions and abandonment as the solution to promiscuity? We are outraged by the expanded access to legalized gambling. We are appalled by so many more open doors to pornography. How quickly the secular worldview changed how we view homosexuality and same sex relationships! These alarming trends influenced a wide range of societal ills, like the traditional family flailing and failing, the rising popularity of false religions, and an even greater indifference about hunger and poverty, prejudice, hatred. The prevailing secular worldview seeks a compromise of biblical convictions. Really, there is not enough time or ink to list all of the contradictions to clear Biblical teaching as Satan promotes the elevation of the secular worldview over the biblical worldview.

"Our days of meeting led us to conclude that if left unchecked, we give Satan permission to cripple what is left of the witness of God's church in this world. We know God has allowed Satan to be a sort of *prince of this world*, in order to challenge His church to be the very contradiction to all these ills aforementioned—to cause us to be His army of redemption and liberation from the attempts by His already defeated, fallen and struggling angel of darkness. We conclude that we were temporarily blinded and backslidden into retreat—no more! I repeat, no more!

"The so-called "downward pull" of evil is intense at this point; so much so that ethics is now being commonly viewed as a case-by-case or situational reaction to the exclusion of God's input. At the same time, absolute truth is seen as closed-minded responses to progressive thinking. Consulting and obeying God through His patterns for obedience in today's world is perceived as an attack to modern intellect and a threat to societal sophistication. In other words, we increasingly view common sense Christian responses as examples of backward ignorance, interfering with personal freedoms, progress, prosperity and pleasure.

"Today, the Holy Spirit led us to see this evil direction. We confirm what God warned about in Scripture, how both Christians and non-Christians alike are inviting the judgment of God, as in the days of Noah; that is, by believing, saying and doing what is right in our own eyes, rather than seeking the absolute truth from the Sovereign Creator of the Universe (see Genesis, chapters six through nine).

"As we prayed and discussed all of this, we couldn't help but see the obvious irony in how those goals of progress, prosperity and pleasure have been eluded throughout human history by all who followed the secular worldview. At the same time, the principles of God's absolute truth consistently brought to all who chose to follow Him the right forms of progress, prosperity and pleasure...as taught by Jesus. We are thankful for the benefits from God that qualify the quality of life: love, joy, peace, patience, goodness, kindness, gentleness faithfulness and self-control... against such there is no limiting their influence on the way we live and move and have our being (see Acts 17:28).

"Our consensus is that while some local churches have made great strides over the years to defend against the fiery darts of the evil one, the overall efforts of God's people to follow Him truly as soldiers of the cross have not reflected our total love and devotion for our Lord. We further conclude that the church has become unable to launch any type of strong, unified offensive against Satan. To the contrary, the church has just been able to put up a rather sporadic and weak defense against Satan and his wiles. We have been far more interested in promoting our self-centered personal goals and focused upon our non-essential doctrinal viewpoints, instead of *being the church*...looking to one another as the body of Christ to join forces in a strong offensive of worship that fights evil with all of our hearts, minds souls and strength. Our churches have become mirrors of the world's values instead of reflections of God. Sadly, we have to admit that in general, evangelism, discipleship, fellowship, stewardship and missional living have suffered serious casualties—We are guilty as charged of not reminding Satan he is already Hades bound, and convicted that we have faltered terribly in showing the world we love and care for them.

"All of this influence by the world upon the church greatly hampers efforts by many mission boards, denominational agencies and other partnering missionary sending organizations. Much of Christianity has internalized, introverted and self absorbed to meet the needs of the church institutions rather than growing as the body of Christ, boldly exporting to the world the glory of God through His Great Commission and Great Commandment.

"We reluctantly face the reality that our moral and ethical disobedience, coupled with our apathy, cynicism, infighting and lack of commitment to genuine worship, evangelism, discipleship and stewardship, have brought the church of the third millennium to a state of decline and weakness, causing us to have the worst identity crisis in the history of Christianity.

"In the missional response of the church to a lost and dying world, we find ourselves constantly experiencing what some describe as an epidemic case of three steps forward, only to counter that advance by four steps backwards. Ironically, this trend has developed at a time when we have more tools at hand and more trained leaders to multiply ourselves to spread the Gospel than at any other time in history. We are actually losing ground daily in the fulfillment of our Great Commission (Matthew 28:18–20) and seeing fewer and fewer victories in the positive obedience to the Great Commandment of our Lord in Matthew 22:36–40.

"You among the press have received a printed copy of what I am about to read to our viewers and listeners worldwide. This will be translated into all known languages so that all of our Christian brothers and sisters can understand what we, as a worldwide church of many denominations, are about to undertake.

"Simultaneously reading in various languages with multiple interpreters, our meeting delegated us to read to you this important statement of faith."

"Roman, this is Agape Love again...let's listen right now to what may be the most historical declaration in the history of Christianity. We will be hearing the English version as read by W. W. Jay Dee. Seated behind him are delegates from at least twelve of the evangelical movements."

"Therefore, to the entire world, both Christian and those who follow other religions or no religion at all, we respectfully ask for your attention as we testify to what the Lord God Almighty has shown us during these days of prayer, fasting and worship. We hereby make this Declaration of Spiritual Warfare against Satan and his demons.

"We are sick and tired of Satan discouraging, distracting and defeating so many of our brothers and sisters, despite those same Christians having access to the living Word and to effectual fervent prayer in order to fight him. Somehow, he has tricked them from reliance in the promises and power available through the Holy Spirit. Enough is enough!

"We are fed up with Satan tempting and testing some of our best leaders to the point that they fall prey to sin and lose their testimonies. Using what Hebrews 12:1 cites as "the sin that so easily besets us", he attacks at our weakest points of resistance—no more! We must be more ready than ever before!

"We are fired up with godly anger and zeal over the growing trends toward a secular worldview, while distorting and confusing people from following the biblical worldview. Satan has successfully launched against the church. He perpetrated these trends through his general assault upon the morals and ethics of the secular world. This has gone on while the church seemed to ignore or to be blind, deaf and dumb to his wiles and our responsibility before almighty God—no more!

"We unequivocally declare that Satan is a defeated, fallen angel who along with his demon followers has no power at all over true followers of the sovereign God, the maker and ruler over all things. All that he has succeeded in perpetrating through lies and trickery must end. We will do all possible to alert God's people so that they will accuse and rebuke the Devil of these lies, in order to realize God's desire for all believers. We stand alert and vigilant, knowing that God awaits each believer's submission to Him before He will show us the final and glorious return of his son Jesus Christ! We want to be ready! We must adjust to be ready!

"Therefore, we commit this day all of our resources to sweeping out evil with true repentance, filling or sowing the void left by true repentance with the fruit of the Holy Spirit—keeping out permanently the Devil's constant efforts to return and potentially reoccupy the repentant heart with even more intense evil. We commit to put on the whole armor of God as described in Ephesians 6:10–18. We know this is possible if we maintain close fellowship with the God of the Word through effectual fervent prayer, while gaining a greater knowledge and understanding of Him by a deeper love and application of the Word of God.

"This declaration comes at a time when we have the possibility to reach out to the very ends of the earth with the love of Jesus Christ. It comes at a time when our level of communication and technology can help us to fulfill our deep desire to see the entire world know the Savior. Therefore, such a leading from God compels us on this day of our Lord to declare that the church of the third millennium, made up of over one thousand different evangelical groups, begin today to educate and offer the orientation necessary for all of God's people:

1) **To know what spiritual warfare is,**
2) **To know who the enemy is,**
3) **To mobilize all true followers of Jesus Christ,**
4) **To fight like we have never fought before in the battle between spirit and flesh and**
5) **To show Satan that we will not bow down and allow him to win any longer!**

"We base this Declaration of Spiritual Warfare upon the following facts that will become the foundation for an all out counterattack against Satan, in obedience to Christ! We would like to ask you in your small groups to announce each of these foundational principles for basic training at this time."

"Roman, that seems to be all Rev. W. W. Jay Dee has to say for now. We will continue to follow this breaking story for weeks and months to come….this is Agape Love, back to you, Roman."

"Well, you´ve just heard the **Declaration of War**, by the church against Satan and his demons. At this time we have been informed that the declaration and a list of foundational principles of spiritual warfare for Christian soldiers is being distributed to thousands here, as well as being simultaneously transmitted by e-mail, website and blogs worldwide. It is being translated into all known languages and dialects that have an oral or written copy of God´s Word. We´ll be watching as we witness a world engaged in spiritual warfare. This is Roman Rhoades for CBS, NBC, ABC, CNN, BBC and GloboSBT, saying good day and God bless!"

OK, I hope this dramatization will help you to get a handle on just how serious spiritual warfare is, how it affects your life. In *Day 4* we will get to know spiritual warfare better, by homing in on some key facts and foundational principles for Christian soldiers. This basic training will help you to understand and apply the principles of *sweeping, filling and keeping out evil* at the most basic and common points of attack.

Sweeping Moments for Today...

Do you remember the report by anchor Roman Rhoades along with on-the-scene reporter Agape Love? Suppose that the church actually did make such a declaration. Discuss the following questions:

1) Do you think that the situation of evil in the world is that serious?
2) What would be the inherent problems of such a meeting?
3) How would you approach your church about the presence of evil influences?
4) What would you suggest that your church do to enter into serious spiritual warfare?
5) What would you add or take away from such a declaration of war against Satan?
6) What would be your response to the indictments made by the fictional Pastor W. W. Jay Dee about the condition of the church, and God's people who make up that church?
7) Just how serious is the spiritual condition of the church today?
8) How is Satan winning his temporary victories? In what ways is it evident that he is actually losing?
9) In general, how are God's people responding to evil in society today, even without such a declaration of war against evil? Relate this response to how your church is responding to evil. Discuss how you personally respond to evil.

DAY 4

❦◌❧

Back to the Basics—Getting the Troops Ready for War!

"Hello again, Roman Rhoades here to resume our breaking news broadcast. As you have probably heard or seen by now, the Christians have declared an all out war on evil, on Satan and his evil army that is. A list of foundational principles was distributed successfully throughout the world. Our reporter on the scene, Agape Love, has joined one of the small groups of a local church here in *Your Town And Country*, to give us a better understanding of just what this spiritual warfare is all about. Some are calling it the *Basic Training for Spiritual Warfare*. Agape, fill us in on the particulars of this training so we all can begin to get ready to fight as Christian Soldiers of the Cross!"

"OK, Roman, I am here with Rob Hefner, one of the coach/ instructors for this group of twelve believers. Let's listen in as he goes over the specifics of spiritual warfare as outlined in the Foundational Principles that were agreed upon in that historic meeting that we have just witnessed. The next voice you will hear is Pastor Rob Hefner, a veteran missionary to Brazil, who will help this group to get ready for war! I want you to imagine that you are in that small group with Pastor Rob right now, as you read these basic facts about spiritual warfare. Some of these basics you will have learned about already during your Christian walk, while others will be an introduction to real, honest to goodness battle against the forces of evil."

"Hi, I'm Rob Hefner, and I'll be walking you through this basic training exercise. These *Foundational Principles* were distributed to all of us just a while ago, so we will go steadily but slowly through them. Please, please stop me if there are any you do not understand, so we can back up and make sure we have the proper orientation to move forward with our main tools: effectual fervent prayer and a love for the Scriptures. OK? Let's pray and then dive right in!

"Father, we love you and praise you! We ask your presence as we seek to become better soldiers in your spiritual army. Guide us to come to an understanding of these most basic of basic principles for battling Satan, so that we might stand strong against his astute, sly and cunning wiles, knowing that not only did you create him but that you can actually use him to grow us into the God-followers that you would so desire us to be! For we pray this in the mighty name of our Supreme Commander, Leader and Chief, Jesus Christ, Lord of Lords and King of Kings....AMEN.

"We'll be going over these steps one-by-one...

1) **Spiritual warfare is the celestial battle for your soul, even though it is fought primarily on the battlefield for your mind. However, that battle is won in the trenches, on your knees.**
2) **Spiritual warfare has as its only objective to honor and glorify the true God as expressed in Scripture. This objective only can be recognized by the way His people respond to evil. Essential to that response is obedience to His commands, instructions and principles as held forth in the Bible.**
3) **Spiritual warfare is all about trusting God to apply in your life what is good, godly and right, in order to**

cancel or crowd out what is bad, ungodly and wrong; that is, what is evil.

4) Spiritual warfare is a process, based upon one basic, singular and unique response to the expression of God's unmerited favor, best known as salvation by grace.

"We call the resulting response to God's free gift of grace salvation. Only after you know in your heart that you are all of the following, can God truly fight spiritual warfare with you as His soldier, fighting for you, through you and in you. In order for all of us "recruits" to be on the same page, ready for war, take time to explain or mentally process what each of these descriptions of salvation mean to you. If you are unsure about any, go to the verses indicated beside each description. If after reading, you are still unsure, go to a trusted believer or your pastor and ask for help. If you are studying in a small group, you might want to invite a pastor or trusted believer to help the group pin down a complete understanding of salvation. No one can "graduate" from basic training for spiritual warfare without first having experienced salvation first hand. That would be like sending a soldier into battle without a rifle, rations, survival gear or even a uniform!

Descriptions of what it means to be saved...

Being born again (John 3).

Being regenerated (Mt. 19:28–30; Titus 3:3–6).

Being reconciled with God (Rom. 11:15; 2 Cor. 5:18–20; Eph. 2:16; Heb. 2:17).

Being redeemed or rescued (Hosea 13:14; Luke 1:68; 1 Pet. 1:18; Rev. 5:9; Ps. 107:2).

Being justified (Acts 13:39; Rom. 3:4, 20, 24–26; Rom. 4:25; Rom 5:16–18; Titus 3:5–8).

"How amazing is it that your salvation is all of these descriptions combined, yet so much more than the sum of their implications! No matter how you describe it, the same essential and wonderful experience is necessary to be a soldier of the cross. You cannot fight the forces of evil in your human or natural strength alone. You can try, but sooner rather than later, you will fail as all others before you, that tried measures other than salvation to fight the good fight against evil. Only through faith in what Jesus did on your behalf are you saved from an eternity dominated by evil, spiritual darkness and separation from God and all God desired for your life. If you do not know with absolute certainty that you are saved, take a moment to read these verses and pray to receive Christ as your Savior...right now!

Here are some key verses to study:

1 John 5:13; John 3:16–18; Luke 22:39–24:9;

Romans 3:23; 5:8; 6:23; 10:9–13; Romans 12:1, 2;

Galatians 2:20; 5:16–25.

"After reading these verses, talk to God in your own sincere and honest way, telling Him that you are sorry for making yourself the boss or centerpiece of your life. Confess that you are a sinner, as well as bringing before God all of the sins you can recall, asking for God's mercy and forgiveness, even for those and sins you will commit in the future.

"Tell the Lord that you desire to accept what Jesus did on the Cross as your free gift of grace, knowing that there is nothing you could do to save yourself from eternal separation from God, apart from God doing it through His Son. Just tell God that you want to be— *(Fill in this space with all of the terms you have just read about from the salvation verses. Be absolutely sure that you know the meaning of each description before moving forward).*

"Now take the time to talk to God, expressing how much you want Him to control and guide your life from this day forward, making Jesus *the* Lord and *the* Master of all you think, say and do. Now if this section of the book is stirring your heart right at this moment, then we both know why He led you to pick up this book in the first place!

"There are church members and churchgoers among most all bodies of believers who have yet to experience this stirring of their hearts. So if this fact of omission or incompletion has been your best-kept secret for days, months or even years, don't let pride or embarrassment be Satan's tools to rob you from this most basic and most awesome of steps as a soldier of the cross! Just pray right now, let go and let God save you as you pray this prayer with Him."

Your Voice: "Lord, I know that I am a sinner by nature and by choice. I know that there is nothing that I can do in or of myself to resolve this condition. It separates me from your desires for my heart here on earth as well as my destiny for all eternity. Only the free gift of Jesus dying on the cross is sufficient to pay the penalty for my sins. I believe in my heart that He arose on the third day in order to bring victory over the grave. I will confess to all that will listen that I accept Jesus as my Lord and Savior. I confess my sins and ask forgiveness based on what Jesus did for me at Calvary. I invite Him into my heart and life. I know that at the moment of my salvation, that God himself in the person of His Holy Spirit will come into my heart to guide me through life's challenges. Thank you for coming into my life right now, and for saving me. For it is in Jesus' name I pray, Amen."

"Be sure to tell someone who is a believer of your decision to follow Jesus. Use this book each day, in your devotional moments, with God, along with your Bible, of course. If you are not already a part of a church, visit churches until you find one that preaches the Bible as the Word of God, and is involved in living out the Great Commission (Matthew 28:18–20). The church should be one that offers you opportunities to live out your faith through evangelism and discipleship. When you find that local body, request that you be baptized in order to make public your profession of faith in Jesus. You may already know of a church like this.

5) Spiritual warfare is the process of the Christian being and doing what honors and glorifies God.

"He loves us and wants to include us in this spiritual warfare as His instruments. God could have blotted this evil darkness out at any time in history. However, He chose to commission us, His followers, in this process, to be the instruments to dispel, dismiss and defeat evil. This is so amazingly cool! God fights the battle against the contrasting darkness or evil that He permits to exist for a determined time frame known only to Him. Even more amazing, He allows us to be actively involved in the spiritual warfare! When good wins over evil, God is glorified. God created you and me to honor and to glorify Him. This honor and glory cancels darkness and permits light to shine. That light can be physical or empirical light, but in its perfect form is symbolic of the light of the world, Jesus Christ, to whom is given dominion to reign and sustain when we call on Him. That personal relationship with God enables us to resist temptation from evil, evil influences or spiritual darkness. God's Spirit, living in the saved believer, fills the believer with the necessary ammunition, for resisting daily attempts by evil to invade our daily walk.

6) **Spiritual warfare depends upon the believer acknowledging the indwelling presence of God.**

"Jesus promised this in John 14: 16–17, 26. This Holy Spirit is God entering your life to give you what you will need to fulfill His purpose for which He created you; that is, to honor and to glorify Him (see Acts 1:8). In Galatians 5:22–25 we see what the Holy Spirit makes available to the believer. This *fruit of the Spirit* exists so that you can live supernaturally, or above what the world's evil principles offer. Those offers by the Devil and his evil band equal enslavement to all sorts of evil influences. The attacks by evil are described in Galatians 5:16–21 as the *works of the flesh.* Those evil works are just the short list of the many other works of the flesh. Spiritual warfare, then, is the battle for your heart, mind, soul and strength. It confronts and seeks to neutralize the godly and perfect attributes as described in Galatians 5:22–25, best known as the ***fruit of the spirit.*** We will deal with these in greater detail, as we learn and grow as soldiers..

7) **Spiritual warfare is the appropriation or permission by the believer for the fruit of the Spirit to operate in the way you think, walk and talk,** in order to win or to have dominion over the influence of the works of the flesh. God won´t *make* you engage in spiritual warfare, but He will *empower* you to win every time if you give Him the chance; i.e., permission!

"You can read volumes of material about spiritual warfare. If you wanted, you could **"Google"** *Spiritual Warfare* right now, and spend countless hours following up on the entries about it. I did this, but did not expect to see spiritual resistance by Satan so abruptly! So intense is Satan's hatred for sincere servants building blogs and sites about spiritual warfare that I found one of his "influenced by evil" examples as I surfed. Someone had hacked a spiritual warfare site! As I searched, I randomly clicked on links, which led me to churches and organizations that had posted sites or blogs about the topic. I clicked this one site, put up on the web by a small church. The first link the church listed for reference to warfare led me to a stolen link with invitations to enter pornographic sites. Apparently, their simple site had been hacked by some evil people, so that every time someone went there, sincerely seeking help with spiritual warfare, that person was thrust into the heat of the battle by being redirected to a smut site! Satan is desperate to influence in any way he can. *Do not ever forget about his desperation to hang on by harassing your desire to glorify God.*

8) **Spiritual warfare is the expression of your faith in Jesus Christ in the face of an evil world. Your expression includes practical expressions of all of the nine attributes collectively known as the *fruit of the Spirit*, in Galatians 5:22–25.**

9) **Spiritual warfare is all about winning the victory over evil influences by developing a godly pattern for responding to temptation, tests, trials and actual involvements in sinful thoughts, attitudes and practices.**

"Since Adam and Eve, we have been infected or inflicted with the inherited sin nature. At the same time, God has given us free choice or free will to make evil or good decisions. Following God's influence in making the right decisions is the victory, because those decisions bring honor and glory to the one who created us. They reflect or give testimony of that influence to a world that so needs that living hope for daily living.

10) **Spiritual warfare is the battle on both individual and corporate battle lines.**

"Whether alone or in the larger context of the church family, the goal is resisting and overcoming the inherent evil that God has allowed Satan yet another attempt to test His soldiers. We can only overcome that evil through a close relationship with the Almighty God who loves us so much that He has gone before us onto the battlefield. God fights the battle for us as we march on His orders and carry out the battle plan. Never reverse the order of these two principles: God fights as we follow, trust and obey His instructions, counsel and direction for life.

11) **Spiritual warfare has certain limits as set by God, as to how far He permits the Devil to attack a faithful soldier who is actively seeking God's power.**

"In your spiritual battles against evil, how long will God permit evil to tempt and to test you? Sorry, but the answer to that is with the Almighty, only known by the Sovereign God, according to His will and purpose for your life. However, we do find in 1 Corinthians 10:11–13 that we must be alert at all times and not overconfident or cocky in our spiritual warfare. We are comforted as Paul reminds us that no temptation has come upon us that someone, somewhere, sometime has not already endured. He reminds us that the test or temptation will not be more than we can take if we are following orders to be alert and staying close to the Commander, who will provide a way to victory or a way of escape from the evil, but only if we listen up for His instructions. The Devil can't *make* you do it...he can only suggest that you turn a spiritually deaf ear to the spiritual battle weapons available to you!

"One pervasive question haunts all soldiers of the cross. Why has God permitted us to confront and endure temptation and testing by Satan? We discover the answer to this question by examining the lives of many Bible personalities from the perspective of how they dealt with evil. Adam and Eve, Cain, Joseph, Job, David, Jonah, Simon Peter are a good start at understanding the why of evil. The list could include many Christians throughout history right on down to you and me.

12) **All soldiers become better soldiers after seeing action on the front lines.**

"After you have battled the Devil in some real challenges to your moral, ethical or spiritual being, you emerge with experience in trusting God, and practical applications of the promises of God. That experience advances your rank to veteran! That time spent battling evil makes you an invaluable soldier! Your sharing or passing on your battle experience is the best description of what we call discipleship.

"Nevertheless, you still might be asking, "What does God expect me to learn from spiritual warfare?" From both biblical and contemporary incidences of battling evil, we learn that in spiritual warfare, we have as our supreme commander the omniscient, omnipotent and omnipresent God who permits us to confront evil. This walking with God through the trenches of temptation happens often, in order for you to become familiar with God's strategy. It enables you to recognize His warnings, His disciplines, His teachings, so that you understand His process for bringing you to a more mature stance against evil. Your spiritual sight and hearing are sharpened. Instead of feeling guilty and helpless all the time over falling prey to evil, God sharpens your senses to allow Him to place you under conviction instead of guilt. Guilt leaves you defeated, downtrodden, hopeless and helpless. Conviction from God leaves you aware of the problem, repentant and ready to seek God's direction for moving upward and onward. This means that you will understand sooner what is going on with evil, and understand how God wants you to correct and recalibrate your focus. This experience better equips you to resist, rebuke and defeat Satan's attempts. How awesome it that!

13) **Ultimately, the result of spiritual warfare is to test God's true church. While God desires that we always trust Him to resist temptation and testing, He knows our weaknesses and the chinks in our spiritual armor. So like in the case of Job (read chapter one), He will even use the fallen angel of darkness to bring you to a point of greater spiritual strength and resistance to evil. God can use those moments in which we are tempted, or even cave to the point of sin.**

"The true soldier of the cross will have a closer relationship with the Lord. That relationship will allow the soldier (you) to see how God tests our metal and refines us in the fire of testing. The test is used by the Lord to confirm whether we will continually submit to evil and suffer the consequences, or trust God to lead us into a state of repentance and contrition. The test affirms for the Father that we have trusted Him enough to do battle for us, with us and through us.

14) **In passages like James 1:2-4, we learn of the many blessings derived from the process of Sweeping Out the Demons.**

"As you develop a love and a growing familiarity with Sweeping, Filling and Keeping, you will readily identify many passages of Scripture in which these principles actually function. In this passage from James, we see that the result of genuine repentance includes some great character builders. We fill the space left empty by that genuine repentance with qualities like perseverance, humility, complete brokenness, total submission to God, along with many more. The filling moves your life toward genuine maturity as a believer. It is a *letting go of control and letting God have control of a specific area of your life.* God sent that message to biblical figures in the form of both Joseph (positive) and Jonah (negative) type lessons! Likewise, God allows the skirmishes and brushes with evil in our lives, in order that we might humbly recognize the Lord God as the *only* source of strength, comfort, joy and lasting peace. Only then can we as a church give God our undivided attention and our unlimited honor and glory. In addition, this growing maturity changes the very way we view temptation and testing.

15) **Spiritual warfare, ignored or poorly fought, can result in the soldier becoming a worthless or unfit follower of Christ**. That condition can endanger the spiritual lives of many of our fellow soldiers. They can become confused and discouraged by your disobedience or negative reaction to life's bumps and bruises. Even worse, as Paul described it, that soldier could become a castaway, with self-styled weapons that are obsolete and useless against the fiery darts of Satan (1Corinthians 9:27 and Ephesians 6:10-18). While one's salvation is secure in Christ Jesus, one's march as a soldier in spiritual warfare can be rendered useless by a growing distance from the commander-in-chief, our Lord.

16) **You cannot fight spiritual warfare well without a clear understanding of the enemy's core value...evil. What is evil?**

Evil is the opposite of what God desires for you.

Evil is the negative response to the positive King of Kings and Lord of Lords.

Evil is anything that contradicts what would result in the Father's ultimate and comprehensive best for His redemptive purpose.

Evil eventually leads to an all or nothing response, even though the evil process itself may appear to be only a partial denial of what is good, godly and right.

"To understand that fact you must be reminded that the half-truths or half-lies of Satan result in a partial denial of Gods absolute truth. They always result in a gradual or eventual all out dive toward evil. That momentum of evil is a force that will take you farther from God's purposes than you ever intended or imagined. This is a principle I like to call the *downward pull*. Like gravity, evil has a very firm pull on your heart, mind, and physical energy to draw you away from what you really know to be right, godly and good. Evil always has as its goal your total destruction. That is, *only* if that power is permitted to keep on pulling you down or away from God's desires for your heart, mind and strength. You as a soldier need only apply the principles of Sweeping, Filling and Keeping in order to resist and neutralize the downward pull. The starting point for that process is an inner resolve to let go and let God have control of that area of your life you have deemed to be out of control.

Evil can evoke a series of wrong or inadequate choices for how you invest your stewardship of the three *"T's" (Time, Talent and Treasure)*. Your life here on this planet is comprised of three commodities: *time, talent and treasure*. God presented you with a threefold stewardship identity: another way to describe this triune of blessings is to describe your life as who you are or whose you are, what you can be and what he entrusted to you as the means to invest your time and talent—three "T's"! Satan will mess with you daily by seeking to gain control of one or more of those "T's". Watch out for signs of his interference!

Evil always results in eventual harm to relationships with God, with others, and ultimately, with one's self.

Evil violates the principles of common sense and genuine wisdom, as well as affecting the relationships between your entire physical world and your Maker. It impairs how we discern absolute truth by distorting it with the truth as perceived by the world, the flesh, and the Devil.

17) **Spiritual warfare must be fought based on the premise that the believer recognizes the enemy is a created being named Satan.** Satan's greatest deception is that people believe and declare that he does not exist. So do not fall for the sophisticated *theologs* or the enlightened *philosophs* who would suggest that evil is only poor choices. Others will state that evil is simply unfortunate circumstances, a question of chance or just dumb luck. Others claim it to be "bad karma" or negative energy or the changing momentum of life— please don't fall prey to these inadequate rationalizations for evil influence from and evil supernatural being.

"Satan, the Devil is real. Knowing who he is the first step in spiritual warfare, and will go a long way to prepare you for confrontations with his influence and astute tactics. Admission of the reality of Satan can protect you from his efforts in manipulating you to fall for his half-truths. The principles of **Sweeping, Filling and Keeping** will provide you with the adequate tools for discerning the character and objectives of Satan. Please remember one more thing. For heaven's sake (pun intended), do not fall for the mythological images of good and evil as being fought on level ground, from the perspective of two equally powerful sides. Satan is *not* an equal and opposing force to God, as many civilizations and world religions have purported in their traditions, myths and legends. God is, was and always will be, immutable, ageless, boundless and limitless. God is the creator of all things, including matter, time, structure, substance, visibility and invisibility and yes, evil in contrast to good. Satan is a created being, as reported in Scripture, as a fallen angel who vaunted himself up in pride and arrogance to consider himself equal to and even more important than God (see Isaiah 14:12–15, Luke 10:18 and Rev. 12:7–10). The Devil is not omnipotent, omniscient or omnipresent. Jesus confirmed the existence of his fallen angel army as He dealt with demons. However, make no mistake: the Lord is always in control and always totally perfect, completely powerful and in total authority over all of His creation, including Satan.

"You must deal with the problem of good and evil in theology, philosophy and practical daily living. There is a conflict in how each of these "schools" deals with the problem of good and evil. Never be mistaken or deceived into entertaining for even a nanosecond that God is not supreme and in control of the Universe. Satan was defeated when God cast him out of heaven. His existence began when God created him and it will end when God expels him into the lake of fire. Satan has been given certain powers and capacities here on Earth, but only as much rope or leeway as God allows, giving all humanity the opportunity to choose life abundant and everlasting or to give in to the efforts of evil to turn us away from God's best for us.

18) **Spiritual warfare is dependent upon a full understanding of whom we are battling.** The Bible itself refers to that enemy as Satan fifty-two times. That name means "adversary". His existence is verified in seven Old Testament books and

in all of the books in the New Testament. Jesus himself refers to him in the gospels twenty-five of the twenty-nine times while teaching about him; whereas, he is referred to as the Devil thirty-five times. That name Devil means "slanderer or maligner". In Scripture, we find many other names for Satan, such as the Evil One, the serpent, the dragon, the tempter, Beelzebub, the prince of demons, he that is in the world, the prince of this world, the god of this age, the deceiver of the whole world, the ruler of the kingdom of the air, the power of darkness, the spirit that operates in the sons of disobedience and the accuser.

19) **Spiritual warfare is fought best when you can clearly identify the enemy and his host of demons.** Military basic training illustrates this well as a popular movie illustrated several years ago. The sergeant takes his ragtag squad of recruits out for a run. He slips away from them momentarily, only to ambush them with gunfire. Scared to death, scrambling for cover, the men finally see their sergeant emerge from behind a bush to declare that what they have just experienced is the sound of enemy gunfire. It has a distinctive sound when fired, and is the preferred weapon of your enemy.

"Likewise, Satan has many preferred weapons, and you *had better* get to know the distinctive sound of each one of them. Like recognizing enemy gunfire, knowing who he is and what he is capable of can give you the edge for victory over temptation and testing. As coaches urge their players to know the every move of their opponents, so you must know Satan's every potential move. This knowledge can make you *own* him! Even though he is a defeated foe, he wants to cause you serious setbacks or sideline soldiers of the cross like you. In so doing, he surmises that his days might be prolonged before his final destruction. This should give you a clue as to how desperate Satan is to survive a bit longer. My friends, there is nothing more dangerous than an opponent who is feeling threatened, desperate or fearing defeat.

"You can and you WILL win repeatedly if you will focus on God and recognize the Devil's desperate efforts to pick your vulnerable or weak moments to tempt, test, influence, discourage or confuse you. Such an offensive by Satan must be defeated with your counter offensive of effectual fervent prayer, along with a deep passion for the Bible. So what do we actually know for sure about our enemy?

Facts That We Do Know About Satan

"He was apparently a very prominent angel in heaven, but chose to raise himself above the Almighty. In so doing, he and his angelic host were expelled from heaven (Isa. 14:12-15; Rev. 12:7-10).

"We can ascertain that this celestial demotion occurred prior to the creation of man, as evidenced by the evil one impersonating a serpent in the Garden of Eden (Genesis 3). His activity throughout time has been spent wandering all over the earth, seeking to exalt himself above God in whatever way possible (Job 1:7).

"He is under the dominion and power of God, as evidenced in Job 1:7–12, when God placed Job in his dominion so that Satan could test Job's limits. God did this so that Job could fulfill his created purpose: that his life might bring honor and glory to the Lord. Through enduring terrible suffering and loss, Job honored God as he learned many lessons about his relationship with God, with others and with himself. Again, Satan was rebuked as Job's life response reminded him of God's sovereignty.

"In his temptation of Jesus in the wilderness (Matt. 4:1-11), once again Satan is shown to be under the dominion of Almighty God, unable to tempt Jesus with any of his primary strategies, namely, catching his prey while at an emotional or physical disadvantage. This time he used hunger and fatigue as the context of vulnerability for tempting Jesus. Then he used his most impressive arsenal of temptations, like presenting half-truths or shrouded offers appealing to ego, pride and power. Then Satan tried presenting Jesus with the possibility of becoming greater than God. Note in the passage how Satan made this attempt using one or more of the senses and catalysts for the temptation.

"We know that a key tactic in the temptation included compromise. Satan offered Jesus gratification of self at the expense of full obedience to God.

"We know that his attempts included an offer for exaltation of self at the expense of testing God's instructions.

"We know that his goals included the necessary condition of Jesus engaging in some form of idolatry at the expense of worshiping God.

"In the case of the Apostle Paul, Satan was used by God to test Paul with an affliction that served to show others how much Paul trusted in Christ (2 Cor. 12:7). On another occasion Satan hindered Paul from visiting the Thessalonians a second time (1 Thess. 2:18).

"The works of Satan are summarized by the promotion or instigation of temptation with the objective of influencing lies, false witness, false doctrines, works of the flesh (Gal. 5:16–20), idolatry, or any violation of any biblical principle that exalts God. Examples of these biblical principles are the Decalogue (Ex. 20:1–17), the Sermon on the Mount (Matt. 5-7), the Great Commandment (Matt. 22:37–40 and the Great Commission (Matt. 28:18–20).

"One of Satan's greatest weapons is to sidetrack or detour your mind so that your focus upon God is distracted. One way spiritual warfare can be derailed is by engaging in meaningless debate about his existence or about the attitude of the believer concerning his evil influence. This pointless debate introduces another tool of Satan, gossip.

"Another way he sidetracks the believer is by using extremes about his existence. For example, some might dismiss the Devil as superstition or archaic ignorance on one extreme, while others might exalt the Devil's importance to the degree that one places Satan on an equal plain as Almighty God. Both extremes need to be avoided by basing your stance upon what we can learn from Scripture, both statements about Satan and implied facts about him in the context of Scripture.

"Theory and philosophical rambling about Satan, demons and evil in general hinder spiritual warfare. Meaningless debate about such matters should be left to bars and godless classrooms. Since only the One Who Always Was, Is and Ever Will be can explain these questions, let's make sure we all know what those questions are, and avoid wasting valuable moments of spiritual warfare by giving undue attention to them.

"As you talk about God, Satan, good and evil the following is by no means an exhaustive list of the many ways to become hopelessly sidetracked...but it is a good start!

Why did God permit evil to enter the world in the first place?

Is God sovereign if there is evil in conflict with His divine nature of justice, goodness and perfection?

Where is Hell or Hades, according to the Bible? Is it a literal place or an invisible state of separation from God?

Why would a loving God engage in eternal punishment instead of universal acceptance?

Who decides what is evil and what is good?

What is the difference between absolute truth and conditional or situational truth?

Would evil even exist if everyone chose to make the right choices in life?

"So right now, why don't you just get this debate out of your system? Take a stab at trying to tackle these ageless issues. Then, take time to talk these questions over with the *one* who controls the controls, so that finally you can relinquish to God the responsibility for answers to these age old questions. While you are at it, go ahead and give over the other debatable questions that may have crossed your mind.

"If you will acknowledge and relinquish to God the outcome or possibilities of these matters, you can trust that He will guide your mind into much more important spiritual matters. This is a great example of how to work through the process of **Sweeping, Filling and Keeping!** The issue of meaningless debate over serious focus on what really matters could be an excellent test sweeping for you to get your feet wet in using this formula to battle evil and temptation at its most basic level. Follow the process as follows:

What needs to be swept here? Questions that you have no control over, yet take expansive amounts of thought and energy, subtly and astutely stealing that time which could be spent considering matters for which you can wage spiritual warfare.

How do I allow God to sweep this time and energy draining issue from my life? I have to identify the specifics of the sweeping. As we mentioned earlier, these are the most prominent of the unfathomable questions for which I can only debate, arriving at only possible solutions, with no real answers. The filling is giving this time spent on these to practical applications of the fruit of the spirit, knowing God alone will answer them in His time and in His perfect wisdom. Filling with the fruit will avoid Satan's attempts to reoccupy by bogging you down with any of these questions.

"The rest of your orientation will continue as you keep out this sweeping from returning. Like all sweepings, effectual, fervent prayer and a deep connection with Scripture will help you to maintain your position. Fight the good fight, and declare resistance with persistence and insistence that Jesus is *Lord*! So friends and fellow soldiers worldwide, from this day forward, you need to follow carefully what the Apostle Peter admonished us to practice in order to maintain this sweeping."

Wherefore gird up the loins of your mind, be sober, and hope to the end for the grace that is to be brought unto you at the revelation of Jesus Christ; As obedient children, not fashioning yourselves according to the former lusts in your ignorance: But as he which hath called you is holy, so be ye holy in all manner of conversation; Because it is written, Be ye holy; for I am holy. (1 Peter 1:13–16 KJV)

"Thanks, Rob, for allowing us to listen in on your preparation of the troops for battle. You really did go back to the basics today, and gave us a lot to ponder over as we continue our basic training. I believe that you will continue tomorrow with a more up close and personal look at spiritual warfare...is that correct?"

"Yes Agape, as a matter of fact we will be sharing about my own spiritual warfare and how God has taught me how Sweeping, Filling and Keeping is the key to really winning this war on a daily basis."

"We'll look forward to hearing about these very personal and real conflicts...This is Agape Love turning it back over to our anchor, Roman Rhoades...Roman..."

"Man, Agape, what a challenge to take in all that Rob has shared today. The leaders have distributed a sheet with some questions for the spiritual mentors like Rob to use with their local groups. I believe I am also going to need to go over them before the next broadcast. This is Roman Rhoades signing off for now. Good day and God bless!"

Sweeping Moments for today...

After joining in with this "broadcast" from over in the fictional *Your Town and Country*, recall what you have read about these basic training facts about spiritual warfare. Discuss within your group or if reading individually, with a friend, which ones stand out most to you as essential to truly Sweeping, Filling and Keeping out evil.

1) Fill in these blanks from the first statement in of basic training about spiritual warfare: Spiritual warfare is the_____ battle for your_____, even though it is fought primarily on the battlefield for your_____, and won in the trenches on your_____.

2) For you, which of the nineteen basic training statements are the *most* basic to being a great soldier of the Cross? Why did you choose them over the others?

3) When we talk about getting back to the basics, the fourth statement and the subsequent explanation is the most basic of the basics. Are you "squared away" on this one? Do you know anyone that is not good to go on this most important of basics? If so, begin now to pray for that person and for persons of peace to come into their lives so that they might be saved.

4) Look at basic training statement number sixteen again, re-examining the basic training statements about evil. Now, play a game in which you and your group try to recall as many statements about evil as possible.

Now take a few moments to pray, asking God to show you how Sweeping, Filling and Keeping can be applied here to cancel out those statements about evil.

5) Number 16 and 17 are all about recognizing your Enemy. Take a few moments to look back at those basic training statements and describe our Enemy. Now take some time to describe God, listing all of His amazing and wonderful qualities! Then recite out loud this verse like you mean it from the depths of your heart: "...for greater is He who is in you, than he who is in the world." (1 John 4:4b)

DAY 5

Spiritual Warfare, Up Close and Personal

"Rob, this is (<u>place your name here</u>). I have started this book but I'm more than a little bit skeptical about all of this Sweeping, Filling and Keeping business. Ok, let me get this straight...so what you are saying is that spiritual warfare fought as a so-called faithful soldier of the cross (you know, the way God would have me to fight), will literally change my whole life?

"Oh, come on **now!** I have read just about all the "How to" books, and participated in many Bible studies about spiritual growth. So please forgive me, but you can imagine how doubtful I am that this book has any more to add to all our small group studies and twelve-week series at church. I mean, hey, they all promised pretty much the same thing and I have to tell you, they have been interesting and a real blessing and I learned a lot from them. But, they never live up to the promises for results in my life. You have heard it said, "If it's too good to be true, then it probably is". Well, what you are claiming in this book sounds too good to be true!

"Nevertheless, Rob, hear me out before I move on, because, what you have proposed sounds very sincere. You take me to Matthew 12:43–45, like it's some kind of Holy Grail. From that passage, you go on to say that a positive response to what Jesus tried to teach those Pharisees will result in sweeping out, or truly repenting of temptations, bad habits, poor attitudes and other destructive behavior. You explain that the man in Jesus' story is cloaked in a metaphor of a house. His "house" was the man's personality and how he responded to the world. You are saying that my life is cloaked in that same metaphorical "house"! The house also describes my personality and lifestyle. In Jesus' example, you state that the man swept his "house" (or life) clean. Then you associate such repentance as basic and essential to spiritual warfare—all right, I get that.

"Then you are saying that is not enough, that such repentance that has swept the "house" clean will only temporarily lead me away from anything that contradicts God's desires for my life, leaving Satan room to reoccupy that swept part of my life. I understand how Satan re-enters and causes a worse mess than before. Then you reiterate that the original audience of Pharisees heard what Jesus was trying to teach them about their own "houses", but would not listen. Finally, you conclude that we don't have to respond negatively like those stubborn religious people. Rather, we are to not only repent, but also fill the empty space left by the repentance with something far better. In the case of the Pharisees, that positive response would have been truly worshiping God, developing a relationship of loving devotion. This was in contrast to a hollow, empty set of religious rules and regulations to follow. OK...so far, so good. But you state that I can apply this principle to any situation in which evil is on the onslaught and emerge victorious...well I have got to say *whoa* here...hold on a minute.

"After all that I've studied and read on spiritual warfare, you mean to tell me that the simple key to true spiritual transformation and soundly defeating Satan's evil desires for my life is to permit God to fill those empty places where bad stuff existed with godly attitudes and actions? And am I understanding correctly that you are seeing this accomplished by submitting to God so that my life can be armed with the whole armor of God, as instructed by Paul in Ephesians 6:10–18? I hear you saying that this armor will make my life available to God's Spirit, in order to make room and give the permission necessary for Him to guide me to make practical applications of His fruit of the Spirit in Galatians 5:22–25. In addition, do I understand correctly that it is all about asking God to guide me to fill or to sow into my life something far better, so that evil is effectually crowded out and evicted from my walk and my talk?

"Then you say that any time Satan attempts to revisit my life where God has swept clean and replenished (filled) that space with actions and attitudes based upon the fruit of the Spirit, that evil can no longer have access to the same sins and temptations in my life.? Finally, you are implying that by staying in the Word of God, freely talking and really listening to the Lord in my prayer life will permanently keep out any junk involving those same evil desires? Man, I'm sorry, but don't you think that's somewhat simplistic?

(Now imagine that I am talking directly to you.) "Well, **(Your Name)** that is exactly what I hope to help you to understand! For one thing, most of those studies that both you and I have been involved, approach these scriptural truths from many different perspectives...and do this quite well, I might add. It's just that I have been very blessed to receive this truth in a way that was easy for a fellow struggler like me to understand and apply. Any biblically based book or study on spiritual warfare is important and I encourage you to read and study as many of them as possible. But what all those works will teach you can be more easily and effectively put into practice after you begin to apply the principles of sweeping, filling (or sowing if you prefer) and keeping out (or reaping, if you will).

"Therefore, I would like to inspire you in today's section to understand how and why I know this to be true, by sharing from my heart to yours about some spiritual warfare victories in my own life. Possibly a word of testimony about how I have battled the enemy using these principles of sweeping, filling and keeping out will encourage and inspire you to see why I know these truths to be proven and powerful. My heart's desire is for you to get out there and sweep, fill and keep out evil while experiencing God's desire for you...consistent and permanent victories over evil!

"After losing to Jesus when Satan tried to tempt our Lord in the wilderness (Matthew 4:1–11), the Bible testifies of a defeated, scared and humiliated Devil, as evidenced at the cross. In Colossians 2:15, Paul reminds us that Christ "having spoiled principalities and powers", i.e.: disarmed Satan and company, "he made a shew of them openly, triumphing over them in it (KJV)". Another words, Christ made them a public spectacle, soundly defeating them with the cross. Actually, long before that, like from the very beginnings of battle with God, Satan had a growing dark cloud of dreadful desperation as he impersonated a serpent in the Garden. In Genesis 3:15 we see that the deal had been sealed already as to his sure and certain demise.

"However, (**Your Name**), this is the kicker and a comforting key to spiritual warfare: Satan has always been under the dominion and power of Almighty God! His arrogant stand and boundless pride makes Satan unwilling to admit the lordship of Christ, the sovereignty of God the Father, or the pervasive and all invasive presence of God's Holy Spirit indwelling the believer. Knowing and trusting in that overarching key changes everything for all who seek to fulfill the Great Commission. This key is above, below and surrounding the spiritual warfare soldier's every attitude and action!

"I am sure that you might be asking yourself at this point, (**Your Name**), why in His world God would permit such exponential growth of evil during the ensuing years of history.

Throughout Scripture, we see intense spiritual warfare has resulted in dynamic spiritual victories for God's people. Culminating with the mandates of the Great Commandment (Matthew 22:36–40) and the Great Commission (Matthew 28:18–20), we can see our marching orders for this final stage of the intense spiritual warfare of the third millennium. In the twenty-first century, God allows the worst evil as both warning and challenge for his people. The warning flashes boldly in this escalating level of evil, as a reminder for all humanity of what happens when people disobey God's desires. In like manner, this evil serves as a bold challenge for us to draw ever closer to the Lord through God's communication system of Scripture enjoined with effectual fervent prayer.

"His perfect will is the same as in the beginning: that His creation would honor and glorify His name in all we say and do. The tension between good and evil is God's instrument to mold us into His likeness and image. That is the same image and likeness that all humanity has possessed since man was created (Genesis 1:26). The image of God and the mission of God both advance as God's followers engage Satan in spiritual warfare, day in and day out, until all is fulfilled that God has allowed to occur, in preparation for the Glorious Appearing of His Son Jesus Christ...WOW! And to think, (**Your Name**), you and I are vital and important soldiers in that battle!

"Fighting evil with the orders to go as missionaries into all the world had to make Satan know that the end is imminent. Then to declare that God followers like you and I would act out of a complete love for God...well, it's no wonder we have experienced so much resistance from Satan over the years.

"Spiritual warfare, my friend, *is* up close and personal, because any spiritual victory over evil during our thirty years in Brazil was met by evil attempts to tempt us, test us or discourage us into whining for mercy and quitting, so that we would retreat in defeat back home to the USA. These attacks, often very intense, showed us vividly that the evil one was threatened over Kingdom advances that we were witnessing. For the Devil, I suppose that this reminds him that he is arriving ever closer to the final conflict. I tell you, Satan has tried his best repeatedly to send us packing and begging for the intensity of the spiritual battle just to cease fire for but a moment! However, in war, the final battles are always the most intense, so we have seen and experienced that intensity in our spiritual warfare in Brazil's Amazon Basin and then later in the idolatrous northeast. Perhaps the battles that await us will make these previous ones seem tame and weak attacks, so no matter how hard it has been at times, my wife and my son and I know that we must trust God even more than ever. As the old chorus reminds us, we need to prepare ourselves for even more intense spiritual warfare...:

> *I wish we'd all been ready,*
> *There's no time to change your mind,*
> *The Son has come and you'll be left behind.*

Or, as we are reminded in Jeremiah 12:5:

> *If thou hast run with the footmen, and they have wearied thee,*
> *then how canst thou contend with horses? and if in the land*
> *of peace, wherein thou trustedst, they wearied thee, then how*
> *wilt thou do in the swelling of Jordan?*

If you read the entire context of chapter twelve, then you will see that what God was reminding Jeremiah, and us, is best summated in the "Rob Hefner Southern Colloquial Paraphrase Version":

> *Soldier, if you think it was tough up until now, and you are*
> *all worn out, then you had better get more ready than*
> *ever before, because you ain't seen nothing yet!*

"So please, (**Your Name**), allow me the privilege to share
with you in the next few pages, how this warfare has fleshed out
in our lives on the mission field of Brazil. Then maybe you will
see more clearly how God can sweep doubt and feelings of defeat
from regular folks like us. And I'm talking about intense battles
that communicated what Jeremiah was feeling in chapter twelve
when he asked the Lord why so much evil was winning and how
much longer He would allow that evil to persist.. I'm talking
about battles that made us actually hear the voice of Evil telling
us to give up and quit before something even worse happens.
God filled the empty space left by our repenting of feeling sorry
for ourselves, complaining and looking back at home, family and
the familiar with His positive message in Philippians 4:13, and
the affirmation of victory in 1 John 4:4, leaving us with a clear,
sharp level of thinking so that we could move forward in victory.

"Of the many experiences we had during our wonderful years
in Brazil, God used this experience perhaps as no other, to keep
us from ever again allowing Satan to defeat of destroy hope in us.
And believe me, he has tried very hard over and over again long
after this account I am about to share. He has tried to reoccupy
that place of defeat and discouragement that his demons so wanted
to return to. But this experience served as an irrefutable example
of God's amazing promises to lead us, guide us and direct us when
we follow Him. It was at that time that Matthew 12:43–45 was
shown to me during some deep soul searching Bible study.

"In 1987, when we lived way out in the Amazon Basin, our
nine-year-old only son was bitten by a little tiny "doggie" named
Guerreiro (Warrior). A few days later, the dog, which had been
kept hidden in the house of his owner, our neighbor, was already
very sick, unbeknownst to us.

"After a few days, while cleaning house one afternoon a
compelling urge that she still cannot explain turned Phyllis' eyes
toward the window at the exact moment when the dog escaped

into the street. She was able to see the dog briefly, as he spun, wobbled and fell, retching and foaming at the mouth. Phyllis immediately knew it was rabies and we freaked! We now know with certainty that the urge to look out the window at that exact moment came from God's angels, because she also saw our neighbor quickly scoop up the sick dog and rush back in their little house. Friend, you are NEVER fighting evil on your own. ALWAYS, God is engaged and involved in your spiritual warfare.

"Not only had the dog bitten our son Ray and badly scratched Phyllis several of days earlier...but also had bitten or scratched several of our neighbors as well. Since time was running out for protection against the rabies, we were horrified of whether or not we could beat the infection and its fatal symptoms before too late.

"At that point, Satan seemed to audibly whisper to me something like", Look what you have done! You have taken your little family out into the middle of nowhere and gotten them killed! You fool!"

"At that very moment, I was overwhelmed with feelings of panic and despair. They were more intense than anything I had ever experienced, so all alone in the bathroom of our house, I stopped and prayed, hands shaking, my mind only able to imagine the worst. But at that same moment, God reminded me of Philippians 4:13, almost audibly saying, "Rob, you can do all things through me strengthening you!"

"I suddenly felt a calm flow over me that I cannot explain. Panic subsided and I began to think clearly and decisively again. In an instant, I just *knew* exactly what steps to take. First, I convinced our dear neighbor and friend to go with us to a "vet" and get help for her dog. I drove us to a guy's house that had an extremely makeshift veterinarian clinic, in the front room of his little house. He recognized the rabies right off. He convinced our neighbor that she would have to leave the dog with him and that it would soon die. We took our neighbor back home, all of us now in tears. We saw her to the door and then frantically packed to get out and board a plane..., which is another miraculous story in itself. We lived in Marabá, out in the southern portion of the Amazon Basin, hours from the capital city of Belém. Travel out of Marabá was very limited and difficult in the late 1980's...but not for God!

"While Phyllis waited with Ray and Nazaré at the vet's little shack, God made a miracle as we prayed for a plane going out of Marabá to Belém, the closest base for this kind of medical treatment. God clearly told me to go to BR Central Airline's little office. I forced every step to get there, because Satan was sending all kinds of negative, discouraging messages to me..."they'll be closed, and it's almost impossible that they would have one of the six seats available on such short notice." God would not allow me to listen to those dark whispers in my mind...He just kept making me hear repeatedly, Philippians 4:13, as though God's Spirit was whispering them right in my ear as I almost ran down that street! But they *were* open and there *was* a small plane going to Belém, but the few seats were already booked. However (I just love God's *however messages),* the guy that usually worked there was gone, and another guy that I had worked with previously was there! I had gotten them a lot of business via our American teams from Arkansas that had visited a few months earlier. Nervously, I explained to him about the situation and he declared it a crisis emergency convincing three persons to wait for another flight two days later so that we could fly out that evening!

"So that night we were met in Belém by other missionary colleagues who took us to the most modern hospital available, where they informed us that it was just too late. They said that the rabies had incubated too long, so what would be our best move would be to go home and make my wife and son as comfortable as possible, until all the symptoms of rabies began to ravage their brains and nervous systems. I was numb. I was in shock. Phyllis was in tears and little Ray just did not know what to think at this point. "This time, Satan almost seemed to yell in my mind's desperate rambling."

"Fool! You ought to have known that you could not get them here and win over this disease. Give up, take them home and just admit it...they are going to die! It will be easier this way. You all three are so tired and it is so late, so why don't you just call it a night? Tomorrow, go and get passages for the USA, fly home to North Carolina, so that Phyllis and Ray can get proper care and die surrounded by family."

"We were all devastated. In the restroom of that hospital I began to weep and pray, pleading with God. I will never forget the almost audible voice I had ever heard, in all my days as a believer. In my *mind's ear,* as I love to reflect on such God-moments, our wonderful Lord reminded me through a sort of personalized paraphrase, of 1 John 4:4.

"You are mine, (Rob, Phyllis and Ray), my little children, and you have overcome all of this, just you wait! Hold on a few more hours, because greater is He that is in you than he that is in the world."

I was reminded at that challenging moment that God uses His Word to fill the spaces where true repentance has left Satan empty, void and homeless! I regained my composure and most of all, felt a powerful restoration of my spiritual fruit—all that love, joy and patience that God had given me when, just hours before, I had asked Him to sweep out the doubt and fear, replacing it with love, joy and patience. It came flooding back to my troubled heart that some weeks before, while studying Matthew 12:43–45, God had given me a Word of knowledge as to what these verses would mean to me and others in years to come.

"I just instinctively *knew* what to do next—the exact opposite from what Satan had whispered in my ear earlier! I asked the other missionaries if they knew of any other doctors in Belém that might have more experience with rabies. Our dear friend, who is a missionary nurse, knew of a doctor who had just arrived in the city weeks before. His specialty was infectious diseases! She made some calls to Brazilian friends and finally was able to contact him. Within hours, he was injecting Phyllis and Ray with their first of many anti-rabies shots. About two in the morning, he called the "vet" in Marabá to gain more information about the situation. The vet was summoned to the community phone. He told the doctor that the dog had died shortly after we left his house. He said that he had already contacted the health officials of Marabá who informed him that there was no more anti-rabies vaccine available in the city due to other rabies incidences that had recently been reported to them. That meant that all of our friends who had been bitten or scratched were going to die if nothing was done. The doctor told the vet to cut the head off the dog and put it on ice so that I could bring it back for pathology at the state health department. That dear doctor then packed me up with enough anti-rabies serum to treat fifty people. The next morning I left Ray and Phyllis in Belém and flew back to Marabá on a *very* small plane, where I retrieved the dog's head, packed in a Styrofoam beer container. You should have seen the looks of terror I got when the pilot asked me what was in the Styrofoam container I was holding so carefully!

"Upon returning to Belém, the miracle continued to grow, as the health officials diagnosed this rabies as a very rare variety, very deadly in nature. The persistence that God gave me in that bathroom thirty-six hours earlier had now saved not only Phyllis and Ray's lives but also all of our neighbors who had been in contact with the rabid dog. Our neighbors were very primitive and very superstitious, not to mention very angry over having to line up and receive the vaccine that the doctor had sent back with me. Their superstitions reasoned that because we *thought* that the dog had rabies, that our suspicions had caused it to be so! Even after these victories over evil, Satan was trying to work through the situation to destroy our witness among our jungle neighbors with whom we had been trying to witness and plant a church.

"But we had experienced decisive victories! Phyllis is still by my side in the battle nearly thirty years later. Ray is grown with a precious wife, our daughter-in-love, Laura along with our two amazing grandkids, Mia and Jake. Always a missionary, even as a child, Ray felt called to youth ministry, where God has used his gifts and talents alongside his wife Laura.

"As for our neighbors, they were all saved from rabies and eventually all saved from eternal separation from God. A church they lead exists and flourishes to this day! Several months later, it came the time for us to go home on furlough. Realizing that God had saved their lives through us, their attitudes changed as well. the attitudes of our neighbors were inverted from anger to gratitude. After mentioning to them that we would like to take ONE Brazil nut shell (like a coconut shell housing three to five Brazil nuts) back with us to show folks in America, we were surprised and deeply moved by their outpouring of love. On the morning of our departure for the airport, we awoke to see on our front porch DOZENS of Brazil nut shells! It was their way of saying thank you. We just cried and thanked them and most of all, thanking God for how He had transformed our insecurities and fears into blessings. Five churches were planted during those three years in Marabá. Many leaders were trained. Sweeping out the demons was now entrenched into the depths of our spiritual warfare, and was promoted to the lead strategy for how we would battle evil forever more!

"God again reminded me of a verse that I knew so well that it had become perhaps too familiar; that is, until that day when God spoke it to me in a new and fresh breathing of His Spirit. Romans 8:28 came to mind as God whispered to my heart, "Rob, all things *do* work together for good if you keep loving and serving me. If you continue to obey and affirm that you are called according to my purposes."

"I will never forget that moment boarding the plane in 1989, for our first furlough in the states. I recall like it was this morning sitting down, closing my eyes for a moment, and recalling how God had brought us through a battle no less intense (or deadly) than soldiers of the cross are experiencing right now, all over the globe...(**Your Name)** and in your life!

"Spiritual warfare is all about sweeping out what would get in the way of God's unchanging purposes for us. It is all about filling the areas left empty by the sweeping repentance, filling that void with attitudes and actions consistent with the fruit of the Spirit as listed in Galatians 5:22-23. Though the entire list of nine is considered a singular "fruit" of the Spirit, each of the nine attributes of the fruit complement the others and build upon one another.

"Some years later Satan would test whether or not he could reoccupy my "house" with that same evil. Only this time, he would use depression, defeat and discouragement, at a time when our work was beginning to flourish. We had moved some years before to the northeast of Brazil, to the beautiful state of Ceará, living in the large coastal city of Fortaleza. Although the northeast is the most idolatrous and difficult turf upon which to evangelize, the people are wonderful and very receptive to hearing your witness. God was beginning to move in the hearts of many and leaders were being discovered and equipped.

"Then one night I was preaching at a church my seminary students had planted a couple of years earlier. My mom had died about a year before and I was still experiencing a lot of sadness from time to time. All of a sudden, I felt like I could not breathe! I was preaching but felt like I was suffocating. I told no one, kept on preaching and made it home. The panic attacks kept on persisting for months. I began to have stomach trouble, depression and feelings of such inadequacy that I did not even want to answer the phone, let alone go to the churches to preach. I just wanted to hide and sleep, while God wanted me to guide and keep! I prayed, I wept, I whined, and I slept when I needed to be awake, yet I could not sleep during the night when I should have been resting. Even though I was desperately praying for relief, my spiritual walk was faltering. My Bible and devotional times were feeling empty and without power. It was awful! Phyllis was consoling and encouraging but neither of us could take this much longer. It was so out of character for someone as happy and joyful as I usually am.

"So we prayed for a spiritual breakthrough, day after day, until God led me to start reading the book *The Purpose Driven Life*, by Rick Warren. I was desperate, so I figured I would read the book to get my mind off the panic attacks, trouble breathing, nervousness and stomach pains. In spiritual warfare, God often points us to indirect beachheads where we can prepare for battle. That book was one of those indirect beachheads where a fortress was planted. I didn't get very far into the book before I was reminded of the two egalitarian essentials of spiritual warfare, first realized years before in the Amazon jungle:

Key scripture leads to effectual fervent prayer, while at other times effectual fervent prayer leads to key scripture.

"Rick Warren wrote that book with hundreds of references to Bible verses. Each time he would call my attention to a verse, I would open my Bible and go there. Well, just like in previous times, it was like God audibly said, "Rob, stay here awhile and read the cross references to these verses in the center of the margins of that Bible that Phyllis gave you for Christmas, the first year after you met." It was very well marked with other notes that I had entered during the ensuing years of ministry. So I started cross-referencing the cross-references of the cross-references! Verse after verse just seemed to come alive again! At the same time, *I* was coming alive again! Before I knew it, I was remaining over in the Bible far longer than Rick's excellent book. A few months later, I collapsed during an evangelistic mission in another part of Brazil. I had to go to an emergency room where they treated and released me with a glucose I.V. I was losing weight rapidly and had lost my appetite. I was fearful that I had some dreaded disease—the stress and the anxiety continued to attack me, while I continued to work and to stay in the Word. I was seeing such fresh and inspiring insights in passages I had read and studied many times before. God was working a transformation in my heart, so I kept on trudging through these unexplained attacks upon my health.

"Six months later, I finally finished *The Purpose Driven Life*. Meanwhile, God had shown me how to pray for this healing and for the comfort that I really needed—**which was** not comfort at all, but rather equipping to return to battle, like a wounded soldier returning to war. He led me to a godly doctor while stateside on a Christmas vacation. Dr. Bob was able to diagnose me with Type 2 Diabetes. That was a miracle also, since I have never exhibited any of the classic signs of diabetes. I had been losing weight at a dangerous level for months when we got home to NC. He first assured me that I was not dying from some rare, dreaded disease, and then challenged me to change my diet, got me on the right medications and within three months I was completely well.

"Satan had worked on me during those previous months in ways that still scare me as I look back over those dark days. During those days of crisis, he brought to my mind some of the most evil and vile thoughts that honestly had never even crossed my mind—even before I was a Christian! He tempted me in ways I cannot describe, especially during the nights when I could not sleep. Satan is metaphorically equated with works of darkness in scripture, but I have to tell you that he works his wiles in physical darkness as well. For example, he seems to be best at such attempts to rattle you at night or when you are alone, isolated or feeling lonely. A couple of times he even made me think that I was dying. But sweeping, filling and keeping finally kicked in when I was spiritually conscious enough to remember this lesson and *react to the attack*. The same principles that had knocked Satan out of my "house" years before came back to give me a great victory. Satan is very astute at making you forget what you should remember, while helping you to remember what you really should forget.

"I had muddled along at times, continuing the work, even during those awful months, while God continued to build my health back. I do believe that even before I remembered about how I had worked on the Matthew 12:43–45 passage years earlier, that the need to sweep, fill and keep came into my consciousness as the way that God was performing a sweeping in my life in the form of the spiritual fruit of faithfulness. He helped me to continue to go through the motions of many of our missionary tasks even though I did not have my heart in them, wanting instead to focus on my physical ailments. God gave me just enough joy and peace during that time, and at the precise and perfect moments when I was ready to give up. Shortly after I got well and my heart was hot for missions again, the work took some unexpected turns that at first seemed like defeats. It turned out that those turns became the basis for the rest of our thirty years of ministry, and motivated me to begin writing and teaching the material which became this book!

"Our state convention split over who would control the Baptist Hospital. In order to sustain the momentum God was giving to the work, we had to leave our church we had help to plant, because they had taken one side of the convention division. In order to remain faithful to all the churches of the convention we had to remain neutral in their politics so that we could continue to preach, teach and plant among all the churches. So God chose this as the perfect moment for us to begin house church planting. It was a dream of many years, but I feared stepping out in such a bold and different direction. I had a sweeping to deal with, the fear of change and working outside the box for the added fear of losing the approval of those around me—a larger and more overarching sweeping called pride and dependence upon approval or recognition. So repentance began, and in came the filling of the void left by true repentance of that fear of being rejected. This filling resulted in the launch of what would become well known to most of the entire northeast of Brazil as **Igreja No Meu Lar... The Church in My House.** Godly partners back home contributed with prayer and material gifts and soon we were launching more house church starts than we had ever dreamed possible!

"God gave us a ministry tool called *Church Planting Jump-Start Kits.* We commissioned a "kit" of one time equipping materials to any church planting team that came to us with a viable project for how to plant and maintain a new mission work. Bibles, tracts, discipleship literature, a dozen or so plastic chairs and a portable sound system made up most kits. Satan went crazy over this, because he tried everything from car breakdowns to shipping and travel snags to keep these kits from going as far as a thousand miles away. Nothing worked for him—nothing! When we left for our final stateside assignment in 2015, one hundred and ten of those kits had gone out to teams. Those teams planted both house and traditional churches, which became bases for multiple church starts. After a couple of years, we could no longer keep accurate records of all the evangelistic groups, mission points and mission churches that came from those one hundred ad ten "kits", due to the rapid multiplication!

"Even today in North Carolina, in our retirement, our teams are requesting kits and requesting prayer for new mission points, all of which began when God graciously gave a missionary the idea to do a plan that would encourage young church planters to get started while not stunting their spiritual growth by creating dependency. However, know this: it all started by sweeping, filling and keeping out the evil of prideful desire to conform and to be recognized and approved by others. That all started when the Holy Spirit showed me something deep within a passage of Scripture that I had probably read many times—Matthew 12:43–45. This same way to fight in spiritual warfare can launch your spiritual warfare to the heights, if you will follow along and apply the process to the totality of the biblical message. It is truly one of those diamonds in the rough, which can make everything else in the Word, in the church and in your life move from the paradigm of good Christian living to great biblical obedience!

"So now that I have shared with you this up close and personal backdrop, let's enter into the personalization of the three principles for spiritual warfare in the twenty-first century. They come to us as a rediscovery from the first century. They come from the mouth of our Lord Jesus. The original audience, a group of proud and arrogant religious leaders called Pharisees, flatly ignored and rejected this message from Jesus. But you don't have to follow their *Jonah example*. Instead, you can react in the opposite manner from those religious leaders, and embrace what Jesus invited them to hear and embrace. Do not be just a religious person who does things out of legalistic duty. Hear the Word and obey it in your heart! Let the words penetrate your heart, change the way you think, act, and speak! Do not permit Satan the easy victory of lulling you to spiritual slumber with numbing religious activity. Be a God follower, a disciple of Jesus, not a mere church member! Read Matthew 12:43–45 again, right now. Make special note that your "house" as described in Jesus' story is **you**. You can be religious and try to do the right things by eliminating and even repenting of the bad stuff. That's a great start toward getting closer to God through obedience. However, when that repentance is complete, what about the space created in your time, talent and treasure by that genuine repentance or reform? Empty time, talent or treasure "space" will exist where the pride and arrogance once stood tall. With the availability of that emptiness or that void, Satan and his demons would love to take down the "vacancy" sign in your heart and occupy that space with even worse attitudes or actions than were there before you tried to make things right. OK, that is the quick start guide for Sweeping Out the Demons. Now let's get in there and take the process apart, step-by-step, to gain a thorough understanding of what it means to Sweep, Fill and Keep out anything that gets in the way of honoring and glorifying God!

1) **Sweeping** – God swept out depression, negative attitudes, offensive thoughts and unthinkable temptations as he led me to scripture verses of comfort, encouragement and victory. For example, the Spirit led me to see the real *enemy* of David as Satan, every time I read of David's many references to his *enemies* in Psalms. This led me to see sweeping is not of our many "demons" or affects of evil, but it is sweeping of the broad brushstroke attack by *the* Enemy! Deal with that Enemy and you will consistently sweep out all those smaller, more specific "enemies". The sweeping comes in the form of *genuine repentance,* in which I was not only truly sorry for my attitudes and thoughts, but also willing to become completely dependent upon God to sweep the larger source of the evil out of my life. I knew that my best efforts on my own would only provide temporary solutions and partial victories. Such efforts are commonly called willpower, inner strength or even such colloquialisms as when people tell us to "suck it up", or "man up", or even "grow up". Only when God is permitted to do the sweeping out of my willingness to place it in His hands, can I experience complete forgiveness

and complete restoration. But left right there, with mere repentance, standing upon its own, you have the potential for the evil to reoccupy that empty space left by the forgiveness and the restoration. Why is that? The answer, my friend is that you have an empty space or void in your attitudes, actions or behaviors, once occupied by the stuff for which you repented. This means that you must continue on, beyond that repentance into the next step in the process.

2) **Filling Or Sowing** – When genuine repentance takes place, it is a special and wonderful experience. One of the great things about true repentance is that the undesirable attitude or action is swept out of your personality and the way you relate to God, others and yourself. But at this point there is room or space for you to grow and to include the fruit of the Spirit in the place where you used to spend time in that negative attitude, habit or activity. Empty space will be filled by something, so be foreknown and forearmed that Satan is looking to fill it repeatedly with any one of a zillion versions of the works of the flesh as seen in Galatians 5:19–21!

"You must ask yourself and ask God, "How will I fill that void?" Only the best is fit to fill. Fill it with the love, joy and peace that come from forgiveness and restoration. Those fruit will build a basis for further filling with the fruit of kindness, gentleness and goodness. Those fruit emerge when I truly have space to listen for how God desires for me to involve in the Great Commandment and the Great Commission. I can begin to listen to God to sense where and how I might demonstrate His loving kindness, goodness and gentleness to those around me. This kind of filling effectually crowds out or makes impossible the re-entry of Satan and his demons as the fruit of self-discipline is permitted to flow. At that point, resistance to the so-called *downward pull* by

Satan is put into your warfare. This can disarm or disable Satan and his demons from making a return to that undesirable behavior that has been swept clean.

"The patience, faithfulness and self-control are then permitted to kick in since your repentance has left the necessary time, talent or treasure space open for good stuff. At that point, I should be experiencing a greater desire to wait upon the Lord. When the temptations occur and when the Devil attacks my most vulnerable weaknesses at the most opportune moments, I will feel a "nudging" to permit the Holy Spirit to give me the self-control to patiently assess the situation and return in prayer to Him. This will cause me to have that moment with God before saying, thinking or doing something that I might deeply regret. Soon those thoughts from the Holy Spirit dominate my thoughts so that when confronted with a similar situation, I allow God to show me the way of escape (1 Cor. 10:13).

"Remember I mentioned about David and his enemies earlier? Well, the Lord showed me an excellent practical application for the fruit of self-control, using the Psalms. As I read the Psalms, the Lord showed me how many times David pleaded for his enemies to get off his back, so to speak. There are also numerous passages where David is condemning his enemies, asking God to smite them or show them the error of their ways or even praying for their destruction. God showed me that David and me and you don't need to consider the *enemies* of David but rather the cause of all those enemies—that is, *The Enemy* who was and is at the root cause for all those other *enemies* that David had to deal with. The desires that David had for his enemies are the same feelings I can have about Satan when he seeks to make an assault upon my emotions, my health, my wealth, and ultimately, my relationships with God, with others and with myself. This is huge! It focuses our filling the void upon the one who wants to refill the empty space, rather than focusing upon the enemies with whom he wants to fill that void. If you sweep him out, you will effectually *sweep out all the the demons!*

"For me, God filled the depression and the panic attacks by showing me how to personalize some additional verses, like Proverbs 3:5 and 6, where He told me again, almost audibly, "Rob trust in me with all of your heart during this tough time. You are trying to lean upon your own understanding—don't! In all of *my* ways, acknowledge *me,* instead of fretting about dying, or giving permission for Satan to nurse and encourage all of those dark thoughts—like the ones that were coming to me in the night or when I was alone. This filling is realized when I begin to see how God is making my pathways straight.

A special note is necessary at this point: be sure to evaluate or assess how the practical applications are helping you to fill the void.

3) **Keeping Or Reaping Continually** – God can and will sweep out the attack as you genuinely repent, and He will crowd out the possibility of its return through the filling of the empty void left by repentance with practical applications of spiritual fruit. However, Satan is persistent and desperate to reoccupy your life, so he will just keep looking for chinks in your spiritual armor. As it turns out in my case, God has kept my life free of those panic attacks and depression as I pray and search the Scriptures daily. If you can think of this step as the process of maintaining the victory, it will make more sense and you will see continuous agreement with this concept throughout the scriptures. You will see this agreement in both Jonah type examples and Joseph type examples.

"In order to resist and keep out the counterattacks, *effectual, fervent prayer* moments with my Lord have led me to a *loving desire to seek out those special places in God's Word.* Through revealing many of these spiritual gems as I prayed, the Lord has instructed me to memorize them, so that I could call them up for active duty like troop reinforcements. I can recall them into sentry duty, to guard my mind and heart when Satan finds a weakness—for example, in the sweeping of late night temptations, the Spirit would convict me to keep off the TV and take the time to pray and go over my memory verses. Before I would know it, I was asleep again! Other weaknesses surfaced as ways for evil to attempt counterattacks of the worry, impatience and pride that had been previously swept and filled. Under the false security of darkness or the interference of stressful circumstances, Satan would try to guide me to make excuses for worry by throwing up past events when uncertainty and selfishness had been my coping mechanisms. Effectual fervent prayer and a return to loving devotion for God's Word seemed to vanquish Satan's attempts to bring me down to his level. This is an amazing experience!

"A frequent battle tactic of Satan is to use anything against you that you to manipulate your responses to spiritual challenges. Be aware right now that he will use everyday things like your computer mouse or cable TV remote for evil in the right context or environment, like in my case as deadly weapons when I was having trouble sleeping. He worked on me subtly during the night, when I was alone and convinced by him that no one could see, hear or know what I might try to click or watch.

"At first, it was difficult for me to see God's hand in all of this. Now I know that God permits these kinds of spiritual battles as tests. With me, He permitted this temptation in the night so that I might have but a brush with this evil danger in order to realize what the Devil was up to, before it was too late. Through times of effectual, fervent prayer He called to mind Bible verses like 1 Corinthians 10:13, in order to remind me that He would never tempt me beyond what I could withstand, and comforted me with a way of escape. My application of the third principle for *Sweeping out the Demons* has been the most rewarding and exciting! It has blessed me repeatedly, to know that *Keeping Out Evil* completes the triune formula for spiritual warfare in this evil time in which we find ourselves. It became the most powerful weapon for spiritual warfare, because prayer and the Bible become the foundation for the sweeping and filling to become ingrained and permanently, indelibly sealed into my spiritual warfare.

"Practicing effectual, fervent prayer, in order to develop a deep love for the scriptures, alerted my mind to yet another verse that I had taped to my desk years before, from Proverbs.5:7–9:

Hear me now therefore, O ye children, and depart not from the words of my mouth. Remove thy way far from her, and come not nigh the door of her house: Lest thou give thine honour unto others, and thy years unto the cruel:

"For me, late night television and the computer could have been the temptress described in Proverbs 7:6-27. For you that temptress can come in many forms. Solomon only described one, but she comes in many forms to many people. Satan uses her wiles to destroy holiness. My temptress is but one example. Satan always has a long and intricate skill set to trip up our soldiers of the cross. Long before my battle, in a subtle and astute strategy, the Devil was behind the influence of the minds that were able to drag TV content and web temptation to the despicable levels that we find in the twenty-first century!

"In my context of spiritual warfare, practical application of spiritual fruit had filled the void left by **genuine repentance**. My consistent time with the Lord led me to an application of love toward my Lord and to His church and to my wife, as ultimate and non-negotiable accountability partners, in order to destroy the risk value of the temptation. This third principle for sweeping also led me to put into practice the spiritual attribute of self-control. Conviction over the implications of such a situation gave me strength **not even to go near that potential temptation any more.** After that skirmish and possible ambush in the night, God allowed me to learn to retreat and regroup in times of tempting, testing and evil threats. God showed me that the result of these late nights would surely bring back all the panic and depression through regrets and potential consequences for falling prey to such a simple evil weapon as darkness for subtle attacks through everyday devices like TVs and computers. Meanwhile, God continues to heal much of the insomnia with the keeping out essentials of effectual, fervent prayer and Scripture memorization. Evil was kept out once again, and I was able to reap the victory on a continual basis. To God be the glory!

"The Devil will *never* give up on a weakness that you might have revealed to him at one time or another, so be on your guard by staying in the Word and keeping consistency in your real conversations with God. He will use such instruments of temptation as sniper weapons on your vulnerability. As it turned out the TV and the computer were the very things that helped to cause my insomnia to persist. I have to just exercise the spiritual fruit of self-control and cut them off at a certain time. The Holy Spirit has helped me to fill in those hours when I do find it difficult to sleep. Prayer and Bible reading returned as God's best, for filling the void and keeping out the evil onslaught of nighttime temptations and thoughts in the darkness of night. That sweeping dovetailed to prepare the way for another sweeping—binges of late night snacking. This culprit was how Satan could short-circuit principle three from having any chance for success. That tendency for massive late night snacking has been an ongoing sweeping over many years. It definitely has been what I could call a major stronghold, causing all sorts of health threats. The sweeping was responsible for elevating my blood sugar, thus causing more insomnia symptoms, thus making me more vulnerable to seek ways to fill in those hours when I could not sleep. That sweeping is what I call a chronic or critical battle line, definitely a tool for other evil skirmishes. But I am seeing God win this battle! Effectual and fervent prayer brings me to my knees and reading the Bible during those weak moments causes me to feel a deep relaxation in my body and soul that creates the environment for resisting the snack binges and resting in the Lord. This comes after years of difficulty going to sleep. I can sleep after I clear my body of excess snack carbs, and my mind of stress, worry and other evil clutter. The old Ray Conniff song that we played for years at Christmas time, pretty well sums up where effectual, fervent prayer has taken me during those long hours:

When tired and worried and I can't sleep, I count my blessings, instead of sheep, Then I fall asleep, counting my blessings....

A favorite memory verse of mine, Psalm 4:7–8 (KJV), states this same sentiment:

Thou hast put gladness in my heart, more than in the time that their corn and their wine increased. I will both lay me down in peace, and sleep: for thou, LORD, only makest me dwell in safety.

"Yet another tool God has used for keeping out evil is **prayer walking**. All of this healing came when God continually confirmed our prayer walking ministry. For nearly thirty years, it has been our mainstay for removing spiritual strongholds and strengthening us as soldiers in battle for God. As we walk we talk, pray, we visit with folks along the street, encountering all sorts of persons from all walks of life. Spiritual fruit grows in intensity for keeping out the evil as we submit to being prayer warriors. God has helped us to deal with a lot of junk while prayer walking, talking it through as He guided us along. Prayer walking is definitely a way to nourish your hunger for effectual, fervent prayer. Prayer walking reinforces important truths that God has shown us during our devotional Bible times with Him.

"Prayer walking improved our physical health (your "house" or "temple of the Holy Spirit") over the years. About one thousand miles or more a year is just how far we did walk over various routes all over our city and other towns. I experienced healing as a direct result of our prayer walking. Prayer walking strengthened our faith muscles beyond our fondest expectations, as we encountered all sorts of challenges and dangers along the way. Encounters with the street people were divine appointments. Some of them make a living by begging; others are either on drugs or selling them. As a result, some often steal on the side for survival, so we survived and thrived through three muggings, an attempted kidnapping and saw God protect us from many wrecks, robberies and other dangerous encounters. Most of all, we could end each day knowing the sense of peace and joy which comes from being obedient to that which God called us. Every ministry in which we were involved was affected by prayer walking: one-on-one evangelism, church planting, discipleship, Bible and literature distribution, benevolence, counseling and yes, even my seminary teaching was fortified by divine appointments we met along the way. This book would not reflect as strong of an offensive or defensive against evil had we not seen God guide us through some of the most frightening and intimidating of spiritual battles. Our very call to Brazil was entrenched after more than a few prayer walks in Elm City, North Carolina, where we were in our first pastorate when we felt God's call to international missions.

"So, (**Your Name**), you can be sure that what I am sharing in each of the "Days" of this book is true, steeped in effectual, fervent prayer, saturated in God's Word and tried in the fire of experience—testings from Satan himself, many times. He made all kinds of attacks upon me to prevent this book from being finished in the Portuguese version. He failed miserably—it is being used by many there to battle evil. He flubbed it when he tried to prevent me from teaching it there and in the states. I taught it many times there as well as preaching from its precepts. He tried making me sick, causing more panic attacks, and even causing my mission car to falter on more than one occasion. He tried to make me less confident in speaking the language with which I had been communicating for years. He *really* failed in that attempt, since the Holy Spirit frequently gave me grammar, vocabulary and special phrasing of sentences while preaching, that I still shake my head over when I am finished with the message. This wasn't me, it was the very breath of God flowing through me and it so humbled me, yet emboldened me. Then Satan has tried to keep this book from being published here in America— buzzzz! Wrong again, Evil One! WestBow Press has taken this on, after many rejections and suggestions that this material was just not what they were looking for. He does everything in his power to feed one of my most chronic and difficult chronic sweepings (so far, that is...), ***procrastination***. But the very fact that you are reading this right now shows he got the boot on that one!

"So please do not stop—**read on**! Then take what you have gleaned to go out and wage spiritual warfare, knowing that God has commissioned you and sent forth none other than (**Your Name**). You have now been commissioned to do front line fighting against powers and principalities—another words, against an enemy who is not always easily identifiable, intent upon winning, even after the final, glaring, humiliating and wonderfully glorious defeat at Calvary! (**Your Name**), right now, read the following section aloud, or as if, you are talking directly to me."

"Well, Rob, I think I can really see what you are trying to share with me about being a soldier of the cross. All I can say to all this is, *"Where do I enlist?"* I'm ready to begin learning more, perfecting my military skills as an effective soldier, so that I can begin: *sweeping through genuine repentance, filling the empty space left when I repented, with some attitude or action that is much better, and keeping out evil by engaging in effectual, fervent prayer while developing a growing love for Scripture.*

"I am excited and humbled that God would choose me to fight this fight, coming from such a long line of brave soldiers like the ones in His Word, and those throughout Christian history. Rob, this is so awesome! Show me more, and pray with me that I will equip, train and mobilize to fight evil on a day-by-day basis. Pray that I will do my part in obedience to God, as together we move Satan that much closer to the stark realization that his already determined demise will come in God's perfect timing. Pray that I will be a faithful soldier, doing my part to diminish all of Satan's attempts to prolong his time as Prince of this world. You know, Rob, this is really agreeing with God's Word in another sense as well. As we study eschatology and see how the Bible teaches about the end times, being a sweeping, filling and keeping out soldier against evil causes our lives to move in the same direction with how God is desiring for us to move, toward the final victory and His glorious appearing!"

Sweeping Moments for today...

1) Thus far, what have you read which is still difficult for you to comprehend?

2) Discuss with your group anything that you have read thus far, that is difficult for you to accept as practical truth rather than mere theory from yet another "fix-it" book.

3) Do you have serious questions about whether Sweeping Out the Demons is even possible? Please take time with your group to discuss these questions and pray through them together.

4) Reconstruct and discuss your impressions of the testimony about our encounter with "Guerreiro" in Day 5. What impressed you most about it? Have you ever had a similar brush with danger in which Satan tried to discourage or defeat you?

5) What role did prayer and God's Word have in your previous brushes with evil?

6) What did you learn about spiritual warfare in Day 5? Were there any lessons that will help you battle day-to-day temptations, tests and difficulties?

7) Did you identify with the dialogue between and Rob in Day 5? Did you prayerfully read the response to "Rob" as if it were you? If so, how did this change your thinking about spiritual warfare?

8) Go back to the three *sweeping principles* and attempt to memorize them. Repeat this activity daily, whenever you have a moment to think, i.e. waiting in line, driving, etc.

9) Read once more Matthew 12:43–45 and try to share it with someone, in your own words.

10) Try to consider at least one attitude, habit or temptation that you have dealt with continuously. Now try to apply to that situation **sweeping, filling and keeping out evil**. After about a week or so, share with your group or a friend how you are doing with this practical application. Also, solicit someone in the group to become your prayer partner in this sweeping.

DAY 6

❧❀❧

Sweeping = First Things First...

And God said unto Moses, I Am That I am...
Sweeping is bigger than I am, but
not bigger than *the "I AM"*!

Now, during the next three "Days", let's assemble your spiritual warfare battle plan, one-step at a time. The first principle of spiritual warfare is:

Sweeping out evil through genuine repentance.

We have discussed sweeping at length in general terms, but now it's time to get some basic training in the area of *sweeping* as the first spiritual discipline in real spiritual warfare.

In order for you to truly battle Satan, you must begin by sweeping out that which is being used by the Enemy to defeat your best attempts to overcome temptation and sin on a daily basis. But you are probably saying to yourself, that is information straight from Captain Obvious, right? You already know that. If you are like me, you have been there, and done that so many times that you could write the book, chronicling all of those times you decided to repent, reform or resolve to do better.

Genuine repentance is what sweeping is all about. If you will allow genuine repentance to sweep out the "demons", or the evil temptations, tests and influences that allow evil to permeate your everyday walk, then you will have armed yourself with the "silver bullet" of spiritual warfare! It can change everything and cause you to turn a corner in the way you deal with attitudes, actions, habits and generally destructive behavior. Sweeping repentance, if permitted to operate freely in your situation, is a profound paradigm shift in how you can even overcome temptations that we consider chronic, stubborn, difficult or even repetitive tests by the Devil. They are the sweepings that he uses to influence or confuse your mind into going where you neither wanted nor needed to go with your choice of words, actions or thinking. Repeatedly, many of these chronic sweepings have been beating up most of us, spiritually, emotionally and even physically.

So why not get a real handle on how to arm ourselves with this silver bullet! We know that it is no secret weapon, since God has called His people to genuine repentance throughout history. However, most of us operate in the realm of genuine repentance like it is some unheard of exercise that seems strange and foreign. Since most of what we attempt is only partial repentance instead of genuine repentance, our attempts are self-styled, rationalized compromises. So when applied to evil influences or outright disobedience, repentance is frequently misused or poorly handled. So how can you appropriate God's desire for your heart in your life, in order to *really* sweep out those influences that are causing you to lose your temper, repeat bad behavior or move you back into the downward spiritual spiral against that habit you so desire to kick? This one area can cause you so much spiritual frustration, since this usually involves a sweeping that you thought you had moved beyond in the battle.

For a few moments, consider a situation in which you find you have given in to an evil influence, one that you have succumbed to more often than you would prefer—it could be a habit, or it could be an activity or just the way you have been reacting to life's inevitable bumps in the road. In addition, consider how you feel after the fact. The worst part of it is that you want so much to respond or react in a way that will honor God and help others to see Him in you. This particular chronic attack in spiritual warfare has so frustrated your attempts to repent or reform or repair behavior that you have run out of your own solutions, tricks, "How to's" and quick fixes. You are finally coming to the uneasy yet liberating point that you have come to the end of yourself. You have become desperate for a miracle to stop this (**you name the sweeping that you are considering**). Your best ingenuity, religion, philosophy, therapy or self-made remedies no longer seem even close to permanently breaking free and attacking evil. Instead, you find yourself in a stalemate, enslaved by this chronic battle.

When you come to the end of yourself and can actually admit or confess, "I hate the way I am responding over and over to this evil influence in my life! I really hate who I am when I say, do, or think this way." At that point, you are ready to graduate from the basic training of spiritual warfare and enter battle as a true soldier of the cross.

You are letting go and letting God control what you cannot. You are surrendering to the right enemy (your pride or your inability to let go and let God take over the command post of your heart). Now you can enter into battle ready to allow God to take over your inability to make anything happen of any lasting or significant impact on that which Satan is attempting to use to defeat you. At this point, any reader that has serious problems with control issues will find this sweeping very important to your future victories in spiritual warfare. Before you can move forward, you must deal with this sweeping by letting go and letting God be your GPS, your pilot and your navigator. To paraphrase an old hymn, if you don't give this to the Lord in prayer, oh, what peace you're going to forfeit, and oh what needless pain you are going to bear! I speak from experience in this, believe me!

When you include God as the General, the Master, the Chief and the Boss/Mentor/Coach of your approach toward *(fill this in with your most difficult spiritual battle ridge you need to take back for God)*. If you can take this step in genuine repentance, the equation of battle strategy is complete! You have become superior to the Enemy, *"because greater is He that is in you that he that is in the world." (1 John 4:4b KJV)!*

A peace will flow over your battle weary soul as you admit that you are no longer able to handle the problem without divine intervention. You will be arming yourself with the nuclear weapons of spiritual warfare—humility and brokenness, that permit God to do the sweeping—not you or your best efforts, but God!

But my God shall supply all your need according to his riches in glory by Christ Jesus. (Philippians 4:19 KJV)

My friend, only God is big enough, knowledgeable enough, wise enough and powerful enough to handle your chronic spiritual failures and strategy flaws. This is *the* silver bullet or key battle maneuver for actually satisfying the biblical definition for genuine repentance. Biblical repentance is submitting to an about-face change of heart and mind, in order to be in agreement and in harmony with God's desired outcome for that chronic attitude, behavior or action. The result of genuine repentance is a response that will honor and glorify God. Let's describe genuine repentance.

Genuine repentance involves the act of surrender or a "letting go" of pride's stronghold, formerly directed by the Devil and his demons. Evil influences function as they whisper false solutions and lies in your mind's ear about how badly you will come out on all of this. Evil desires that you refuse to admit your inadequacy and inability to overcome emotional reactions to circumstances—**especially** the mini-disasters that occur daily. In so doing, Satan can hold on to your way of thinking and reacting that much longer. But this is only possible if you permit him to influence your thoughts to be controlled by false or half-truths that result in your inappropriate or undesirable response.

Only then, can he confuse you into a knee-jerk reaction or darkened attitude to what could have been an opportunity to emerge with God in control of your emotions, your physical health, your money, your calendar and your common sense. Instead of another bad reaction or yielding to temptations snare to do it, say it or think it through all wrong, you declare, *"Here it is, God! I am sorry that I have allowed my foolish pride to guide. I repent and desire you to turn me toward the light and guide me home to victory!"*

Genuine repentance is giving up on doing thins your way and giving in to God's way. This kind of pride crushing will make you a submissive and great soldier! God will not lead you into some "pseudo-repentance". He will show you where you have gone astray in your self-made attempts to conquer your junk. He will teach you how to hate sin, how to feel desperate to rid yourself of this chronic condition of the heart, and most of all, how to *abandon* the conditions that Satan was using to keep you out of control while he remained in control.

Genuine repentance is a genuine remorse, regret or even a kind of hatred for the evil influence. You will *never* give up and let go of any habit, attitude or activity that you don't *hate with a righteous hatred*. If there is a way to describe the attitude of Almighty God toward sin, I would have to use the verbs despise and hate. God hates sin because it separates His dear children from realizing the desires of His heart for them (us, you, and me). You must adopt that same level of disdain, distaste, dislike and denouncement of an attitude or action before you will be willing to give it up and allow God to sweep it from your way of thinking and doing. God can heal us from evil in the same way He can heal us from a physical illness. But the healing begins with your willingness to give God permission to restore you from any prodigal or rebellious behavior.

What most of us attempt is incomplete repentance, or "pseudo-repentance", in which we do develop a kind of hatred for the negative behavior or attitude. This is followed by a kind of self-made attempt to correct the habit, attitude or activity on our own, as if we can help God battle this with our own ingenuity and "wisdom". At that point, most of us don't back up and back down from our prideful desire to help God do what only He can do. What must happen, however, is for you to stop right there and begin from that moment forward to give God control of the repentance. Ask Him to kill pride, and ask Him to guide you to relinquish control of the situation to Him. This happens through the right kind of conversation with God, which henceforth, we will call "effectual, fervent prayer" as we see modeled in James, 5:16 (KJV): *Confess your faults one to another, and pray one for another, that ye may be healed. The **effectual fervent prayer** of a righteous man availeth much.*

Effectual means with purpose, with direction and with focus upon a desired outcome. Prayer should always be more purposeful than any important activity you have to do during your day!

Fervent is a Latin derivative, which literally means to boil. In English, however, fervent means hot, glowing, showing marked enthusiasm and intensity. Such words as zealous or impassioned can be used for fervent. In the sense of prayer, all of these need to be a part of the environment for our talks with our Loving Heavenly Father! For James, God led him to instruct the early Christians to be confessional or honest and open with God. Repentance in its most perfect form lays it all out on the table for God to see, so He can take your remorse and sorrow and turn it into healing! Let go and let God heal you from that habit, action, activity or way of thinking that is causing you so much trouble, guilt, and frustration. I could never imagine how much God wanted me to begin a sweeping with Him, until I got down and effectually and fervently poured my heart out to Him about _____(the situation at hand, and believe me, there are many that I have knelt with Him to offer).

Genuine repentance lets God be God! Invite God to give you a sense of desperation and admit your arrival at the end of yourself. This humble willingness will give God the go-ahead permission of your will, to sweep out your "demon". God could do this with or without you, but His amazing grace and mercy allows you to participate in the covenant of forgiveness, by demonstrating to Him your willingness for Him to heal you emotionally, physically and spiritually, from that bad habit, attitude or behavior. This act of broken yielding honors and glorifies God, since it acknowledges His sovereignty and your total submission to His power.

At this point, you no longer have the right to go it alone, floundering at solutions that only bring temporary or even no resolve. An example of this sense of desperation, remorse, regret and hatred for a previous pattern of evil we find in the "Jonah type" example of Jacob, son of Isaac, in Genesis 32. Jacob was a real minefield of Jonah lessons, throughout his early years. We definitely learn how not to treat a brother from a glance at the early days of Jacob! He tricked his brother Esau out of his birthright and later on, from his blessing offered by their dad Isaac.

Then came that day of reckoning when the two brothers were about to meet up again after years of separation. Jacob was so sorry for his treatment of Esau, but let's keep it real here. He was also very afraid of what would happen when he encountered his twin. Would Esau still be so angry that he would kill Jacob? At that moment the true hatred and remorse must have flooded over Jacob, as the consequences for his actions finally surfaced. Like Jacob, your consequences for the evil will surface and cause a sense of fear that my son and I have come to call "devil dread"! That level of fear and dread should be sufficient to bring you to the point of contrition, sorrow, desperation and helplessness—that point where God has been waiting for your arrival!

True sweeping was about to take place because Jacob recognized his sin and was ready to confront it while trusting God for the consequences, however scary they were. Consequences are scary, but they also enable us to learn from what has gone down to move forward by God's grace, toward forgiveness and restoration. At that point, Jacob desired to make all things right with his brother, yet he was utterly helpless to do anything about it. He had to rely completely upon God at that moment. God must love it when we come to that point, so that genuine sweeping can take place, resulting in true, not pseudo-repentance. The results were amazing! Esau was so glad to see his brother. He must have buried the hatchet long since, to grudges or bitterness. Now he was just glad to see his brother coming toward him, to have that healing, calming, forgiving embrace with which only God's grace can bring. God wants to bring that same experience to your equation for repentance from evil, temptation, sin, rebellion, omission, neglect or disobedience.

Another example of genuine repentance would be Joseph's brothers in Genesis 44, when they found the silver cup of Joseph in the sack designated for his younger brother, Benjamin. Joseph had it stashed there to insure their return from the Land of Promise. Judah had to do some major backpedaling as he explained the situation about his father's attachment to Benjamin, the youngest son. As Judah explained this to the Egyptian leader, he *had* to be reliving their sinful act upon Joseph so many years before (Genesis 37:12–36). The remorse, regrets and the hatred for their wrongdoing suddenly flooded into his mind as he told this Egyptian, who held their fate in his hands, about how one of the two favorite sons of their father was dead. In truth, Judah had no way of knowing that he was actually speaking to his long lost younger brother, Joseph. Sometimes God, in His infinite mercy, develops circumstances that help to bring us to that point of genuine repentance, even when we are unaware of all the details and developments. We could even call those moments "Judah moments", or "Simon Peter moments". Recall the three denials of Jesus during the Passion. Recall the moment Peter put back on his garment and dived in the water upon realizing that the risen Lord was standing on the shoreline! Have you ever had a "Judah moment", or a "Simon Peter moment"? They are special and we need to watch for them in order to experience all of the genuine repentance moments that God so desires for your heart.

At that moment, all of the evil that he and his brothers had exacted upon Joseph made him feel so sorry. As the events of years before flooded his memory, the jealousy-driven act of selling Joseph to Midianite traders seemed so foolish. Feeling regret and remorse reminded him how prideful and immature they had been. Judah was shouldering more of the guilt and remorse than he had ever experienced—he had come to the end of himself and was ready to let go and at least seek God. That deception had caused Jacob to cherish the youngest, Benjamin, that much more. Now Judah knew that the request of the Egyptian official to bring Benjamin back with them to Egypt would surely finish off their already grief-stricken dad. If you were in Judah's shoes, how would you have felt at that moment? He was truly sorry and ready to do anything to relieve this guilt and sorrow over the consequences of their sin. That is the degree of regret and remorse and yes—hatred for sin, that is necessary for true repentance to take place. Your evil does not have to be even one-millionth as bad as this example. It really does not matter about how bad the habit or how serious the attitude or how destructive the behavior, but rather, how much you have come to despise the consequences and the ramifications of the evil. Has it grown into a "demon" strength burden? Have you arrived at the end of yourself with that sweeping you used to fill in the blank, earlier in this section?

If your response is a resounding "yes" to those two questions, congratulations, because you have arrived at the beginning of true repentance—the kind that will turn you about-face from the sin, in order to face the music of the consequences, and declare yourself *totally incapable and inadequate* to remove it on your own. The desperation for true repentance will bring you to a prayer similar to this one:

*God, I cannot resolve this on my own, even though I have tried and tried! I just hate it being in my life. Please take back over the wheel, and guide my regret and remorse to eliminate this from my life, no matter what it takes or how long. I am letting go and letting **you** have permission to sweep out a force that has become like a demon in my everyday life. I feel like a slave to it, and I know you are greater than anything in this world is. I genuinely desire to repent from this and walk away from it from this day forward, but I know that on my own, I will be like Peter walking on the water! Guide me not to look back or to the right or to the left Lord, but to look directly to **you** when the weakness or the vulnerability seeks to creep back in like the demons in your story that Matthew reported in 12:43–45. I am ready to repent and follow you to fill the empty place that I will joyfully have, where this mess existed up to now. Fill me with the fruit of the Spirit, and confirm that I have on all of your armor. In Jesus' Name I pray, Amen.*

Now my friend, if you used your own words, and spoke to God from the depths of your heart, that is effectual and fervent prayer. Now God will sweep out this "demon" from your life—my friend, you have experienced and modeled genuine repentance!

Genuine repentance depends upon specific confession, in order for you to experience the desired outcome of that repentance—ultimate restoration!

Let's look at yet another example to understand, beyond any shadow of a doubt, about the essential nature of confession for ultimate restoration. Move forward in the Old Testament a bit to 1 Samuel, chapter seven. There we will witness an actual application of sweeping which results in genuine repentance. Talk about a Jonah type lesson! The Ark of the Lord had become something that it was never meant to be. Captured by the Philistines some years before, they returned it to Israel. The Philistines had seen it as a bad luck charm. They returned the Ark to Beth-shemesh, but the men there did not know how to reverence it, so they used it as a sort of curiosity piece. Like any curio, they would look into it to see just what the big deal was about this sacred box.

Of course, they were killed for mistreating the place of reverence for God. So that part of Israel wanted to get this strange box down to Kiriath-jearim, so the men of that town came and got it. They put it off on Eleazar, the son of the man who owned the hill where they wanted to place it, so that they would no longer have to deal with that Ark of the Lord—*or so they thought.* They did not deal with any of their sin or with how this would affect their relationship with God. They just wanted to dump it off over there, and make Eleazar in charge of dealing with it. (*Does this sound familiar? Have you ever tried to get rid of sin simply by not dealing with it, hoping that the consequences and the real problems would just disappear?*)

So for twenty years they just ignored it, placing it on a hill over to the side of their city so that they would not have to mess with that problem anymore. You know—out of sight, out of mind, right? That was bad enough, but when we are talking about not dealing with Almighty God, well, that is a top-shelf kind of serious! In 1 Samuel 7:2–3, we read of how all Israel mourned. They felt that because the Ark remained neglected and ignored, there was no joy when Israel worshiped—none. They were so full of regret and remorse over their relationship with the Lord that they mourned as though someone had died. In fact, something had died...their zest and zeal for God!

Samuel saw that *they had come to an end of themselves*. They could go no farther in their self-fashioned religious ways to deal with their relationship with God and the damage done by their own sinfulness. Samuel took that moment to explain to them, to you and to me about *sweeping*!

And it came to pass, while the ark abode in Kirjathjearim, that the time was long; for it was twenty years: and all the house of Israel lamented after the LORD. *And Samuel spake unto all the house of Israel, saying, If ye do return unto the* LORD *with all your hearts, then put away the strange gods and Ashtaroth from among you, and prepare your hearts unto the* LORD, *and serve him only: and he will deliver you out of the hand of the Philistines.* (1 Samuel 7:1–3 KJV)

For your application of this Jonah-type lesson, personalize this sweeping by substituting *"the Philistines"* from 1 Samuel 7:3, with the sweeping that you are desiring to deal with right now. In a kind of fill-in-the-blank exercise, prayerfully, sincerely, humbly and honestly include your need right now: *and he will deliver you out of the hand of* ___. This substitution is a confessional step in repentance, so that God can truly sweep it out of your life. Those "sweepings" in your life like the one you have been filling in the blanks with today, are your "Philistines" that threaten to attack your peace of mind and your joy. Your enemy is *The Enemy!* He has cheered on this interruption to your peace and joy by whispering in your mind's ear that such sweepings are just the way it is and that they are impossible to change—*what a liar Satan is!*

At that moment, Samuel led Israel to a genuine repentance and victory over an evil that had plagued them for over twenty years (see 1 Samuel 7:2). He told them to gather at Mizpah so that he could pray for them to the Lord. Why did they need to gather? Samuel needed them to focus on the problem to confess the sin of neglecting their worship and ignoring God. Only when they came together and truly made the effort to focus only on God would they truly be in a mental and emotional posture to fight Satan and truly allow God to sweep out this sin from their lives.

In 1 Samuel 7:5, when Samuel used the imperative "Gather all Israel to Mizpah", we can best get the intensity of what he said by phrasing it as an emphatic, urgent command. "Gather!" can help us feel how important this assembling for repentance was. We cannot forget that also, this command was a collective one, best expressed as "Gather together!" My take on this is that Samuel was indicating for them and us, to *"Come to the Lord with your "demon" influence that Satan is using to short-circuit your capacity to be joyful and at peace, no matter what life slings your way!* " Quit trying to go it alone and go to the only place where God can truly sweep it clean from your heart and life. Go to the Lord in *effectual, fervent prayer!* Right now, if you are serious about fighting the good fight and ridding yourself of some evil influence in your walk, your talk or your thoughts, bow your head and go to God. Talk to Him, confessionally, and be **absolutely honest** with our Lord, explaining exactly what is going on inside of you. Be **obsessively specific**. Give details to Him. After all, He already knows, but that humble, submissive posture best expresses how our loving Lord desires for us to come clean and unashamedly to Him.

I am warning you in advance, when you open up to God, be ready for some strong emotions to come forth. In my private prayer place, I really wept when I poured out about past battles as a child that were the real cause of my inner battles with worry, depression and anxiety. I cried out for forgiveness as the Lord showed me how all of this had been used by Satan to make me negative, cynical and a skeptic to absolute truth. The Lord showed me what was *really* going on in my heart, and He will do the same in yours. He revealed to me how I had been lying to myself for ages about the real source of the problem. For me it was that I was placing all the emphasis in my life on pleasing others instead of pleasing God. This was making all of this pressure and guilt build up inside of me. Whatever God shows you, embrace it and allow Him to heal you, inside out!

Don't think for a minute that Satan was not influencing me to view circumstances around me so that I would react to them with more world like cynicism and people pleasing apathy. He did this so I would *fit in instead of standing out for God.* The Devil knew that this attitude would stoke my ego when people liked me, leading me to do all that I could to be politically correct and stand with what the world is standing on. Even if I disagreed vehemently, my silence could appear as an affirmation and agreement with the secular worldview. No matter what people would ask me to say or do as a pastor and then as a missionary, I would say yes of give a nod in affirmation so that I wouldn't be in conflict with them or make waves with the status quo. Then no one would think wrongly of me, and I would be loved, popular, accepted—and miserable!

God showed me through the times of deep and intimate conversations with Him, that what was at the bottom of the most far-reaching sweeping that I have encountered up to now. He helped me to see an ungodly pride at the core of all that I said and did. This kind of pride is evil and has great potential for Satan to rock all you do and all you are. It caused me to develop an insatiable desire to please the world at the expense of pleasing God. It left me feeling that the Devil had manipulated me and jerked me around since childhood. Eventually, when I gave my heart to Jesus at fifteen, those prideful tendencies carried over into my early Christian walk. It caused me to have periods of superficiality in my commitment to Christ and His desires for my life. This kind of pride is a tremendously powerful joy robber!

Confession can bring restoration, if you allow God to be in control of the results. I came away from this letting go and going to God with a sense of freedom that even now I cannot fully describe—probably because it is a work in progress, even years later. Such restoration experiences can bring you back to those original sparks of enthusiasm and excitement like when you accepted Jesus as your Lord and Savior. The newness of life returns when you allow God to sweep you clean and eliminate all the invasions that Satan has attempted to make into your life. Something very destructive was swept from my life during those moments with God. I have been overjoyed to know that the rest of the formula for sweeping (filling and keeping out evil) caused a permanent sweeping of that destruction. The freedom and permanence of this process was largely due to a continual indwelling of the Holy Spirit that fills me to the joyful point of overflow! The confidence of permanence in the sweeping came through a thorough filling of the repented "space" with spiritual fruit. Today, the battle lines are clearly marked by a continuous sentry of maintenance, armed with the discipline of effectual, fervent prayer, coupled with a growing love for Scripture. So you see, this sweeping has gone full cycle, from sweeping to filling to keeping out the evil. I know that the Scriptures clearly teach that this is God's desire for you in all of your spiritual warfare in the twenty-first century!

So do you have a handle on genuine repentance, in which you permit God to sweep out those demonic influences? While those influences cannot have complete dominion over a true believer, acknowledge that they can make guerilla attacks and sniper fire from time to time. The Devil is unrelenting in his desire to hang on a few days, months, years, decades or even centuries, before being cast into that lake of fire. He is subtle. He is astute. But he is not an omni being. He is not a god. He is a fallen angel, limited far more than he would want you to know, even though the Bible and Christian history are replete with crushing defeats from godly saints.

In my case, I was a dedicated servant of the Lord. As a staff minister serving a church in North Carolina, I was a young believer with zeal and a zest to grow spiritually. During that time, Satan attacked me with an illness called Meniere's Syndrome, causing vertigo and panic that the attacks would reoccur unexpectedly. Some depression over my limitations set in and voilá, he had me in a downward spiral. As a child, I had experienced some anxiety and panic attacks, but these had long since disappeared. Nevertheless, make no mistake; Satan never forgets a point of vulnerability that became exposed in past days. Such vulnerability serves as a chink in the spiritual armor that he attempts to use much later. All of these incidences, along with a dysfunctional broken home, meant that he pretty much had all he needed to attack, using my prideful desire to be liked with an ever growing false sense of insecurity, that I would *not* be liked and accepted.

Nevertheless, ever since I experienced that sweeping so many years ago, I have felt cleansed and ready to turn the page when all that inner stuff seeks to scratch its way back to the surface. It never affected my teaching or preaching, my ministry to others, but inside I knew that it affected why I was doing what I was doing. That inner conflict caused great spiritual insecurity that could have crippled me as a missionary. Oh, if it were not for God's unlimited and amazing grace, where would the believer be?

For me, it was nothing short of miraculous and awesome. Like any great model or pattern one discovers, I placed other chronic situations that had the potential for evil into the same model for sweeping, filling and keeping out. But none of those short-lived or chronic sweepings that I have since brought to God would have been possible without the honest and sincere time with the Lord. Satan's best attacks can be laid away before they develop when you immediately go to the Lord in total confession. You see, it is only then that God can guide you to get alone with Him and examine what is deeply rooted at the core of your problem. Those moments of sweet time with your Father can uncover any hidden weapons for evil. Before you know it, God is revealing to you the root causes for sin, guilt, confusion, frustration, stress, depression or even physical illness.

You will be blessed with a greater spiritual clarity as God receives honor and glory through your undivided attention. God will clear your mind to see how He can use all those experiences. He will place along your daily pathway persons of peace, counsel and encouragement. For example, my doctor explained to me the relationship of stress and anxiety to type two diabetes symptoms. He will place both Joseph-type teachers and Jonah-type teachers in your pathway, as reconnaissance soldiers to pave your way to spiritual victories over previously insurmountable obstacles. And it will happen because you chose to get along and get real with your King!

For all of us, these confessional moments should remind us of Adam's experience after the original sin, when God came in the cool of the day to have fellowship with Adam and Eve, only to find them hiding from Him. "Adam, where are you?" was God's way of inviting His children to come clean and confess what He already knew to have been the case. God knows your heart and all you say and do, yet we hear the echo "(**Your Name**), Where are you?" Like with Adam, God already knows your spiritual and physical whereabouts. I could feel in my heart the same deep questioning from my Lord, calling for me to reveal my whereabouts, so that He could lay bare my wounds caused by Satan while I was trying to go it alone. God knows what we have tried to use for spiritual first aid too! He knows when we have bandaged our broken hearts with false pride or stubborn pride or devil dread that fears God's presence...He knows it all!

But for me, revealing my spiritual whereabouts was what confession was all about, causing me to spill my guts to the Lord about everything—and I mean *everything* that was causing distance to grow between me and God. All I could feel through my long overdue tears of repentance was an indescribable sense of how much He loves me. Somehow, I began to see again for the first time in many years, how much He wants this child and all of His children to experience the freedom and victory that comes from confessional, sweeping repentance.

He is asking you right this minute as you read this section of the book, "Where are you?" He knows your whereabouts, to be sure, but He wants more than anything for you to tell Him your exact spiritual location, like an updated GPS would pinpoint the exact latitude, longitude and map coordinates to the minute and second. The same wisdom that caused you to pick up this book will lead you to tell God in detail the sordid story of how your situation came to the point of displeasure, disappointment and disdain. That wisdom will lead you to share how it all started with a habit, an attitude or an undesirable behavior that kept on messing with you mind, your clock, your wallet, your marriage, your work or your body. Based upon the description in God's Word of how God loves us with an everlasting, unconditional, just and perfect love, you can know that He really wants to hear every word and thought of how this evil influence is robbing you of His joy, which is your strength.

"And now let's learn the rest of the story", as a great newscaster used to say. In a great ceremony with Israel at Mizpah, Samuel did something symbolic that spurned the people to respond to God in a most powerful expression. In 1 Samuel 7::6, they took water from a well and poured it out on the ground before the Lord. This was symbolic of what He wanted all of His people to do in their hearts—to pour out their sin and evil tendencies, their habits they didn't like and all of their reactions to life that were contrary to God's desires for their hearts (see Ps. 37:4–5).

As for you and me, we are no different from those Israelites. God wants us to pour it all out before Him and then just let go of it! Let go and let God is a theme we hear a lot in preaching and teaching these days, because it is an essential element of spiritual warfare. For me, however, it did not really hit home until I actually poured out my heart to God about what was bugging me to the point of spiritual distraction. If you get nothing more from the book than this, it will have been a worthwhile basic training exercise for your service in God's army.

Pour it out to God, right now! Don't wait. Don't be embarrassed. Just get alone with God and get right with Him, because He loves you so very, very much. He will not accept the excuse that you are uncomfortable with opening up to Him. He opened his heart completely at the cross. He sent His son from heaven to die for us. Therefore, he won't be very impressed with such lame excuses as "I'm a man or I'm a woman with better things to do than getting in a closet or a bedroom or out in the woods by myself to be alone with you, God! I simply cannot pour out my every thought to you, Lord, now can I?" Such excuses just will not cut it!

When you pour water on the ground, it is gone. Pouring out to God your sense of remorse and regret, your brokenness of pride and your sorrow about anything you do not like about your relationship with Him, is the same as pouring out water on dry ground. It soaks or beads and then spreads out on the dry dirt. But soon it's absorbed into the fiber of the earth to be used by roots, bugs and even by the soil itself. You cannot take a sponge or a rag and reabsorb it from the ground. In the same way, God uses your genuine repentance to grow a new heart, mind and strength in you.

Because Christ died in payment for your sins, you can confess them freely to God and pour your heart out to Him right now, on the dry ground of forgiveness at the foot of a cross where the blood of Jesus was shed. It fell to the ground, absorbed by the earth to express His loving substitution for you! Remember that this blood was appropriated for all mankind, but its power only absorbed through the lives of those who have chosen to accept His loving, free gift of grace. None of this will ever make any sense to you unless you have clothed yourself with the whole armor of God as described in Ephesians 6:11–18. Take a moment to read those verses, and then to personalize them with my version of their meaning as follows.

"The armor protects the soldier from the weapons of the enemy. The armor emboldens the soldier to fight more aggressively. The armor helps the soldier to move forward and to advance to the desired position on the battlefield. The armor gives the soldier a sense of identity and decorum with the other soldiers. The best armor helps an army to emerge victorious. But the armor must be properly worn, and properly used in order to help the soldier. One piece of armor is usually dependent upon the functionality of the rest of the armor. That is why soldiers usually all wear all the armor distributed to them. Each piece has that very specific purpose, but the overall purpose is a life marked by resounding victories, not just survival or temporary advances over enemy strongholds.

"God's armor is absolutely the same in character. You must wear it all in order to withstand the wiles or strategies of the devil. Your enemy is subtle and astute enough that the entire armor will be necessary. After all, you are not fighting just any enemy...certainly not the flesh and blood type. Your enemy is invisible, a force of evil, and an army of fallen angels under the Prince of this World. His territory is paradise lost by his own evil nature. Your enemy has certain powers, and rules over rulers of the dark kingdoms of this world. Your enemy seeks to lead certain evil rulers in the world as well, so that they might exercise evil in high offices of government, industry and instruction. God designed your spiritual armor

so you can withstand the most evil of days. His desire is that at the day's end, you're still standing, still joyful and still advancing!

"Your pants are the absolute truth of God as revealed in His Word, in prayer, through the Holy Spirit, through faithful testimonies, and through the soldier's own experiences on the battlefield. God's guidance in how you live, act, react and interact is like a breastplate or shield of right living and right thinking that is just, moral and genuine in every way. The soldier of God can walk the walk and talk the talk because he/she walks on a preparation of the Gospel lessons learned and internalized, giving the soldier great peace as he/she marches into and through battle. This inner peace causes the soldier of the cross to hold high like a shield an unshakable faith that gives courage and more boldness, to march right toward the Enemy, by faithful confidence in your commander. Satan can't take this, so he is rebuked like his weapons, once fiery, now seemingly doused with water and deemed powerless."

"All of this is made so much more effective because you, the soldier of the cross, has placed over your mind a protective helmet that remains intact throughout all eternity, the helmet of salvation through Jesus Christ. He joyfully and prayerfully positioned this salvation helmet upon you as the most important part of the armor. This helmet enables you to develop this uncanny rapport with the commander as straps on the scabbard to hold the sharpest two-edged sword ever devised!

"It is such an honor to have it strapped around uniform pants of truth, designed by none other than the Holy Spirit of God. That sword of the Spirit is able to pierce bone and marrow, soul and spirit. It is able to discern the deep things of the heart. It is the Word of God, and it just keeps getting sharper, the more the soldier pulls it from the scabbard and uses it.

"Soldier, you are only to speak when the sword of the Spirit is drawn, and only through the wisdom of your supreme commander, our Lord. Your mission is to attack the enemy and by faith, to defend the truth with the persistence that comes only from wearing the protective vest just like your perfect example for righteousness, your ten star general, the Lord Jesus! Why, you're so focused upon God that the Enemy seems

powerless. However, when the Enemy does detect a chink in the armor, he will go after God's army with all he has, often causing temporal casualties. You the soldier moves onward, knowing what the commander has assured you: the Enemy is powerless to win the war or inflict eternal casualties. You and your fellow soldiers of the cross are like the National Guard, a homeland line of defense and protection as well as a servant to the people. Your serve under the rank of guardian, yet ready to attack as an infantryman at a moment's notice. So go into battle, fellow soldier, armed with celestial power and might from the Almighty!" (Expositional Paraphrase of Ephesians 6:11–18, by Rob Hefner, 2015)

Feel free to use this version any time you desire for discipling and equipping more soldiers of the cross. Now here is the actual equipment requisition, as drafted for us by order of the commander, by the Apostle Paul.

Put on the whole armour of God that ye may be able to stand against the wiles of the devil. For we wrestle not against flesh and blood, but against principalities, against powers, against the rulers of the darkness of this world, against spiritual wickedness in high places. Wherefore take unto you the whole armour of God that ye may be able to withstand in the evil day, and having done all, to stand. Stand therefore, having your loins girt about with truth, and having on the breastplate of righteousness; And your feet shod with the preparation of the gospel of peace; Above all, taking the shield of faith, wherewith ye shall be able to quench all the fiery darts of the wicked. And take the helmet of salvation, and the sword of the Spirit, which is the word of God: Praying always with all prayer and supplication in the Spirit, and watching thereunto with all perseverance and supplication for all saints; (Ephesians 6:11-18 KJV)

Sweeping brings many lasting and satisfying results, but only when enjoined and completed with filling and keeping out evil. I have shared my most enduring and endearing sweeping today. However, there are many more victories just like mine that sweeping can make in your life, regardless of what needs to be swept.

To follow is a rather extensive list of incidences where sweeping is necessary for you, the soldier to be free to fight with persistence and win with consistency, against the fiery darts, wiles, temptations, or influences of Satan. Many with whom I have talked see the following list as the most frequently encountered sweepings. Evidently, Satan uses these as obstacles in the lives of many potential soldiers of the cross. Certainly, you should add others as they come to mind as enemy strongholds in your life.

You might want to underline the ones with which you know to be sweepings in waiting for your spiritual warfare. A brief examination of Galatians 5:16–21 is a good starting point. The list will require you to begin the soul-searching self-examination that will reveal your need for sweepings related to the works of the flesh. Examples are the likes of selfishness, jealousy, envy, vengeance, impatience, prejudice, double mindedness toward absolute truth, or any activity or attitude that contributes directly or indirectly in the neglect of one's relationship to God.

Another list could be personal excesses like overeating, substance abuse, negative talk or gossip. Yet another list might include unhealthy habits like smoking, drinking, recreational and prescription drug abuse or gambling. Still another category might include sexual immorality, adultery, pornography, virtual sins on the internet. Your list must include sweepings related to pride, such as greed for money, time or power. At some point your list should include making better choices in diversions like bad programming on TV, as well as literature, video gaming and PG13 to R-rated videos that have questionable moral, ethical content. The question to ask in the case of media is "Does my viewing, reading or playing of this media honor God?" There really needs to be a list for uncontrolled emotions, provoked by

your interaction with your world. Satan can use the everyday stuff
to draw you into inappropriate expressions of anger, fear, anxiety
and worry. You could spend a fair amount of time on a list of
misplaced priorities that damage relationships, like overwork,
obsessions with certain leisure activities. Sometimes you can be
subtly drawn into over involvement in activities that take away
from family roles as a spouse, as a parent, as a close friend or even as
a child. Of course, there needs to be a list of unethical practices in
business and money management, like lying, dishonesty, cheating,
lewd or vulgar talk and profanity.

Whew! The lists can go on and on, can't they? If your specific
problem was not on a suggested list, add it now. Up to this point
in the twenty-first century, I have seen persons confront directly
or indirectly every one of these evil tendencies. You can deal with
every one of them using the three principles: **Sweeping through
genuine repentance, Filling/Sowing with something
better, and Keeping out evil through effectual, fervent
prayer and a love for Scriptural Truth.**

Well, let's go back one more time to Samuel's example for
repentance. It must have made a profound impression upon the
hearts of those present, because the account goes on to report:

*And they gathered together to Mizpeh, and drew water, and poured it out
before the LORD, and fasted on that day, and said there, We have sinned
against the LORD. And Samuel judged the children of Israel in Mizpeh.
(1 Samuel 7:6 KJV)*

The time of worship and the message they had witnessed
caused them to change their behavior toward God. In reverence,
they fasted. Fasting has all sorts of Scriptural applications, but the
meaning behind the practice of fasting is unchanging. Fasting is
a time of focus upon God, denying self in order to accentuate
that focus. It is an offering of self to God for a temporary period.

While fasting from food or drink is the most common application in Scripture, there are contemporary applications in your life and mine that can be more specific to the context of whom or what you are dealing with.

For example, you could fast before God from a habit, an activity, a behavior or anything else in order to make more room for more time with God. A period of fasting could even begin the sweeping of a habit, attitude or activity. As you pray for God to sweep it out, you could fast from it during a time of prayer and Bible study, in order to gain a deeper focus upon God. This focus can contribute to making you a more prepared soldier in Satan's attempts to reoccupy your "house". This could be *the* time for demonstrating to God your sincere desire for Him to sweep this evil from your *life house, that earthly tent or dwelling for your heart, mind soul and strength.* Remembering that ultimately, only God can sweep, you can abstain for a period of hours, days or longer, as an act of worship. This will also make more room in your "house" for God to speak to you, teach you, admonish you and encourage you. This type of fasting agrees with a well-known passage, Romans 12:1, 2 (KJV):

I beseech you therefore, brethren, by the mercies of God, that ye present your bodies a living sacrifice, holy, acceptable unto God, which is your reasonable service. And be not conformed to this world: but be ye transformed by the renewing of your mind, that ye may prove what is that good, and acceptable, and perfect, will of God.

You see, it is like an offering that you are giving to God, to show Him that you want Him to take over. You are saying something like,

"See, Lord, I am serious about not wanting this in my life anymore. I want it out so much, but I can't remove it on my own. I can do it for a few minutes or hours or days, but I know that one or more of my weaknesses

will invite it back in. With this pouring out and fasting, I am showing you my desire to worship you and my desire to repent from this. By faith, I will now be willing to allow you to do that which I can't do on my own. Please sweep this from my lifestyle, from the way I act, react and interact with You, with others and with myself."

Today we have begun the process of spiritual warfare training with the ultimate weapon: a threefold offensive designed to defeat Satan in his efforts to tempt, test, discourage, suggest, influence or otherwise mess with you mind as you go about your day-to-day experiences. Have you begun to memorize them and to personalize them?

1) **Sweeping through genuine repentance;**
2) **Filling or Sowing a new attitude or action to fill the void left by your genuine repentance;**
3) **Keeping out or maintaining the sweeping and filling through effectual, fervent prayer and a growing love for Scriptural truth.**

From today's discussion, I hope that you are well on your way to permitting God to *sweep* something out of your life that you have wanted out for a long time. For some, this sweeping could mean improved mental, emotional or physical health. For others it could mean the beginning of increased freedom to enjoy your daily life, while for others it could mean success or fulfillment at home or on the job. The effects can be far reaching. This could mean significant improvements in the way you relate to others and a breakthrough for some of your most important relationships. For all of us it means a deeper and closer relationship with our Lord.

Sweeping means that you do not want just to improve, to reform or make some lame resolution. You want the real thing, genuine repentance full of confessional, emotional and personal contact with the living Lord! So just in case you are still unsure what the outcome of sweeping will look like, let's view three scenarios that reflect incomplete or inadequate sweeping...

Scenario One: Sweeping began well, but then the old behavior returns to replace the new way, leaving you discouraged or disillusioned. You feel like, "It is no use to try sweeping out this—**it was** probably a bad idea anyway". In this scenario, Satan could succeed in discouraging you from ever trying again. This is junk from his infernal inferences to your freshly swept spiritual ears. One of his best strategies is to drop low your expectations of lasting results from sweeping repentance. He will try to deceive you to rationalize that it's O.K., and that no one really expected you to win anyway. Besides, he continues to whisper, you can always start over soon or someday or whenever...but not right now...kick back and go back to the way it was...it wasn't so bad, really, was it?

Scenario Two: You really are keeping the old way out, but Satan is battling continually with your sense of victory and resolve by intensifying the temptations that would lead you to fail and fall back into the old ways again. He does this by separating your thinking from your new hiding place in the cleft of the Rock, to a worrying obsession with the problems and cares of the day. This leads to a constant, nagging dread that kind of looms over your shoulder, causing you to doubt your ability to continue. It suggests the possibility that you might soon weaken in willpower or resolve, causing another failed attempt. Since it is God doing the sweeping, not you, this is actually a very well prepared web of lies, designed to make you forget that God sweeps, and you obey. A relapse to the old way seems inevitable, because you feel so alone and powerless...what a lie! Satan can shake your confidence, making you feel like you are nearly at the end of your rope, out on a weak limb or teetering on the tightrope of insecurity. The attack by Satan results in an assault upon any inner peace or sense of victory that you already have begun to experience. Where is God in all of this self-doubt and fear of failure? Wake up! He's just as close as He was when the sweeping began!

Scenario Three: Satan fosters a sort of jealousy or envy that divides how you feel about the new way of thinking and acting. While glad that it is behind you, you begin to begrudge those who are still doing or acting in the same old way. Instead of focusing upon what you have gained in the victory, you begin to wonder what you are missing. This can lead to a wistful longing to go back to the old behavior. This scenario is most common when you are almost at the point of total abandon from the carnal style of Christian living, to being completely convinced that nothing can separate you from the love of Christ. Your influence from the world seems almost equal to your influence by the Holy Spirit at this point—Satan has done a kind of con game on your mind. To eliminate this scenario you must decide to move forward toward the filling from the Holy Spirit, never looking back at whatever junk the world had filled you with previously!

What about moving forward to a fourth scenario? Of course, I'm referring to your abandonment of the other three false scenarios, choosing the real deal. No matter what, pick this one—don't you dare let Satan leave you hanging in scenarios one through three! Letting go and letting God do the sweeping requires genuine repentance, or an about face, 180 degree turn from one attitude, action or behavior to one that completely cancels out the effects of the previous condition. It is a process of transformation from one way of thinking or acting to a completely different way. Now that is a pretty tall order to expect from you, is it not? No wonder Satan is able to sling those other three scenarios at those who cling to trying to sweep on their own steam!

To accomplish sweeping, first you must recognize that sweeping is much bigger than you are. It is a *God sized* task reserved only for the Almighty to accomplish in you. It requires your cooperation with God to submit to Him your desire to repent, while at the same time confessing honestly and openly all that is involved in getting to how you arrived at this evil or frustrating place. You pray with purpose and power, and you describe the sweeping specifically to God. Sweeping will involve relinquishing the ownership of that evil so that God can defend you. You just have to confess you inability and helplessness to resolve this on your own. You must remind yourself that sweeping is the starting point in spiritual warfare. In order to reach the finish line, you must realize that sweeping is bigger than you or me, so as you let go and let God handle the genuine repentance, you must allow Him to guide you through the next two steps in spiritual warfare. Only in this sweet submission will you emerge a hero soldier, a victor, a winner! For many that I have talked with, this relinquishing was likened to when you are holding onto a heavy load for way too long. Just when your muscles and bones are aching to let go of it, you are suddenly reminded that you can lay it down on a nearby shopping cart, table or chair! The burden is nothing for the cart, chair or table, and it was there all along, yet you just kept trying to hold on, carrying it yourself a little bit farther. That cart, chair or table is the cross of Jesus Christ! You never had to hold on that long! God had it all along, but Satan wanted to see you weaken and drop in discouragement. The cart of the cross wants to roll your burden away. The table of grace is so large that you can't find the end! Just as you accepted Christ to table your sins with His forgiveness, He wants you to daily repent and keep laying down those daily burdens on that table of grace and mercy! And that chair is where you can place the seat of your emotions, guilt, pain and shame! It is so sturdy and strong that nothing will be too heavy for it. That chair is none other than the throne of God, where someday you will bow in His presence, and hear the words, "Well done, thou good and faithful servant." Go to the throne daily, table the weight of sin, and let the cart of redemption roll away the penalty and accusation by Satan and his world!

In "Day 7", we will focus on "Filling", the key to sealing repentance permanently, by removing the possibility of that evil influence from ever returning to take up residence in your "house". This part of the formula takes us back to Matthew 12:43–45. Let's recap the key passage. The "house" Jesus described in that story is the man's self—his personality, attitudes and way of interacting with his world. The man in the parable swept his house clean, but left the cleaned spaces like empty rooms. Jesus inferred that something was going to fill that empty, void space. The demons that had been swept from the house were bent upon returning and bringing all their friends! Jesus stated that scenario would end up with his "house" much worse off than before the sweeping.

Filling is best understood by the synonyms of "sowing" or "refurnishing" your "house" with something far better, far more enduring, far more godly and far more enriching. Filling is the key to genuine repentance remaining intact. So that's where we will go from here. As we leave genuine repentance, the *Sweeping Moments* are a bit different today, so pay close attention to some of the potential demonic influences that can invade your life, even if you are a saved, strong and serving soldier of the cross. Though incapable of dominating or possessing the soldier, Satan will use all of his astute and cunning to slow or impede repentance. Throughout history, he has been known to cast an illusion of soundly defeating believers through what has been historically chronicled as the "Seven Deadly Sins". And make no mistake about it, my friend; these "Seven" are broad brushstrokes of evil, which have umpteen zillion variations, sizes and shapes from which they can emerge.

Sweeping Moments for today...

1) Today was all about sweeping. Take a moment to look back in Day 6, listing at least three major facts that impressed you most as you seek to begin letting God sweep out the demons.

Share these major facts with your group or journal them if studying on your own. Be sure to explain why each fact impressed you, and how each could be of great help to you as you move forward as a soldier.

2) Have you begun to reflect and pinpoint areas of your life that need sweeping?

How many of them are chronic (you have dealt with them repeatedly, with only limited or low success)?

Which ones do you consider high priority sweepings, i.e. those that are having a damaging, frustrating or even destructive affect upon your life?

3) To follow is one of the most challenging Sweeping Moments that you will encounter in the entire study, but one I promise will be the most rewarding as you become more and more serious as a soldier in the fierce conflicts you have already faced and will be facing in twenty-first century spiritual warfare.

Remember the sweeping facts gleaned from Day 6 as you take this time for prayerful inventory. Set aside enough time to do this in a prayer closet kind of setting, uninterrupted, honest open, just one-on-one with your Lord. OK? Here goes....

Nearly all church history books, spiritual warfare books and Google searches touch on what became known in the first century church as the so-called "Seven Deadly Sins". Apparently, early church Fathers concluded that these general sin areas represented most of what Satan is up to in his spiritual warfare strategy. The purpose of these destructive sin categories was the same then and now: to destroy the church, one member of her body at a time. Obviously, Satan concluded that such a strategy of temptation would delay his ultimate demise upon the glorious return of Jesus. Almost without exception, the specific sins that you may be currently battling in your spiritual warfare relate directly to one or more of these seven collective areas of temptation.

From my own experience, the most helpful element in this basic training exercise is to open your Bible. Search and study the Scripture references, which I have compiled from places like various biblical reference chains, as well as other Bible annotations. From these and other Bible study tools, you will be able to winnow those that do not directly affect your life as much as others do on the list. Upon returning to the small group (or to your journal or study notes if studying alone), you might take time for an extra meeting just to reflect on what went on during your time alone with God, wading through these powerful weapons of Satan.

Some might share their favorite "power verses" to apply to a sin on the list that you need to deal with. Another idea could be to use the Scripture references in your personal devotions for the next week or so. Finally, before you begin this kind of spiritual warfare exercise, know God is with you and the Holy Spirit will give you understanding as you permit Him. Also, remember that this kind of time investment is very threatening for Satan, and he may just choose you in his prowling as a roaring lion to hassle you or interrupt you so that you will not arm yourself with such powerful spiritual ammunition!

Much of the training in which you are about to engage will enhance your understanding of Day 7 and Day 8, as we will focus upon the second principle, *filling the void by sowing the fruit of the Spirit.* This entire exercise *is* the application of Principle Three, *keeping out evil through effectual fervent prayer and a love for the Scriptures.* You will be old hat at that important focus when we spend time on honing the principle in Day 10.

I. **Pride, Arrogance, Boasting, Haughtiness:** 1 Samuel 2:3; Psalm 10:2; 31:23; 73:6; 101:5; 119:78; Proverbs 6:3; 8:13; 11:2 16:18; 21:4; 28:25; Mark 7:22; 2 Corinthians 12:20; 1 Timothy 6:4; Titus 1:7; 1 John 2:16.
    After searching these and other verses from God's Word, here is where I am currently facing potential temptation or actual spiritual battles that are Pride Based:

II. **Lust**: 2 Samuel 11:2–4; Job 31:1; Proverbs 6:25; Isaiah 16:6; Matthew 5:28; 1 Corinthians 7:9; Galatians 5:19; Ephesians 4:19, 22; Colossians 3:5; 1 John 2:16.
    After searching these and other verses from God's Word, here is where I am currently facing potential temptation or actual spiritual battles that are Lust Based:

III. **Anger, Fury Or Wrath:** Genesis 4:5; Exodus 34:6; Numbers 14:18; Deuteronomy 29:28; 1 Samuel 18:8; 2 Kings 5:12; 22:13; 2 Chronicles 16:10; Esther 3:5; Psalm 30:5; 37:8; 78:38; 131:1,2; Proverbs 14:17; 16:32; 19:11; Ecclesiastes 7:9; Amos 1:11; Matthew 5:22; Luke 4:28; 6:11; Acts 19:28; Romans 1:18; 2:5; Ephesians 4:26; 1 Thessalonians 5:9; James 1:19, 20; Revelation 14:10.

After searching these and other verses from God's Word, here is where I am currently facing potential temptation or actual spiritual battles that are Anger Based:

IV. **Envy, Covetousness Or Jealousy:** Genesis 4:5,6; 26:14; 37:11; Exodus 20:17; Numbers 16:3; Esther 5:13; Psalm 10:3; 37:1; 73:3; Proverbs 3:31; 14:30; 23:17; 28:16; Jeremiah 6:13; Ezekiel 33:31; Daniel 6:4; Micah 2:2; Habakkuk 2:9; Matthew 27:18; Luke 12:15; Acts 13:45; Ephesians 5:3; Colossians 3:5; 1 Timothy 3:3; Hebrews 13:5.

After searching these and other verses from God's Word, here is where I am currently facing potential temptation or actual spiritual battles that are Envy or Jealousy Based:

V. **Sloth Or Laziness:** Proverbs 6:6; 12:27; 18:9; 20:4; 24:30, 31; 31:27; Ecclesiastes 10:18; Ezekiel 16:49; Romans 12:11; 2 Thessalonians 3:11; 1 Timothy 5:13; Titus 1:12; Hebrews 6:12.

After searching these and other verses from God's Word, here is where I am currently facing potential temptation or actual spiritual battles that are Sloth or Laziness Based:

VI. **Greed Or Avarice**: Joshua 7:21; 1 Samuel 8:3; Proverbs 1:13; 1:19; 15:27; 21:26; Ecclesiastes 5:10; Isaiah 56:11; Jeremiah 17:11; Amos 2:7; Micah 3:11; Zechariah 9:3; Matthew 26:15, 16; John 12:6; Acts 16:19; 24:26; Romans 1:29; 1 Corinthians 6:10; Ephesians 5:5; Colossians 3:5.

After searching these and other verses from God's Word, here is where I am currently facing potential temptation or actual spiritual battles that are Greed or Avarice Based:

VII. **Gluttony Or Self-Indulgence**: Genesis 9:21; Numbers 11:1-5, 32; Deuteronomy 21:20; 1 Samuel 25:36; 2 Samuel 11:13; 1 Kings 16:9; 20:16; Esther 1:10; Proverbs 16:26;

18:20; 23:1-3; 23:20, 29-35; 25:27; 26:9; Ecclesiastes 6:7; 10:17; Isaiah 5:11, 22; 28:1,3; 29:8; 56:12; Hosea 7:5; Joel 1:5; 3:3; Nahum 1:10; Habakkuk 2:15; Luke 12:45; 21:34; Romans 13:13; 1 Corinthians 6:10; 10:31; 11:21; Ephesians 5:18; Philippians 3:19; Titus 1:12.

After searching these and other verses from God's Word, here is where I am currently facing potential temptation or actual spiritual battles that are Gluttony or Self-indulgence Based:

DAY 7

Fill it up with the Good Stuff! Filling the Void Where Satan Wants to Reoccupy...

If you had grown up in western North Carolina during the late 1950's and the 1960's, then the title for Day 7 will ring a note of familiarity. Gas stations were better known as "filling stations" for most of us. Cars had *big* V-8 engines that required a lot of octane in the gasoline to purr and effectively haul those huge cars down the highways. Around our part of the world, many a customer would pull up to the pump and tell the attendant (who pumped the gas for you, by the way, just as they still do in Brazil) "Fill it up with high test." High test or high-octane gasoline was full of refinery kick, but also full of lead, so that when the spark plugs fired, they fired with authority! Most cars had to have the "high test" or they would not run at peak performance. Filling the tank with that good stuff restored an empty tank with powerful fuel for a trip to the store, the school or on that family vacation. Refilling an empty tank with the good stuff made it possible to ride in style!

Today we want to fill up with the good stuff, but not the tank of a Chevy, Ford or Chrysler. We want to fill the areas of our lives that are running on a near empty level after the great "ride" of your life made possible by sweeping, through genuine repentance. Swept clean from your heart and life are all of these "demons", which in our use of the word in this study means those temptations, trials and tests from the Devil via his evil influences. After Day 6, I hope that you are already experiencing some sweepings. Now let's begin to fill those voids left by effective repentance with "the good stuff"!

With God guiding and sweeping out that evil influence, you enter the next stage of the battle. Inevitably, the Devil will attack with what you learned from our key passage. Having repented and experiencing God's sweeping, Satan has no other recourse but to resort to his "plan B" for regaining his dominion in your "house". In his story, do you remember how Jesus explained to the Pharisees of the man sweeping his house clean of demons? Well, that was where that fellow stopped in his spiritual warfare, at sweeping through genuine repentance. The evil was vacated from the premises, but was lurking just outside the property line, gazing at all that nice, clean space in those rooms of that fellow's heart. Evil saw this as unoccupied space, just waiting to be filled by something or someone. Ergo, the Devil's plan B—*to reoccupy your life after repentance*, where the empty void and cleanup seems complete. It is as if the Devil is saying to his band of liars,

"Well it looks empty to me! What does it look like to you guys? I see no new activity or spiritual furnishings that would give us any hassle, so why don't we invite some more of our gang and reoccupy this place? Why, it will be better than ever since he has swept out all of that fake religious clutter that was in there before he cleaned up!"

Many a soldier has stopped in spiritual warfare at repentance, allowing God to sweep clean, considering the sin or temptation problem solved. Life goes on, and the soldier feels that problem is now a "done deal", as we say in our part of North Carolina. But to stop there is to follow to the letter what Jesus warned about in Matthew 12:43–45. The truth of the matter is that you have only just begun the battle.

Satan would want you to think; *"Now I am home free and on my way to victory over this bad habit, attitude or act of rebellion. I am so over with that destructive behavior."* However, he will still seek to reoccupy your "house". You are falling for the same trap that Jesus warned that original audience to understand; namely, that mere repentance or reform, in and of themselves, does not change the attitudes of the heart. Jesus was seeking to open the eyes of those stubborn and legalistic Pharisees to see what He yearns for you to see. It was not enough just to do the right actions, or to follow their complicated web of rules—and the intricate interpretations of those rules. Jesus desired them and He desires for u to understand that mere reform or even genuine repentance cannot be the finish line for spiritual warfare.

Where all those "no's" and "do's" and "don'ts" were rigidly placed as a set of regulations, those pharisaical hearts were not firmly filled with love, joy or peace. Despite all of their strict obedience, there was no room for God's continual guidance. Instead, "demons" of negativity and judgmental attitudes filled the voids left by empty obedience to rules, many of which had long since lost their original meaning. Through legalism and hollow ritualism, they had forgotten their position in God's plan as God's redemptive people. The same can happen to you and to me if we don't finish the process of genuine redemption.

No, God is not yet finished with you after a victorious sweeping. You have to allow the Holy Spirit to fill that void left by your most sincere and dynamic experiences with genuine repentance. This filling will complete God's sweeping measures upon your heart. At this point, you have definitely experienced the victory over that troublesome and frustrating evil that has had such a negative effect on your daily life. But like the story

I told in Day 1 about the game between Satan and God's team, the "demon" as we are calling those evil influences, is not done with you. Satan and his demon army are not ready to vacate permanently a place left vacant. They won't be evicted until something so much better, purer and higher occupies that space. When that occurs, evil cannot bear to show its ugliness even near that kind of godliness. Satan finds your emptied and cleansed heart as he prowls. That is just how he rolls! After his "Plan A" type temptations and tests have failed, he will employ his "Plan B" ideas via his demonic army. He will use whatever vulnerability or weakness he can find from your daily living, in order to reoccupy (**not possess**) your life. He will prowl during a tough, frustrating or vulnerable moment. Though swept from the picture, he will seek to slow or even prevent your continued repentant sweeping from leading you into a dynamic and permanent victory. Filling with the any one of many practical applications of spiritual fruit will validate your repentance and permit God to sweep. At that point, principle three will need to kick in. Only your continued vigilance in spiritual warfare will fortify the filling, making possible containment—keeping out evil. Principle three will assure this permanence—effectual fervent prayer enjoined with a true love for God's Word. With time, the spiritual fruit will soundly trounce the works of the flesh from having even a microscopic spot in your thinking! Now that is a pretty amazing thought to ponder, isn't it!

Here is a good way to illustrate this process. In 1981 my mother's house burned. She got out with her life, but all of her possessions and furniture were destroyed. The fire department placed a sign on the property that it was condemned, deemed unsafe and uninhabitable. They did this so that all would be safe from the fire and water damage. You see, the house burned, sending my mom away from a horrible situation. God was using this arson tragedy to give her a wake-up call from years of alcoholism and poor choices. Not only was the house vacated in order for her "house" to experience repentance and healing, it was abandoned, boarded up and left behind. Her life began to be totally transformed to the godly woman she had once been. She relocated to a rented place that placed her close to new friends, family and restoration from her previous problems.

Like my mom, we all have to go through a process of abandonment, distancing ourselves from past demons in order for God to employ His healing and restoration! When I consider what blessings my mom would have missed, had she gone back to that burned and condemned house, it makes me shudder. The rest of her years were spent in victory, living a life of prayer and devotion. Is there an empty, burned and condemned house that you need to abandon in order to move forward with sweeping and filling? Move out! Relocate your heart far from that place, lest Satan attempts to reoccupy and hold you back from a completely new way of thinking and living!

You might ask how Satan works this kind of strategy. From my personal experiences and my observations of others, I have surmised that he will capitalize upon disappointments and frustrations. He will influence you to obsess or focus upon discouraging words from someone you value, like a loved one or a coworker. While Satan did not cause these incidences, he will seek to develop mental "whispers" of doubt and confusion. One of his strategies is sidetracking you from God's desires for your stewardship of how you invest the three "T's Time, Talent and Treasure.

Distracted by a disappointment, for example, the Devil and company will do what they can to mess with your schedule or daily routine (Time), your activities or the how you perform those activities (Talent), or how you invest your resources (Treasure). One of Satan's "Plan B" strategies might be to reoccupy territory using some previous circumstance to flaunt the temporary pleasure, security or convenience that this old habit or attitude promised before Christ entered your life. The web of evil influences is a master at tempting you to look back upon the old life, so that it appears as though you are somehow missing a possibility of enjoying any one of your three comfort zones: ***convenience, comfort or security***. Before you know it, he has cast a grenade-sized doubt upon your repentant victory. You begin to drift back into the old way of thinking or acting. He does this repeatedly, if you let him. But remember, you don't have to let him!

The "Why" Behind Filling/Sowing

There is so much more to spiritual warfare beyond the victory of repentance. It's kind of like the infomercials on late night TV. Infomercials have this extended pitch for their product, but just when you think that they are through and you can get back to a favorite show, they come out with a "clinch offer" in order to seal the deal. Clinch offers sound something like this: *"But wait! There's more!"* At that point, they either offer something even better than what they were originally pitching, or double the offer, or even lower the price one more time. This tactic has proven to be one of the most effective sales tools ever.

God's Word is full of honest to goodness "clinch offers". They are His promises and His exhortations! He uses them at perfect moments to fortify your spiritual muscles so that you will continue to ask, seek and knock on the door of His desire for you. God constantly desires you to join Him in what He is already preparing all around you. As Henry Blackaby so masterfully explained in his book, *Experiencing God,* the Lord wants us to seek Him first and really examine how He wants us to join Him in what He has already prepared all around us (Blackaby). It is as though God is constantly preparing us for something better during the moments of temptation and testing—as though He is saying, *"But wait! There's more!"* He wants to fill the void made by the sweeping out by true repentance, with something far better! When Satan seeks to cast those dark thoughts of doubt and discouragement, keep telling yourself, *"But wait! There's more!"* Keep reminding yourself to ask the question during frustrating or difficult moments, *"Wait! Lord, what are you trying to show me or teach me here? What is it that I am not seeing, that you want to do in my life with this sickness, pain, or spiritual attack?"*

Filling with the practical application of the fruit of the Spirit is the *more* that we are talking about in spiritual warfare. Moses saw that *more* when he paused at the burning bush, instead of moving on. Mary pondered in her heart the words of the angel of the Lord concerning just who her child would be—in her heart she probably reflected many times, on what Jesus said and did as He grew in wisdom, knowledge and stature. *"But wait, Lord, there is more that I need to see about my son Jesus...show me!"* Peter, after hearing the rooster crow surely reflected back upon his three denials of the Master—as he retreated in tearful despair from the scene of the Passion, could he have been saying to himself something like, *"But wait, there's so much more to my Lord than I have yet to see!"* The Roman soldier at the foot of the cross, upon Jesus breathing His last, definitely had the change of heart that could have contemplated, *"But wait! There's more to this Jew being crucified!"* For all around him to hear, that centurion actually declared, *"Surely he was the Son of God!" (Matthew 27:54)*. Scripture is replete with many other examples of how God desires to fill the emptiness left by repentance if only we will ask Him what He wants us to see, hear, sense and feel from life's undercurrents.

No matter what the repentance you have made, there is a clinch offer for you from God! But wait, my friend, there is so much more than the repentant abstinence, or the freedom from the addiction. But wait, there's more to repentance, beyond breaking free from destructive behavior or speech patterns, questionable business practices or relationship breakers. That repentance opens your life up to a *free fill-up with the good stuff, the high test of life!*

If you stop at repentance, you will miss the time of your life with God—it's just as simple as that. So praise God that He has guided you through genuine repentance, and praise Him who has swept clean the places that were hindering your relationship with the Lord. Whether in your life-walk, your life-talk or your life-reactions, God's unlimited clinch offers invite you to live life with expectancy. Watch how God wants you to continually ask—*"But wait, Lord! What can I learn from this repentance? How do you want to fill that empty void where you swept this evil from my life?"* Your repentant heart can be a blank canvas for God to paint a wonderful, spirit-filled life! Looking in God's Word for our battle plan for filling, let's go to the pump in this twenty-first century spiritual warfare. But wait! There's more! Since spiritual warfare has not change one iota, now you can go to the pump to fill your life with the good stuff at first century church prices!

After repentance, you have an "empty tank", so to speak. Now where all that junk was integrated into your life, all those habits and attitudes that you so wanted out, there is all this space in your time, your talent and your treasure. That space will be filled up again by **something**. Satan's filling station wants to offer you a free fill-up of all the trashy fuel that God has swept from your walk. His slick talking sales pitch includes anything he thinks you might want to hear, in order to get back your business. You surely don't want that to happen, but honestly, Satan will make his offers pretty tempting. Remember, he is desperately hanging on to his territory, to his very existence outside of that lake of fire.

Sweeping repentance is a struggle with the world, your fleshly nature and the Devil. However, it does not have to be if you submit to God and relinquish your sweeping to His filling. Think about it—it's no wonder people fall away from the church, or worse, from the Christian life altogether. Without a filling of the empty space after experiencing real repentance, the Devil works overtime to call to your attention the old *demons*. In many cases, he gets back in and causes a re-hash of the same ole frustrations, discouragements and spiritual disappointments. The carnal Christian, with one foot in the world and one in the church is the most vulnerable to this drift. But hey, we are all vulnerable to Satan's wiles if the eternal security of the salvation of your soul does not include the sanctification of your heart. The grace of God and His redemption is forever. But the way you live out the life on this side of eternity can be an unnecessary struggle caused by a life that is empty of spiritual fruit, but full of the world. But wait! There is so much more!

During our years in Brazil, on more than one occasion, I witnessed persons stop at a service station requesting the attendant to fill it up (in Portuguese), not indicating which fuel to use. In Brazil, there are many more choices for fuel at the station: gasoline, 100% ethanol, diesel, biodiesel and natural gas pumps all stand side by side. Suppose you pull up in a newer model car, and the attendant assumes which fuel to use, without consulting the customer. He goes with his default choice of gasoline, to the dismay of the customer who is driving an alcohol powered car! I never hung around for long, knowing that they would have a couple of hours of siphoning all that gas out of the tank!

In like manner, Satan will try to refill your life with his default fuel—evil influences. In the event that he does re-enter your sweeping, you must be swept clean, emptied of the wrong "fuel" in the form of evil influences. Repentance must be permitted to allow God to siphon out that which would impede your start-up and acceleration forward in a life fueled by God's Holy Spirit. Spiritual warfare gets intense at this point. The Devil would lead you to choose the wrong fuel from many choices out in this evil world. Thus, your empty, clean tank is vulnerable, without the old bad habits or misguided behavior. Make no mistake: your salvation and eternal life is not vulnerable, but your abundant life this side of eternity is very much up for all kinds of choices for how you will allow God or the world, the flesh and the Devil to fill your tank/house/personality/lifestyle.

Counterattacks by Satan are common, especially after we have allowed God to clean some area of life of the world's influence. Filling or sowing with spiritual fruit based upon your armament with the whole armor of God (**see Ephesians 6:11–18**) can seal the deal and make your armor impermeable. Those swept areas of your life should be so armed or "filled" with the "good stuff" that Satan can never again return to badger or attack with any degree of success. If you refurnish your "house" after allowing God to sweep, your house is under new management! Now you refurnish your life from a godly and Holy Spirit controlled perspective. Your submission to God will open the way for the Spirit to fill your swept and open house with *practical applications of spiritual fruit*. Satan will continue down the evil road with his prowling, seeking someone else more vulnerable. But wait, there's more! You have just rebuked and denounced the Devil, as you have reaffirmed you salvation! You're more aware than ever of the free gift of God in Christ Jesus. Suddenly you have returned to the dead...dead to sin, that is! Your grace and redemption, justification and reconciliation have emerged from their exile as religious words and churchy rhetoric, because sweeping and filling have awakened you to be alive in Christ with the old stuff crucified (check out Galatians 2:20).

Preparing for Filling/Sowing

You must allow God to arm and ready you for any unexpected guerilla or sniper attacks that evil might attempt. So just to be certain that you have absorbed and comprehended with total clarity the message behind *Sweeping Out the Demons*, let's revisit our key passage, Matthew 12:43–45. Then we can move forward into some smooth and seamless fillings or sowings, making practical applications of God's best lessons for abundant and joyful living, as we fight courageously as soldiers of the Cross.

When the unclean spirit is gone out of a man, he walketh through dry places, seeking rest, and findeth none. Then he saith, I will return into my house from whence I came out; and when he is come, he findeth it empty, swept, and garnished. Then goeth he, and taketh with himself seven other spirits more wicked than himself, and they enter in and dwell there: and the last state of that man is worse than the first. Even so shall it be also unto this wicked generation. (Matthew 12:43–45 KJV)

A heads-up for understanding the situation Jesus was addressing.

Let's move over to a few moments of medium weight Bible study, so that our key passage will be even more meaningful. To do this in summary fashion, I consulted many general reference Bible commentaries. All of them reflected similar light on our key passage.

1) Jesus taught knowing that His lesson would be easily understood by his specific group of listeners: the scribes, Pharisees and Sadducees.
2) Matthew 12:43–45 would have an application for all of Israel, echoing the voices of the prophets as they urged the people of Israel and Judah to do more than window dressing when it came to reforms.
3) Legalism had blinded them to how their religion should affect their relationship with God. Truly seeing this blind spot was Jesus' objective for this important lesson.

4) In the context of Matthew's gospel, we must view the audience as a specific one. Jesus taught this message to a group of scribes and Pharisees. They seemed to be more interested in exorcisms, healings and the like, while uninterested in the transformation in their way of thinking and acting.

5) In this parable type story, Jesus explained that the man's "house" was swept clean, but left empty of any interior refurnishing or improvement. Old demons were cleaned out with the Law, while all of life was strictly governed and controlled.

6) We need a little Old Testament backdrop, in order to understand how Israel, during the time of Jesus, had moved so far away from loving devotion to God, to radical legalism, religious snobbery and a hollow religion.

7) Ever since the time of Ezra and Nehemiah, after the Babylonian exile, nearly six hundred years earlier, their ancestors had rightly reacted to the potential influence from the idols of the pagan religions from all the surrounding countries. The reaction was a hyper-religious and cultural purity, where the Jewish people were prohibited from marrying and interacting with the surrounding pagan cultures. Such legalism began as a good thing to keep Israel true to their devotion to God, in reaction to the drifting of their ancestors from exclusive devotion to the true God.

However, over time, some reactions can begin to be supplanted by an oppressive enforcement of laws, rules and regulations. In order to enforce and refine those legalistic stands, more rules and regulations are enacted. Before long, one cannot even see the original reason for the reaction, and legalism and bureaucracy have replaced a disciplined devotion to God. People had begun unconsciously to worship the laws instead of the Lawgiver, forgetting the real reason for righteousness and obedience, which was summed up for them in verses they recited daily. Deuteronomy 6:4–9 was spoken, written and heard repeatedly, of loving obedience and heartfelt worship of the one true and living God.

8) The legalistic and exclusivist reaction resulted in the groups known as the scribes, Pharisees and Sadducees of Jesus' day. Their continual extensions of rules and regulations to their religious and social practices resulted in their focus on the laws to the neglect of the purpose of the laws. Ironically, the people Jesus was addressing with this story had replaced the feared religious contamination by pagans, with even worse idols, the likes of legalism, pride, provincialism, artificial observance of the Sabbath, insincere fasting and purification rites. These excesses as well as many others had gotten to a ridiculous point by the time of Jesus' earthly ministry. While God was not taken out of the picture through these superficial observances, He became secondary to the outward displays and meaningless interpretations of them. In short, they could not see God for all of the rules for religious practices. The demons spoken of by Jesus in the story were those that led them to religious superficiality and meaningless rituals and rules. They were like the guy who reads all about the rules of golf only to go out and play by all those rules without ever even loving or enjoying the game. He missed the point of the game, and so will we as Christians if we follow rituals, church policies and practices to the exclusion of why we are going to church in the first place!

9) So these verses are a reminder that mere repentance and outward attempts at getting right with God will only

result in leaving the door open just far enough for the evil that once occupied the person to return, stronger and worse than ever. Coming closer to home with this, in our spiritual warfare, sweeping without filling will result in a condition that is inadequate and incapable of keeping out the "demons", or the old evil influences. The original audience, some skeptical Pharisees and scribes, could have been healed from spiritual blindness that day. Religious people are not necessarily close to God. The religious activities can supplant the loving act of devotion to God, resulting in a superficial religion that has supplanted the practice of the ritual in the place of a deepening relationship to God. After trying to remain strong and forming more rules and rituals to help follow the ones that are already in place, the result is a powerless practice that becomes shallow and devoid of any real peace.

10) In the key passage, the central figure is a man who tried to sweep on his own, resulting in ridding his life of the demons. Nothing resulted from the sweeping of the house. The demons were evicted or exorcised without reoccupying the space in his life with true devotion to God. God's strength was not introduced into the space to overcome and "fill" the emptiness of a house or life swept clean. This left room or opportunity for the demons to return in far greater force than before, making the state of the house worse than ever.

11) Like all stories by our Lord, each element had an allegorical significance. The man was symbolic of all who practice religion without realizing the relationship to the object of that religion. The house represented his lifestyle, his thoughts, personality and character. The demons represented...demons. Unlike our supposedly enlightened and sophisticated way of thinking in the

twenty-first century, those invisible forces, powers and principalities were still perceived as they actually are, as real, with a very real influence upon the moral and ethical decisions of life.

12) Jesus spoke of demons and spoke with demons in His earthly ministry. There are instances of His healing individuals while with other healings He cast out demons from the individuals. So the man in the story related to the belief of the scribes and Pharisees in the need for exorcism of evil spirits. They would have no problem understanding Jesus' parable. Their problem was seeing beyond the practice of the casting out of demons to the transformation of the delivered soul. Like people today, they could not put the dots together to incorporate new and better thoughts, attitudes and practices from the God who had cleansed them from demonic forces. This implies that the Pharisaic practices of exorcism were in and of themselves, superficial or even artificial rituals designed to coerce or enforce their intricate set of religious practices. Whether or not that was true of all of their ritual cleansings from demonic powers, the resulting condition of the people cleansed was consistent—they remained empty and void of any deeper devotion or spiritual healing from the God who was originally the object of all of Jewish religion.

13) This is the conclusion drawn by Jesus for the man and his house in the parable. Because nothing replaced or filled the void left by sweeping, his condition would revert to the original evil influence, only worse. The condition would be deemed far worse because the swept house remained disconnected to how the house might be used or refurnished after the sweeping. His house would most likely deteriorate to a worse state than before. The

demons would continually seek rest in some dwelling. Finding their original abode empty, we can conclude that Jesus was inferring of the potential for more demonic influence. Since the man felt he had swept clean the house, we can also presume that he was through with any further attention to the matter. Therefore, the previous occupants along with their cohorts would have an open opportunity to return without opposition.

14) Jesus said that this described the condition of the generation with whom He was speaking. He described that generation (which could describe all subsequent generations, including ours) as evil. Repentance is empty, hollow and superficial, without subsequent acts of loving devotion and reform.

15) Could the parable be speaking to you and me as well? Could it speak to the church in the twenty-first century just as it spoke to the original audience? Absolutely and without a doubt, it speaks to us through the power of the Holy Spirit. Just as all of the teachings of Jesus have both historical and contemporary applications, God's Spirit breathes inspiration and revelation into our interpretation of His Word.

Let's make the practical application to filling/sowing.

So for a moment, let's examine filling as a sidebar or footnote. If you don't allow God to fill the void left by true repentance with His fruit, gifts, precepts, exhortations and inspirations, Satan will fill the void with the works of the flesh, temptation, pride, guilt or any variation of those so-called "Seven Deadly Sins". Here is a huge example of how Satan inflicted a long term, long-range attack, during a time when humanity was gradually turning our backs on God. One of the Devil's greatest strategies is to erode the confidence and authority we have in God and His Holy Scriptures, by casting doubt and skepticism in the absolute truth of God's living Word. The secular worldview has caused many to view Scripture as only a vestige of the past, labeling it as an outdated and outmoded book. The prevailing lie is to perceive the Bible as a book that may or may not contain truth. This premise presupposes that all Scripture is not trustworthy or even applicable to this generation. So there was room to fill a void that had deepened in the church's capacity to trust God. So, in steps Satan, prowling to see whom to devour. The Devil has been working in media, literature and even through some segments of the church, to bring society to these general conclusions about the Bible. Sadly, he has been patiently carving out this secular worldview for just a little over two hundred years.

During years when religious thought was fragmented, there were far more arguments, splits and denominational squabbles than focuses upon the Great Commandment and the Great Commission. Theological haggling with philosophy and science was growing, while the churches were getting more and more casual about the influences of the world. Meanwhile, Christianity was growing less concerned with the influences of the church upon that same lost and dying world. Seeing few revivals and renewals from among the churches, the church experienced only brief flickers of qualitative or quantitative growth. Satan must have seen God's people as floundering and weak. So God in His infinite and perfect wisdom permitted Satan to test and try the church as never before. Like in Jesus' story, God has allowed Satan to see a house empty and open to reoccupation, largely due to the church's apathy and laziness. So the Devil has used what was going on in the secular worldview to change the way people would view life in general. Satan saw it more specifically, as a subtle way to change how the church would view God and His Word in the twenty-first century.

As a major attack by Satan, three important eighteenth and nineteenth century historical movements were used as evil attempts to disrupt how God was permitting humanity to grow and mature intellectually, through those same three movements. The Industrial Revolution, the Renaissance and the Enlightenment ushered in all sorts of new ways for viewing the world. Industry grew exponentially through the mechanization of factories, better forms of energy and new and faster ways to transport goods. Art, literature and music flourished. Advances were made in the inventiveness and development of scientific and mathematical thought. Medical breakthroughs in treatment and care were frequent and life changing. It seemed that God was filling humanity with all sorts of advancements in order to be more fruitful and multiply our usefulness for the betterment of His creation.

All of this was God's creative expression of His image, to advance and improve society, both of which should have been tremendous tools in ministering to the lost world. Yet Satan saw these movements as an opportunity influence humanity to use our own pride and arrogance to relegate God's role in our ingenuity. Then he found it easy to influence those same great minds, already full of themselves with egocentric grandeur, to elevate freethinking beyond all moral and ethical boundaries. He used pride and arrogance to venerate the empirical thinking of the scientific method to the exclusion of the spiritual realm of thought. With this empirical standard in place (*no truth unless it can be scientifically proven*), Satan proceeded to dismantle confidence in the biblical worldview.

Religion in general was demoted to mere superstition and unenlightened ignorance. Satan reoccupied society in such a way that he could gradually bring about a level of thought that would emerge in the twentieth century as secular humanism, elevating man as superior to God. This emphasis upon the human potential over faith relationship with God has come full circle to a worldview that has created its own gods, led in a progression of heretical thinking which spurned a host of ways of thinking and living. Among the most basic is hedonistic materialism. Satan used it to spurn greed and unbridled morality to their limits. Religious and philosophical expression also has furnished some fiery darts for the Devil. The short list includes the liberalism drawn from the conclusions of neo-orthodoxy, the rise of varying alternatives to true spirituality like the Spiritism of Alan Kardec, the New Age Movement, the occult and psycho-socio alternatives like transcendental meditation, yoga and pseudo-interpretations of eastern religions. Always, Satan's strategy has been to break down barriers in order to attract people away from serious consideration of Evangelical Christianity. His ultimate goal in our time is to move the biblical worldview from mainstream religious discussion to a postmodern back burner, and ultimately to a post Christian position—where the Bible and solid theological positions for life choices is seen as impractical, antiquated and irrelevant.

During the past thirty or so years, he used theological squabbling to generate denominational splits and parachurch reactions to Christianity, all attempting to explain the supernatural with empirical or humanistic explanations. The so-called prosperity gospel movement is a prime example of this type or reaction. The point is, look at how many ways Satan has used to fill the void left by the need for repentance and reform in the local church. Every void in our thinking, attitudes and actions will be filled by something. Satan in his mad dash to survive yet a bit longer, is frantically using the secular worldview to move people away from a basic receptivity to the message of the Bible. This is filling the void in empty, seeking and even rebellious hearts with many subtle applications of the way of the world to life's most basic needs and desires. My friend, he is making some advances that are causing a chain reaction of monumental proportions. The most blatant fillings by evil are the aggressive LGBT agendas, pro-choice agendas, advertising of alcohol, drugs and other dangerous alternatives as safe and acceptable and multiple Hollywood agendas to move sex, violence and profanity to complete desensitization by viewers. Not far behind is the filling by legitimized, organized criminal elements with their subtle gambling agenda. For some years now, they have worked through state governments to hook people into the addiction through state sanctioned lotteries and more widespread availability to casinos. These are fillings by Satan of empty voids in lives of everyday people, designed to allow him time to reign just a bit longer over the world.

Another subtle filling that evil has masterminded is a late nineteenth and early twentieth century assault upon the Bible. Respected Bible scholars of the early to mid-twentieth century were highly influenced by science and empirical thinking to prove the Bible. Before anyone knew it, seminaries were purporting methods for exegesis that led to challenges to the veracity of Scripture. Almost like sleight of hand, the Bible was taken on as a book to be dissected by renowned Bible scholars in order to give their "science" a more empirical identity in the scholarly world. I truly believe that most of these fine scholars did not even realize what they were doing to the identity, integrity or authority of Scripture. Yes, filling can be at the hands of evil while appearing as impressive, scholarly and validated by the world it was meant to redeem. Theology began to try to explain the origins of God's Word at the expense of applying its principles and precepts to life. Anything that was not empirically verifiable was seen as suspect, superstition or even as contrived by unsophisticated or under educated minds of previous generations. Spiritual warfare has made significant advances against this strategy in recent years, through faith based scholarship and genuine applications to life's problems through a God-centered apologetic. But to be forewarned is to be forearmed to such attempts at filling with the wrong things. Filling or sowing is huge in its impact for your life and the very redemption of the world.

This is a shorter than desired explanation of how Satan will fill your repentance with the works of the flesh if you do not permit God to fill them with practical applications of the fruit of the Spirit. That Devil will prowl and seek until he finds some vulnerable place to dwell. When he finds a weakness to trip you up, he will develop that evil in a destructive way that could help him to survive a few more generations, before realizing his horrible demise from God.

I hope that you are seeing how his deceptions are designed to lower your guard in spiritual warfare, making it easier for him to tempt, test or otherwise slow your spiritual advancement. So I pray you will consent to a realization of this basic tenet for spiritual survival. Satan has tried to do a number on humanity, even using the church against herself, to further his filling with evil. Therefore, we must permit God to fill us as we repent! We have to deny Satan's lies and repudiate them with God's truth as lived out in how we fill or sow. A great beginning to permitting God to fill your life with practical applications of spiritual fruit is to take this story from Matthew 12:43–45 and treat it like a Jonah-type lesson. Move beyond the sweeping like the man in the story. React in the opposite manner from those stubborn scribes and Pharisees! Fill where the man did not fill his "house"! Take every word in the Word as absolute truth, profitable or useful for your instruction in how best to fill the void left by genuine repentance. In Paul's letters to his "son" in the faith, we are reminded of how he instructed Timothy concerning Scripture. The admonition really helps us to remember where to go first for filling and sowing.

And that from a child thou hast known the holy Scriptures, which are able to make thee wise unto salvation through faith which is in Christ Jesus. All scripture is given by inspiration of God, and is profitable for doctrine, for reproof for correction, for instruction in righteousness: That the man of God may be perfect, thoroughly furnished unto all good works. (2 Timothy 3:15–17 KJV)

Now for the basics of filling or sowing...

Now let's return to your training in the second principle in *Sweeping Out the Demons*: *Filling or Sowing.* Our objective in the second principle is: allowing God to begin **filling the void or empty place left by genuine repentance with something far better, in order to crowd out, evict and permanently displace Satan and his demons from ever again occupying that part of your life.**

The spiritual principle that Jesus implored the Pharisees to understand might be compared to the physics principle of the occupation of space and time. Segments of space or segments of time will always be occupied with something or some event.. Some form of matter will occupy all space, be it solid matter, vapor, gaseous or liquid. You could say it this way. Where space exists or where time passes, there is a spatial and temporal possibility to occupy that space or time, such as the activity of nature, a process, circumstance or event in time. Eventually a hole in the ground fills with something, like dirt, rocks, water or vegetation. Besides solid matter, air occupies space. The air dissipates in order for the solid matter to replace it. Getting more on my level, consider mealtime, as I surely do! Eventually food and liquids will fill your empty stomach (*you hope*). Otherwise, the stomach fills with spatial gassy acids and vapor that beckons all of us at one time or another...hunger. Helping to prompt that bodily understanding of hunger is a glandular and cerebral impulse, sending a message to your senses to satisfy hunger by the filling of that space, better known as your appetite. In spiritual warfare, remember that we have all sorts of appetites. Pleasure or the avoidance of the unpleasant opens up the need to fill/sow with something or someone, in order to satisfy these appetites. Consider how you are filling appetites like physical, emotional, psychological and most importantly, spiritual ones.

Our desires, our will or volition, our preferences and our reactions are all a part of a different kind of spatial filling, called *intellect*. Though invisible, the way we think and the choices we make fill an intellectual "space" that was occupied by an inquisitive curiosity that calls out to all of us to investigate the possibilities for knowledge, gratification or resistance to that knowledge or gratification. What fills a desire or preference toward making a simple decision? Well, that depends upon other spatial and temporal factors, such as circumstances, interpersonal relationships and influences from your surroundings. Every experience in life, involving our sensitivities to sight, sound, smell and touch influence our thinking—remember Eve in Genesis, chapter three? A filling of a void definitely took place that day! A void caused by curiosity, fueled by half-truths from Satan, caused Eve to fill her appetite with evil, instead of good. Look at the factors involved in her choice:

And when the woman saw that the tree was good for food, and that it was pleasant to the eyes, and a tree to be desired to make one wise, she took of the fruit thereof, and did eat, and gave also unto her husband with her; and he did eat. (Genesis 3:6 KJV)

Eve filled the void with the original forbidden fruit, while we have followed suit with many other variations of that forbidden fruit. Many have followed her lead throughout history. We learn what not to fill with from those examples. We call them

Jonah-type lessons—you know, it's as if you say to yourself, "... don't mess up like I did, do the opposite!" The other side of filling sees you make the right decision from the get-go. Many have filled the voids with obedient, loving devotion that leads to decisions based on conviction. We think of those fillings based upon good examples as Joseph-type lessons—you remember, it's as if you say to yourself, "...follow my example and my model for filling, sowing the same way that I responded!" How we fill the emptiness that remains after genuine repentance will determine the degree of victory in spiritual warfare. It will determine the degree of joy and peace that you experience in your daily walk with the Lord.

We will now look at some of the ways to fill the void in order to make your sweeping repentance complete. A synonym for *filling* is *sowing*. The Bible tells us a lot about sowing seed, both in the sense of vegetation and in the context of sowing spiritual seed. The principle of sowing is enjoined with the principle of reaping. What you sow will affect what you reap, how much you reap and how long you will reap. You already know that. So, filling or sowing in spiritual warfare should be easier to implement than the silver bullet of repentance was. Nope—buzzzz, I'm sorry, wrong answer! Filling or sowing the right seed with the fruit of the Spirit is just as challenging as when God sweeps out the demon influences after your genuine repentance. Just as repentance is hard, challenging and humbling, filling or sowing the right seed is a challenging combination of prayer, time in the Word, and the deep faith dependence upon God.

The principle of filling is continuing to trust God to guide you to sow the right seed. Choosing the right seed to sow, in order to fill the emptiness left by repentance, is just as essential as were the steps to genuine repentance. This filling is going to make or break you as an effective soldier of the cross. It will most influence how you deal with how you confront the everyday tests, trials and temptations. You probably are way ahead of me here. Such sweeping and filling are impossible apart from allowing the Holy Spirit to lead you through the filling. After all, my friend, upon your salvation, He already filled your life with His indwelling presence, so why not allow the one who fills you to do the filling.

This filling of empty spaces is what spiritual warfare is all about. Where repentance implemented your attack upon Satan's forces, filling is your battle plan for advancement to the battle objective: *a life that joyfully honors and glorifies God.* How you fill the empty spaces left by repentance is influenced by who or what is most in control of the way you think. How you fill determines how you make all future choices. Either God will influence these fillings through prayer and His Word, or Satan and his forces will influence them with their influences upon your thinking. One or the other will win the battle for your mind. Much has been written about this influence to the mind, all of which emerges from Paul's admonition in Romans 12:1–2. Satan can have some wins here, but not if you change your paradigm for spiritual warfare. You are a child of the King! Remember whose you are (John 1:12), who created you, and why you were created. Most of all, remember who has redeemed you, and why (John 3:16; Romans 5:8).

Look again at the Pharisees with whom Jesus addressed our key passage. It was the same for those Pharisees as it is for you and me in the twenty-first century. God is almighty, sovereign, creator of all, and yes, that creation included Satan. Those religious leaders had a choice to make as they listened to Jesus. They could take what He had said to them and repent, asking God to sweep out pride, arrogance, legalism and closed mindedness filling that void with loving obedience and devotion to God. On the other hand, they could reject what Jesus taught them and continue to live in empty religious ritual. The filling that they chose was allowing Satan to keep them enslaved to their own egocentric power, in order to maintain control of the synagogues. Just thing of what they missed!

In a tone of loving discipline, Jesus tried to reach out to those Pharisees with the essential message of His Good News. He taught them that in order truly to fight evil, the man in the story would have to get close to God and go beyond legalism and empty, artificial religious rituals. He would need to fill the empty spaces with loving devotion to God and others, in loving obedience to God and God alone. By exercising this filling of true devotion to God, they would come to an end of themselves. Their lives would be filled with the fruit of God's Spirit as being taught by Jesus Himself. Instead, they were legalistic slaves to the Law with its complicated pattern of principles and statutes, not to mention all of the varying interpretations that the rabbis had appended to the Law. To continue as they were would mean that they would methodically move along in religious drudgery, trying to follow all that they had included in their list of do's and don'ts, while excluding how those laws should have been affecting their relationship to God as well as to their fellow Jews. Take a minute or two to read Deuteronomy, chapter six. That lifestyle of devotion is what they were missing! Instead, their lives would be filled with self-styled attempts to fulfill the Law at the expense of love, joy, peace, patience, goodness, kindness gentleness faithfulness and self-control. In short, filling on their own would make them discontented, prideful, unfulfilled and worst of all, continually more distant from the God they had replaced, with their rituals and heartless rules.

They chose not to listen to Jesus, but you can use them as a Jonah-type lesson. Hear and heed to the example Jesus gave. Because the man did not fill the empty space swept clean, the demons entered anew in the arid, empty space, returning with such fervor and enthusiasm that the situation was far worse than before his house had been swept clean. Jesus concluded verse forty-five with a warning for them and for us: *"Even so shall it be also unto this wicked generation"*.

So it was for the Pharisees, Sadducees and the scribes, who continued to deny Jesus as Messiah until they crucified Him. Their plight with the Roman government got worse, and eventually Rome destroyed Jerusalem and the Temple. In like manner, you will experience a type of destructive defeat every time you attempt a "DYI" (do-it-yourself) filling or sowing. Any type of filling you try to do on your own will amount to no more than a self-improvement campaign or some New Year's type resolution. Instead of allowing the Holy Spirit the freedom and permission from your own will to filling that void left by genuine repentance, most of us feel more confident and comfortable trying to fill it ourselves with duct tape or super glue type fillings, instead of with the fruit of the Spirit. Why not, we will invariably ask. The answer is permanence and authority. Without God to bless, guide and direct, these efforts, sooner or later, even your best efforts at sowing resolution or resistance to a habit, you will be left with a void and empty frustration, where you have sought to right a wrong, kick a habit or repair a relationship. Either the corrections and adjustments will not last, or the willpower and fortitude of character will be so intense and stressful that you will be miserable in your victory. You will feel just one temptation in a weak moment away from a disappointing return to square one. Before you know it, you'll find yourself going through the same cycle of reform, only with one more defeat to deal with, and a sense of devil-dread that you won't make it to filling victory this next time, either.

Only God is strong enough to do the filling, just as He is the only one strong enough to sweep through your desire for genuine repentance. Filling requires yet another "silver bullet"—it is the conscious act of surrender and submission of your will to God's will. It entails giving God's Holy Spirit permission to do that which you cannot. Actually, you're already en route with this submission, because that process began when you said yes to Jesus and accepted Him as your Lord and Savior. At that moment of surrender to Jesus, the invisible, unexplainable miracle of the indwelling of the Holy Spirit occurred in your life, to remain and reign forever! In like manner, every time you call upon the name of the Lord to fill you with the practical application of the fruit of the Spirit, He willingly and joyfully takes control of that area of your heart and life. Suddenly, you have experienced another invisible, unexplainable miracle. So if you are reading this and have never experienced the first filling of the Holy Spirit, then you can resolve that right now by accepting Jesus into your heart as your Lord and Savior. He will save you, redeem you from eternity in Hades, and fill you with all that is necessary to live the life God meant for you when He created you.

God through His Spirit will not force you to give that permission for Him to fill you with His fruit. Just as you must earnestly seek His gifts that were endowed to you upon your salvation, so you must ask God for wisdom, discernment and understanding in how He desires to exercise His will upon just how He will apply the fruit and gifts of the Spirit. We can know with certainty, that He will make this application in order for your repentance to be filled with the fruit in a way that will influence some action, attitude or decision from some element of your spatial or temporal life base. This life base or endowment is best understood by expressing it as your *three "T's"*—your **T**ime, your **T**alent **or your T**reasure. Another words, God will fill in a way as to influence you through His will. He will do so in how you spend your time, how you use your God-given talents and how you spend or invest His material wealth.

Given permission to operate, the Holy Spirit will release the spiritual weapons necessary for a powerful defense and an overpowering offensive attack in your spiritual warfare. God loves you too much to make you or coerce you into giving Him the permission to appropriate this filling. Even though the Holy Spirit indwells in you the believer every second of every day, ever since the decision to accept Christ, He does not desire to make you follow and be filled. To the contrary, He longs for you to choose to reject the Adam nature as well as appropriate His wisdom. He will continue to guide you to respond appropriately to all the Jonah-type lessons that got you to the point for the need of genuine repentance in the first place. The nature of God demonstrates all through Scripture how He desires that you openly, humbly give His Holy Spirit permission to flow through your mind and give you the knowledge and wisdom to let God fill you with the fruit of the Spirit.

Now at this point in your basic training for filling, you are approaching a critical transition in your spiritual warfare. Like a promotion in rank, you will be advancing from continuing to live under the carnal nature like Adam (and like the lost world without Jesus), to claiming your spiritual nature of sonship as a child of the King. *Claiming your sonship* is the first step toward allowing God the freedom to guide you in filling. Romans, chapters six through eight help you understand the wonderful freedom you have to be a child of the King of Kings. Being a child of a king means that you have special privileges and unlimited access to that king. It means that Jesus loves you with an everlasting, unlimited and unconditional love. It also gives you the relief from having to control all the strings and decisions in life. You have the greatest yokefellow! In Matthew 11:28–30, Jesus invites you His child (*also check out John 1:12*) to allow Him to bear the load of your yoke, be it temptation, frustration, or any physical, emotional or spiritual challenge. He is your Lord! He is your Great Physician! He has gone ahead of you to prepare your place in heaven when you die! Let Him guide you in filling, because He has already filled you with His Holy Spirit. He is available, ready and eager to do that which you could never do on your own. Appropriate the step of giving permission for the Holy Spirit to operate where you have repented and where God has swept clean that evil. I cannot repeat this enough. Please pray right now and sincerely give God that permission. Your salvation will become more real than ever before, because you are giving the God who saved you the freedom and permission to operate freely in the control of your will, your attitudes and your actions. You may or may not know what it means to be filled with the Holy Spirit—but now you can know without a doubt, and best of all, begin to live like it!

A truth you must embrace in order to be filled...

Jesus preached, taught, healed and cast out demons. As we stated earlier, the worldview so dominant today would have you think that demons, evil and a literal Satan do not exist. That viewpoint would have you consider that these images of darkness were symbolic or primitive ways of thinking. In order to fill the voids with spiritual fruit and fiercely battle Satan with great confidence in God's guidance, you must believe that the evil of Satan is real, so that you can declare the greatness of God. As surely as God created you and me, He created an angel named Lucifer. As surely as God is in control of His universe, you must agree by faith that His control includes the activity of Satan. By faith, know that God can even use the evil attempts of Satan for the strengthening of His saints like you and me. In this step of filling, you relinquish fighting solely with your ingenuity and intellect, and allow God to fight before you, beside you, behind you, above you and below you. You are realizing the fullness of the Godhead in you by allowing Him to fill your life with His fruit.

You must trust that by allowing God control of the filling, that He will fill your life with something far better than you could. You may already know this, but I ask anyway, so all readers will be on the same page with regard to the essentials of filling. Just what is it that God will use to fill the voids? He will use practical applications of what we have come to call the fruit of the Spirit. Let's try to learn all we can about the fruit of the Spirit.

The fruit of the Spirit is a collective list of attributes or qualities that enable you to honor and to glorify God in a particular situation or decision. The fruit of the Spirit are more than just good points of character. They come directly from God to equip and permit you to live in the Spirit instead of under the enslavement of the flesh. They are the tools for replacing evil influences and evicting the subtle and astute influences of Satan and his demons from your "house". They can only be appropriated through giving permission for God to replace this fruit for what you have repented of and what God has swept from your life. They are endowed by the Holy Spirit, available to the believer in full measure...all of them. Unlike the gifts of the Spirit, as listed in Romans 12:6–8, 1 Corinthians 12 and Ephesians 4:11–13, the entirety of the fruit of the Spirit are yours as a believer since the moment you were saved. However, one or more of the gifts of the Spirit are given selectively to believers, as God desires for the spiritual needs of His body, the church. Where fruit are qualities of character, spiritual gifts are abilities, competencies and talent based skills that the Holy Spirit chooses to commission in specific lives.

Few persons have all the spiritual gifts, but rather each of us is gifted with at least one gift. I discovered as I taught church planters in Brazil that generally speaking, most would see in their lives a couple of dominant gifts and one or more secondary gifts. In contrast, the fruit of the Spirit is the tool that the Holy Spirit uses to refine and sharpen your personality and character. This enables you to be equipped to confront everyday living in a manner that will let your light shine, your salt season and your personality reflect that you are a new creature in Christ Jesus and the light of the world for all who encounter you.

In Day 9, we will focus more on the fruit of the Spirit. In the meantime, here are the places in the Word where you will find the most prominent attributes or expressions of the fruit of the Spirit: Galatians 5:22–23 contains what is considered the most complete list of the fruit of the Spirit: love, joy peace, patience, gentleness, kindness, goodness, faithfulness and self-control.

Mention of the fruit or commentary about one or more of the fruit are found in several areas of the New Testament. Please take time to read these while you are here, marking them in your Bible or a note journal. Matthew 3:8 expresses a desire to be repentant, a key factor in preparation for permitting the fruit of the Spirit to operate freely in your attitudes and actions. The Beatitudes in Matthew 5:1–12 are the best list of general attitudes necessary for the practical application of spiritual fruit. They can be seen as *shades* or *degrees of expression* to guide you in the effective application of the fruit of the Spirit in daily living. Those general attitudes are spiritual poverty, growing dependence upon God through a genuine sorrow or contrition over the influence of sin. The Beatitudes also encompass such expressions of fruit as meekness, humility, and a righteous or passionate indignation to evil. Attitudes about right living are influenced in the last tier of the Beatitudes. The intensity with which you express your applications of spiritual fruit depends upon a growing hunger or thirst for righteousness (Matthew 5:6). The application of spiritual fruit depends upon an attitude check to include **mercy** toward others (Matthew 5:7, also a gift the Spirit). Other Beatitudes reflect results of the fruit: purity of heart and life, a growing desire to be a peacemaker, and the capacity to endure persecution or suffering in the name of Jesus (an expression of the fruit of self-control).

Other indicators of spiritual fruit are described in 1 Corinthians 13:1–7 (a more complete and profound definition for love), in Ephesians 5:9 (goodness, righteousness and truth), and in Philippians 1:11 (righteousness). In James 3:17–18, we find multiple expressions of spiritual fruit: purity in wisdom, peace loving, consideration for others, submissiveness, mercy and peacemaking. Never forget that at the very foundation of how you will apply the fruit of the Spirit is how well you are wearing the whole armor of God, as described in Ephesians 6:11–18. Read that chapter right now as I walk you through it.

The chapter begins with some practical applications of the fruit of the Spirit, concerning how children should treat their parents, how parents should treat their children, how servants/ employees should treat their masters/bosses and vice-versa (Ephesians 6:1–10). A great exercise in your devotional Bible study would be to mark every passage that answers the question, *"Is this action a practical application of the fruit of the Spirit?"* Then keep a list, and integrate some of these into filling/sowing those voids left by genuine repentance!

Ephesians 6:11–18 focuses on the foundational principles for sweeping, filling and keeping out evil, best known as "The Whole Armor of God". I urge you to read all that you can about this armor. Tons of great teachings have been written on this amazing description by Paul of what is behind your practical application of the fruit of the Spirit. Ephesians 6:11–13 aptly define spiritual warfare. Filling with the fruit of the Spirit is not possible without the building blocks of the Christian soldier's uniform. This armor is essential because of the strength and cunning of this evil angel of darkness. His "wiles" are truly unruly and deceptive for even the most apt disciple. God has meant it to be so in order for His true church to emerge faithful to the test. Describing the fabric or material for this armor, Paul states that truth, righteousness, the gospel of peace; faith for salvation and the Word are absolute necessities for the soldier to wrestle with these "powers and principalities". While the Roman soldiers of Paul's day wore this armor over the body to protect from physical injury, this passage uses those same pieces for outfitting the soldier's inner man. Long before he is outfitted with his weapons and protective garments, a soldier goes through rigorous basic training, which is followed by specific training.

That training is designed to prepare the soldier's mind and body to withstand any assault, preparing the soldier to make appropriate advances against the enemy. Paul uses the analogy of body armor to outfit you the soldier to stand against invisible forces that lurk in darkness in "high places". It is very important that you examine your life right now to determine whether you have allowed God to equip you with this armor. Without the outfitting by the Holy Spirit, you can't move forward in sweeping, filling or keeping out evil. So for each piece of the whole armor of God, you must ask these questions. Am I saved? Have I allowed the truth of the Gospel of peace to free me from sin's penalty of eternal separation from God? Am I ready to permit God to turn my natural, former way of living into His righteousness, or am I trying to do this on my own? Am I allowing the sword of the Spirit, the Word of God, to speak to my heart daily? Answer these questions during a time with the Lord, and you truly will be ready to answer this next pivotal question, and make the scriptural formula begin to transform your spiritual warfare, one sweeping at a time! (Please stop right this very moment and have this talk with the Father, before continuing your journey in Sweeping Out the Demons.

Now you are ready for the home stretch in your basic training for filling. Just as you moved forward in your sweeping by allowing God to do the sweeping as you submitted to genuine repentance, make that same move in filling, by answering this question: *"Am I now willing to let God do the filling?"*

In saying yes to this premise, you are saying that you are good to go on yet another related premise: that you unequivocally believe that Jesus is fighting spiritual warfare on your behalf.

He began this in heaven at the right hand of God, and He sealed the veracity of this at Calvary. From the empty tomb, He filled your life with hope for eternity. And as He ascended into the heavens, He promised the coming of the Holy Spirit (Acts 1:8). So you are a soldier without any reason to fear death. Think about it. A soldier who is fearless and has no apprehension about given up this life is unbeatable. You have been given the hope of eternal life after this part of life is finished. Regardless of how long that is, you know that your life will continue in heaven forever! Are you a slave to the fear of death? Allow God to free you from this bondage. A soldier who is not afraid to die will not be afraid to live life to the fullest! Claim these verses as yours, right now.

Forasmuch then as the children are partakers of flesh and blood, he also himself likewise took part of the same; that through death he might destroy him that had the power of death, that is, the devil; and deliver them who through fear of death were all their lifetime subject to bondage. (Hebrews 2:14–15

So with all of this armor and fruit and assurance of eternal life, are you willing to let God do the filling? If you have prayed thus, then you are ready, my friend, to aggressively go forth into battle, allowing God to defeat anything that might cause evil to make advances in your lifestyle. Your genuine repentance from that which interferes with honoring and glorifying God is abundant living. It is Spirit-filled living. That is living connected to the Vine (John 15: 1-5). Now you are ready to graduate from basic training in spiritual warfare! So what's next?

The next step is giving the Holy Spirit permission to fight on your behalf with the fruit of the spirit, armed with the whole armor of God, against the works of the flesh.

Permission is an interesting concept. We give permission for our kids to go outside and play or watch TV. We extend or make conditional permission for them to play computer games for *just a few more minutes*. We give formal permission for them to go on a field trip by signing a permission letter. On a much more serious level, we might be called upon to sign permission or release forms for a loved one in order for a hospital to perform surgery or some other form of treatment. Permission can be a life or death decision.

At times, we give unspoken or even unconscious permission to other people to act toward us in a certain manner, by what we say or by our reluctance to say anything at all. At times, we may even give the Devil permission to torment us with temptation and testing by our unwillingness to resist him with the spiritual warfare tools at hand, namely, effectual, fervent prayer and a love for the Bible. Permission means consent to a given contract or agreement. It means to allow another to act or not act in a certain manner toward us. Permission always implies that we must adjust —to the conditions that were agreed upon when permission was granted.

The Holy Spirit will always await your permission to act on your behalf. However, He will operate freely from your will... because He is God. He will minister to you in the capacities of teacher, encourager, edifier, healer and messenger. God also sends His angels to intercede on our behalf with perfect timing and discernment. He disciplines us, rebukes us, and even punishes us out of His love for us, apart from any volition on our part (Hebrews 12:5–6).

Even though He is God omnipotent, omniscient and omnipresent, in matters of sweeping, filling and keeping, God yearns for the believer to come to Him. The repentance is responded to by God's intercessional sweeping as He works with your desire for reparation. That reparation because of repentance

173

is what we call filling or sowing. God requires of us that we come to Him in this filling and open heart and life to receive what is actually already available to us. Every omni capacity of God is availed to you the believer when you give God permission or open yourself to be Holy Spirit controlled. Already Spirit filled at the moment of conversion, you must now open the door for God to give you all that He wants to provide. At that point, you can celebrate that you are freed to live in victory over the sins that have so easily beset or entangled you (see Heb. 12:1–2). You can rejoice that you have been liberated from Satan's attempts to defeat or discourage attitudes or actions that would otherwise honor and glorify God. At your request and at your point of permission and submission, God will appropriate the fruit of the Spirit, guiding you to make practical applications of the fruit of the Spirit spiritual.

With **permission** naturally follows **submission**. As you pray that you have come to the end of yourself, you are entering the battlefield ready to submit and permit the General to lead you into battle. In war, it is explicit that you follow His orders and instructions. Regardless of whether or not you agree with them or even fully understand them, you must submit and permit the orders to play out their implicit purpose. God is neither required nor obligated to give me complete orientation about the course of battle that He is leading me to fight. I am not capable of even beginning to understand the will, plan and purpose of God for upcoming spiritual warfare, and neither are you. Sometimes we say to children, to team members or to the small group, "Just do as I say and go with it. Someday you will understand." God requires us to walk by faith on a need to know basis. That is the best way I can think of to describe filling at this point...just go with it and trust God for the victory. This one adjustment will make the greatest difference in your entire walk with the Lord!

You become the optimum soldier when you follow orders to the letter. You are putting your life in the hands of someone else in the heat and dangers of war. God is your leader, your Commander-in-Chief, your boss, your chief, your C.E.O., if you will—go with God and He will take you where you need to go, show you what you need to know, and fight the fight before you strike a single blow. He will even raise your Sword of the Spirit at the precise moments when Scripture can speak loudest! We follow, and as the Israelites discovered, God actually fought the battle before they even lifted shield and sword. So I ask you to make a formal invitation to God Almighty right now to lead you into battle. Your invitation to Him should contain the promise that no matter how difficult the battle, and no matter how the battle is waxing or waning, that you will permit Him to be in control. This will not only be difficult for any strong willed soldier, but it will be impossible apart from a growing dependence upon God's Spirit. Invite God to appropriate the fruit of the Spirit in your fight to complete repentance. Frequently take a mental "step-back" to consider where the battle is raging. Allow the Lord to fill the void where evil once resided. If you will allow your Lord the time and space to do this then you can be assured of continual victories over the habits, attitudes and actions in your life that do not agree with His desires for your heart (see Psalm 37:4–5).

Actually, you should be very excited at this point, as if you are winning some great and valuable prize, or on the verge of seeing a great victory, because that is *exactly* what is happening! Look at Colossians 1:27, where Paul spoke of this process of allowing Christ to live in you and through you, as you agree with Him in this permission to submission.

...the riches of the glory of this mystery among the Gentiles; which is Christ in you, the hope of glory (KJV).

There is no point in the Christian life when you will feel more connected and crucified with Christ (Gal. 2:20) than when you permit and submit to the appropriation of the fruit of the Spirit in spiritual warfare. It is one thing to *read* about spiritual warfare. It is quite another matter actually to be in the *fight* with the Lord leading the way! At this point, it all becomes so real, as so much more than being in a Bible study or hearing a message. You are in the thick of battle, face-to-face with evil—with the Devil and his demons, in person, as you mentally, emotionally and physically march behind the Lord Jesus Christ! Wow! Spiritual warfare is intense and exciting and more rewarding than I can describe, but only if you are following Christ, the hope of glory. Imagine how honored and glorified Jesus is as He makes that heavenly glance behind Himself and sees *you*. If there is a smile in the countenance and glory of God, this is the moment you will feel it as He is permitted to take over, equipping you, encouraging you and challenging you to experience the best life! Prosperity preachers talk about the *best life* as success, position, cars, houses, money and luxuries, but my friend, spiritual warfare, well fought behind the General Jesus is as good as it gets!

In Colossians 1:27 and several other places, we are told about a *mystery* (Romans 16:25; 1 Corinthians 15:51; Ephesians 5:32; 1 Timothy 3:16). In each case, these verses complete key details of how the mystery in Colossians 1:27 fleshes out in your life. This mystery is from God and cannot be generated, invented or imitated by you or me. We just have to permit or allow God to reveal the details of the mystery, one day at a time, by faith in the ability, character and capacity of the General, Jehovah-Jireh—the Lord who will provide! I am tempted to do spiritual warfare on my own, to make it up as I go along, to scheme and to bargain with God. **This is the disclaimer:** do not try this at home or anywhere else without God in control, because it will fail and could cause serious casualties in your spiritual warfare. God has to do it all with you the soldier as His instrument of faith and trust. This should give you great peace knowing that the pressure is off you to be ingenuitive. Your role has become that of just being submissive to God's directives.

No battle plan for filling or sowing is adequate until we understand the potential strategy of the Enemy, to keep you from that filling. Satan is out to gain some control point in your mind as you go through the day, doing what you do. He desires to make your permission and submission just as difficult as possible. He tends to use a kind of subtle frustration or abrupt urging so that you will react inappropriately to life's physical, emotional and spiritual "bumps and bruises". Watch out for this, because it is a primary tactic of the Evil One and his demons as they make their subtle assaults throughout your everyday routine. Battling Satan at this point is combat at the center of the battlefield, where the soldier knows that the fighting will be intense, heated and very fast paced. In your daily routine, *stuff* just happens and you don't necessarily analyze all of it as having the potential for the Devil to pounce with it.

Remember this age-old counsel: *to be forewarned is to be forearmed*! At this point, Satan and his demon army tend to dig in their heels. When you switch over to faith and trust mode is when he will challenge you most. It is the moment when sweeping will be most at risk for losing ground, as Satan tries to tempt you to walk by sight rather than by faith. At that point, many of us express our fears and impatience by claims of abandonment by God. That is all a deception and a lie, based upon Devil induced doubt! Maintain your focus on God and continue to allow the fruit of the Spirit to be appropriated in those moments of tension, frustration and confusion. Many a military soldier has had these misgivings the moment that ammunition is exhausted and bayonets fixed. At that moment, the soldier must trust his training in hand-to-hand combat. Fearless, confident advances can be won in the thick of any battle, where you express your deepest dependence upon God and stand your ground! You stand the potential to gain the most ground in your advance toward permanent victory over that sweeping for which you are battling!

During your daily routine, frustration, confusion and distraction are the weapons most used by Satan to delay or discourage the filling of a void left by genuine repentance. Satan desires that your focus be on other things than being filled with the fruit of the Spirit as you drive, walk, work, play, lead, dine, etc.. It is easy to lose your focus on God when you are changing a diaper, stuck in traffic, or experiencing a computer freeze. You have to remember at those moments that those tests and trials have the potential to be used by God or manipulated by evil intentions.

As a soldier in spiritual warfare, effectual fervent prayer will sharpen your *God-consciousness* of potential dangers ahead. This unceasing time with God will help you to let go and let Him lead you all day long, even when your mind is on other matters. Random consequences to everyday occurrences will demand your attention hundreds of times a day. Many of the devil's most potent attacks will be subtle ones while you are in your daily routine. So begin now to use your basic training by memorizing key Scripture. As you get alone with God every day, be sure to mark and note verses that you feel will help you to stay focused during the lightning pace of your day. For example, to remember how God so desires to be in control of your every moment, memorize and take with you Romans 8:28, so that when crises strike, your first thoughts will not be panic stricken, but more like:

"God, how do YOU want to use this mess? I know how all things work together for good since I am called according to your purpose. So just guide me in what to say and do in this problem, and keep me very calm, knowing that whatever the outcome, you will be glorified and I will retain the ground gained on the battlefield of my soul when you swept out extreme anxiety and panic."

For me, a major sweeping was anxiety and panic. This lifelong need became a sweeping target a few years back. For me this is designated as a *chronic sweeping*. Any sweeping that is not immediate or that you were unable to allow God to sweep the first time you repented should occupy a priority list considered chronic. Greater attention must be given to chronic sweepings. Special weapons are deemed necessary! For me, Scripture memory, rightly applied in real life situations is a gigantic weapon against Satan. He not only hates the Word but is soundly rebuked when you claim its truth by faith. The potential for Satan to use worry, anxiety or panic is huge, so draw in your ranks at that point, take a deep breath and regroup your thoughts with God being given the permission to control your emotions in the heat of that latest skirmish with the car, the dishwasher or with your boss. What if at the end of the day, when you are talking to God, that you could look back and recount how He led you through some potential moments of anger, frustration, hurt feelings or even a couple of *"uh oh"* moments, when your mouth got just a few nanoseconds ahead of your brain. How you allow God to control and even do damage control during the bumps and bruises of the average day will determine how much joy He is permitted to appropriate for you that day. Remember, just because you yielded to temptation or messed up with this influence in past days, you don't have to anymore! Let go and let God!

Instead of giving in to temptation, step back, either physically or mentally, and give it up to God. When you give God's Holy Spirit permission to operate freely, the Lord will guide you through the process of genuine repentance. He will show you how to select the attributes of the fruit of the Spirit necessary to fill the void where the junk once thrived. He will show you from that selection of the right attributes of the fruit how to make practical application of the fruit.

Looking for practical applications of the fruit of the Spirit is a key element in utilizing the fruit in everyday circumstances. Where each attribute of the fruit is an overarching, broad quality, practical application means that you take love, for example, and consider how love can apply to fill the void left by sweeping repentance. It would be impractical and difficult to implement if we just left the filling in general terms like love more, or just love people and that will fill the void. No, it would change your attitude and make you a more thoughtful person perhaps, but just giving broad-brush strokes to life's problems is one of the reasons many do not see Christianity today as bringing anything to the table for helping them live better and deal with life more effectively.

However, Christianity *is* practical and it *does* have much to bring to the table of everyday problem solving and abundant, victorious living. We have to allow God to show us how love is really applied to the life situation that we are asking God to sweep, or how love can fill the void in a viable, practical manner. The three principles of this book are very practical, while being gleaned directly from God's Word. The Bible is a very practical book when read through the power of the Holy Spirit. With the inspiration and teaching from the Spirit, God can show you amazingly practical and useful.

When you think about it the biblical message, practically applied is the basis for the radio and TV ministries. Each offers the unbeliever as well as the believer *a new beginning* and a *turning point* from which to make a *family focus*. The practical application of Scripture can offer *insights for living* your life *in touch* with Him, helping you to live *a life that matters* while maintaining a *power line* with God to direct your *pathways* with His message of promise. Okay, enough of the subliminal commercials for some of my favorite Christian ministries—you get the point, and this makes a a great conclusion to this first part of your training in filling or sowing. Also, it gave you and me a minute to rest our minds before diving into the process for Sweeping and Filling. Take a minute, stretch, and we will be back to prepare for even the most serious spiritual battles in Day 8. Now, it is time to get a handle on practical applications of spiritual fruit.

Sweeping Moments for today...

1) Today, we have focused upon Filling with the "good stuff". This implies that there are all sorts of ways to fill the void left when you truly repent and allow God to sweep out evil—both godly and not so godly. What are some of the not so godly alternatives to filling the void with the fruit of the Spirit? Why are these imitations for the "good stuff" so easily used in daily living?

2) What are some "Clinch Offers" that Satan has used in your life as imitations to *the* "Clinch Offer" from the Lord? Share a bit about how those imitations worked to tempt you, test you or draw you away from God to "buy" into a non-biblical deception?

3) Today, we discussed how Satan could manipulate the Three T's. Make an informal study of how you are doing with your Three T's. Take a day to consider how you used the Time, Talents and Treasure entrusted to you by God during the past twenty-four hours. On a note pad, make three columns with headings: Time, Talent and Treasure. Jot down under the columns the activities for that day, grading each with the following code: **W=Wasted, WI=Well Invested and S=Stolen by Satan.** The study could look something like this:

8:00am: Morning devotion - Time=WI /Talent=WI / Treasure=WI

9-9:30am: Commute - Listened to Christian Radio and prayed while in a traffic jam - Time=WI/Talent=WI/Treasure=WI

1:30pm: Got aggravated at my co-worker and let it really upset my afternoon - Time=S/Talent=W/Treasure=W

4) We looked at Matthew 12:43–45 again today. Try to tell the story to someone by memory. Now discuss how the story parallels some historical or current event you remember. How could a right response have affected the outcome of the decisions surrounding that event?

Apply the principles of Sweeping, Filling and Keeping, commenting on how things this would turn out if only they had followed through and Swept, Filled and Kept out the evil of the situation.

5) True or False: Galatians 5:22-23 is the only place in the New Testament where the fruit of the Spirit are found. Explain your answer.

DAY 8

꧁ ꧂

Fill It Up With The Good Stuff! Part 2: Using the Good Stuff to Fight the Battles!

Some of my favorite resources for Bible study are practical ones, like the Life Application Notes in the *Life Application Bible,* and the Chain References in *Thompson's Chain Reference Bible.* I commend these and other wonderful resources to anyone who is looking for devotional and Bible study materials that help you in everyday living. Both believers and non-believers are searching earnestly for how the Bible applies to their daily lives. They are reaching for solutions to life's questions and life's problems. Preachers are preparing more and more biblical sermons with the purpose of sharing God's practical handbook for daily living in a way that people will see just how the Bible can help them to live in freedom from the bonds of sin, discover how to get closer to God and deepen their love relationship with Him. That is where we will go today. How do you make practical applications of the very non-specific fruit of the Spirit? We have used love as our lead example, so let's continue with that attribute. From this example, I hope that you will see a clear pattern for interfacing any of the fruit in place of love in our model so that you can test each fruit to see just how it might help you to fill the void or sow fruit that will fill the empty space of repentance. That is spiritual warfare for the twenty-first century...biblical, practical and life changing!

To help better understand how sweeping principles work, I will use my example that you read about in **Day 5 – Spiritual Warfare: Up Close and Personal.** (Take a minute to review that example if need to.) I know that it is in the past tense, but this will give you an idea of how I followed the sweeping pattern shortly after God revealed this life-changing message within Matthew 12:43–45, even before I thought about writing it down. From my testimony of victory, you can know without any doubt that these principles work. I can assure you, that they have been tested in the fire of time and trial in my life. Here is the way that I have gone about working through sweeping and filling/sowing. I hope that this will help you as you place a critical sweeping need in place of this one, using this pattern to process the principles to spiritual warfare.

FIRST: What needs to be swept? For my context, it was worry, compounded by a crisis in my family (the dog bites, rabies-causing Satan to jump on my back with depression, feelings of failure, unfounded guilt and more anxiety than I could shake a stick at).

SECOND: How is Satan using the circumstances to fortify his attack? He was almost audibly whispering in my ear, "You fool! You have brought your family down to this God-forsaken place and gotten them killed...why don't you just go home to the states and let them die in peace with family surrounding them."

He was exaggerating the situation and placing such guilt and shame on my shoulders that he was able to get me to question why I actually had the audacity to bring Phyllis and Ray to Brazil, and the Amazon jungle area to boot! Satan knows I am a worrier and have had bouts with anxiety, panic and the likes, so he definitely raised the bar on my temptation to freak out. Pride, guilt, depression in the face of God's power and worry are the items that I needed to ask God to sweep.

(Remember, you must be specific in what you desire to be swept from your life.)

THIRD: Have I gone to the Lord with this sweeping, and asked for His guidance in genuine repentance? Have I asked friends, family and prayer warriors to pray with me in this sweeping? Have I gone into His Word to seek biblical counsel?

As you are being introduced to this level of spiritual warfare today, please note that I was new to this kind of intense spiritual warfare, being a rookie missionary. The year before we had experienced culture shock and cross-cultural communication challenges during language and orientation studies in Campinas, Brazil. It had been a rough year but as a missionary, we had already assembled a mighty force of prayer warriors back in the states. Phyllis, Ray and my mother were my official prayer and accountability partners, just as today thirty years late, less my mom who is in heaven now. Anyway, we had the prayer army interceding on our behalf. As far as going to the Scriptures for counsel goes, the Lord had already convicted me and called me back into Scripture memory after a lazy layoff of several years. As you will recall in reviewing the testimony in Day 5, verses like Philippians 4:13 came to my mind as I prayed in that hospital bathroom, weeping my scared head off. Romans 8:28 readily came to mind when the Lord almost audibly whispered to me, "You know I've got this one, Rob. Even this seemingly horrible crisis can be used for my honor and glory." He spoke to me in comfort, in encouragement and in assurance that night.

Along with effectual fervent prayer, the Bible must be employed in spiritual warfare in order to win. As we mentioned back in the suggestions for your time with God in the Sweeping Moments of Day 2, use your hand to remember the five ways to use God's Word in battling Satan, as well as fortifying your position with God. Key memory verses can really be secret weapons in the heat of a moment.

Here is a short list of memory verses that I love to get you started. Type or write the verse reference on one side of a slip of paper or card, then write out the verse on the other side. Then just start reading it and trying to remember sections of the verse in your own words, the way it speaks to you and make sense to you. Then repeat this process with each verse for at least a month of practice days. After you have gone on from a verse that you feel is a cinch, go back the next month and see if it is still such a cinch! You will be amazed at how many times you must repeat memory before a thought moves from your short-term memory to your long-term memory.

Okay, here's a start-up list: Matthew 5:1–12; Matthew 12:43–45; John 1:1–5; John 1:12–14; John 3:16–17; Romans 3:23; 5:8; 6:23; 10:9–13; 12:1–2; Galatians 2:20; 5:22–23; Ephesians 6:11–18; Philippians 4:4–8; 4:13–19; 1 Thessalonians 5:16–19; Hebrews 2:1; James 4:7–8; 1 Peter 5:6–9; Psalm 4:7–8; 37:4–5; 91:1–2; Proverbs 3:5–6; Isaiah 40:31; 53:6; 51:1; 64:4; Jeremiah12:5; 31:3b; 31:34b; 33:3 (I am sure that many more verses will come to mind, even more meaningful to you and what you will confront as a soldier!).

FOURTH: What spiritual fruit will you employ upon your sweeping in order to fill the void left by your genuine

repentance? For me, in looking back, I used the following practical applications of the fruit of the spirit:

Love was employed as I considered how much I love the Lord who was guiding me through this, and how much He loves me. Another practical expression of the fruit of love was the love for my family, for whom I would have gladly died in their places, if necessary. Smiles, encouraging words and other random acts of kindness came to mind as I asked the Holy Spirit to guide me how best to express love to Phyllis and Ray through this terrifying ordeal. The Spirit also showed me how this could become a living example of His love for those colleagues and medical personnel all around us. These are just a few examples of the practical application of love.

Joy was employed as I remembered that even though we were all suffering at that point, "The joy of the Lord is my strength," only the verse was not coming to my mind, but the song that I had sung with kids through the years! It just came rushing back in my mind.

Peace was not abundantly evident at the outset, so I needed to ask fervently for peace as I worried about my little family. The peace that surpasses all understanding that guards our hearts and minds was what I asked for as we were riding in that cab. Exhausted at that late hour, I reflected on how God had provided that God-sent doctor. I was sitting in amazing peace as I reflected on how our missionary nurse colleague had remembered about him and then how God guided us in miraculously locating him. God's fruit of peace began to flow as I silently thanked Him for this possibility for the healing of my wife and son. This process of prayer caused me to receive this invisible, almost indescribable peace during those tense hours that we had just endured. Finally, it occurred to me that I hadn't freaked out, hadn't yelled or cursed at anyone. I could not believe that panic mode had not taken over in the face of such shocking news.

Patience was in short supply during the crisis, but being a missionary in northern Brazil and later northeastern Brazil, God already had been teaching all three of us this fruit as daily, we had learned to wait for *everything*! In this particular crisis, I think that I failed in this capacity, to trust God's timing. Since that time, I have learned more and more about how Satan attacks me with impatience.

During those difficult days, our missionary colleagues actually modeled the spiritual fruit of kindness, gentleness and goodness in their ministry to Phyllis, Ray and me. We will never forget how these fruits of the Spirit were so vividly lived out on our behalf. I do not think I will ever have any trouble making practical application of these in crisis moments, after God mirrored them for us through those precious missionaries and that special doctor. An attitude of gratitude will definitely go a long way in helping you with the fruit of patience.

Faithfulness was a challenge too, but even before I left Marabá, I had been praying that I would be faithful even though after this crisis I would be tempted many more times, to pack up and go home to America. The year before God had tested our faithfulness with several other crises that we had experienced in our ministry—all of them had ended in miracles or near miracles!

So like building blocks, God was already bolstering our faithfulness, knowing that we would soon confront even greater challenges. In practical application of this fruit, you need to recall how God has guided you through other similar experiences. This fruit was forcefully imbedded in my heart through a love for Scripture, as I looked back on His promises in the Word. Reflecting upon those places in the Bible where it reminds me that I am a child of God, like all of those Bible personalities. Then I just began to praise God for His faithfulness. The power of praise in the midst of events we neither like nor appreciate is God's way of giving you spiritual medicine for your soul. Like in my situation, I pray that the fruit of faithfulness will cause you to forget about the size of the problem and focus upon the size of your problem solving, promise keeping God.

Self-control is an essential fruit to evaluate how you are doing with the rest. In my situation, I requested self-control immediately, as I dealt with the airline friend, the hospital staff who told me they could not help us, and later, with my neighbors back in Marabá, who blamed us for "thinking the dog into being rabid". A practical application of the fruit of self-control caused me to ask God to put me in their place so that I could imagine how I would react to having to take anti-rabies shots for many weeks.

We recall vividly how all three of us had to exercise Spirit induced self-control after Phyllis was shown by God's angels the moment that the dog escaped to the street, manifesting all of the horrible indicators of rabies. Our God-given self-control kicked in full measure so that we would not panic or offend our neighbor. Brazilian culture was still new to us back then, so we had to ask the Lord to show us the right ways to communicate everything.

Of course, our little band of Brazilian Christian friends had already demonstrated godly self-control before us by the way they had to live, so poor, so hot, so deprived of so much, yet never complaining, always exhibiting a smile and positive attitude. I wish that everyone reading this could have known those special friends. But even better, *you* can exercise that kind of self-control, asking God for an extra measure of it the next time you face a crisis, large or small. You can be that godly example of self-control, but only if it is generated by God's Spirit through you.

FIFTH: Have I gone into His Word to seek biblical counsel? Make sure that you have examined the Scriptures for key memory verses to apply. Look for other Joseph or Jonah type examples with which you can identify in your sweeping. Finally look at the teachings of Jesus to see what He says about your sweeping or the general category for your sweeping.

SIXTH: What spiritual fruit will I employ upon my sweeping in order to fill the void left by your genuine repentance? Prayerfully work through all nine of the spiritual fruit to see how each one could be practically applied with an attitude or action that would honor and glorify God while testifying of His glory to others.

OK, was this helpful? Can you now see how you need to process what you are going through with practical applications of some or all of the fruit? I would suggest mulling over all of the fruit of the Spirit as you face your next zinger moment of anger, pride, fear, jealousy, envy, or any one of a myriad of temptations that will arise daily. Memorizing the fruit of the Spirit and understanding well the character and application value of each will go a long way to helping them become automatic weapons for filling the voids left by a repentance and God's sweeping of that sin, temptation or bad influence, habit or attitude.

After reading the next few pages, why don't you use the spaces after each of the three sweeping categories to record those priority sweepings that come to mind? When you are alone and ready to confront Satan eye to eye, begin to walk through the six steps that I have just guided you through, which will take you through each sweeping and filling. If you need help in assessing your potential sweepings in this realm of spiritual health, look back at the *Sweeping Moments* in Day 6, examining the list of the so-called "Seven Deadly Sins". Remember to consult Day 6 for Sweeping orientation. In Day 9 we will focus more on learning about each fruit and how to best internalize them through practical actions and attitudes.

Now that you have done a walkthrough of one of my earliest sweepings, let's set up your battle plan. You have the basic training and background reconnaissance necessary to do sweeping and filling. Our desired outcome has to be total victory. I want you to win and win big over whatever the Devil wants to use to keep you from living under the control and power of the Holy Spirit. You will need each one of the fruit that He has collectively provided for your ammunition, so that you will **own** Satan in that battle, and dominate him in the breaking of bad habits, unwanted attitudes and destructive behavior!

Let's be clear as we move forward. The first step in implementing **Sweeping Out the Demons** is to determine exactly what needs to be swept from your life. We are going to get up close and personal from here on in, so put on your whole armor, especially those truth pants, your righteousness body armor and those Gospel shoes! God's Word must be personalized in order for God to be permitted to operate with power and might in your life. That will require you to effectually, fervently pray for the brokenness of pride, for God to bring you to the full impact of humility, and the God-sent desire for Him to appropriate in you the kind of courage that can only come from supernatural intervention. Perhaps you already have that list of potential sweepings in hand, but if you are still unsure about just which sweepings to approach first, check this out.

In my research and interviews with Christians both in Brazil and here in our part of the states (NC, SC and VA), I have found that there are a few areas that many of us see as potentially damaging to spiritual, emotional and physical health. So let's address those categories of sweeping first. As you read, consider if anything in your life falls into one of these categories. Make a note of it in that section of this chapter, so that you can come back to it later with the formula of sweeping, filling and keeping out evil. The three major categories where there seems to be the greatest need and interest for sweepings is your **Spiritual Health, Your Emotional Health And Your Physical Health.**

A. Spiritual Health - Many with whom I have discussed spiritual warfare see a real need in the area of how easily they are defeated when a temptation arises. Others see a lack of joy and peace as their downfall. There are many who speak of an inner feeling of constant guilt over past sins and backslidings that just won't leave them alone. Some speak of prayer as having become shallow and artificial, having the feeling that at times, their prayer life is just not "getting beyond the ceiling of the room". Some cited their devotional lives as being "blocked" or "stopped up" by resistance from evil distractions, disguised as every day time wasters or interruptions that subtly and suddenly rob them from their time alone with God.

Others described a growing apathy over reading their Bibles or even getting alone to pray and read a few verses. A large number of folks confessed that they had wanted to start a quiet time with God for a long time (some reported for years), but "something" always seemed to get in the way. A large number of folks complained of a nagging negativism in their Christian walk as it related to the church. They cited church squabbles, interpersonal conflicts; hurt feelings or being "offended" by something or someone, and scheduling problems with church activities and daily schedules as issues that had subtly moved them out of regular church attendance. This negative vibe they felt turned into a feeling that church experience had become a mindless routine. They expressed comments like, "These days I just do not feel like I used to about church and Christianity in general". Every one of these scenarios are generated and aggravated by Satan himself. They seem quite benign and simple, but Satan uses such situations to damage spiritual health.

However, by far the greater number of spiritual health threats are cited by people who feel like the Devil is attacking their Christian walk with temptations so strong that they have never felt such a looming sense of evil all around them. TV, books, magazines and especially internet temptations for porn, gambling or social media flirtations seem to be especially strong temptations these days. These are powerful generators for relational, sexual, financial and emotional problems, often neutralizing their commitment to Christ. Some of those I interviewed used examples of how their moral and ethical standards, their speech and social habits and their relationship patterns had gone in a downward spiral over the last ten or so years as a result of these spiritual health threats. None said that they thought the Devil was at the bottom of the problem, but rather shared about how other things going on in their lives probably had brought them to this point of crisis, unrelated to their distance or closeness to the Lord. Satan tries to mask his interference with everyday matters, so that you cannot see his behind the scenes activity. After I asked them to look closer and dig deeper, they seemed to understand clearly the relationship between Satan's subtle interferences with their temptations and tests. They seemed to understand how this connection was damaging their spiritual health. That connection will do the same for you. It will reveal much more specifically, where you need sweeping.

Some disturbing discoveries about spiritual health....

I did not have to read between the lines very long to know that some of these persons were relatively new believers from secular worldview backgrounds, unable to see how little distance they had traveled from their old nature and secular culture. Yet, these were the very individuals who seemed to be truly seeking a fresh and vibrant relationship with Christ. A large majority of those I singled out as Millennial's and "Gen-X'rs" naturally fell into this category or group that had secular backgrounds that still seemed to be very much a part of their lifestyle. They spoke of difficulties in relating their faith to friends and family who still do not know Jesus. They said that many barriers just seemed to develop mysteriously every time they tried to share about their newfound faith. Those identified as long time believers or veteran church members had the same connection to a secular worldview and to the old nature. I was not ready for that finding. Also, many of them held little or no viewpoint on the relationship between Satan and their spiritual health having been damaged. Those interviewed came from small suburban or rural congregations. Many, I am disturbed to report, were leaders in their respective church bodies. Folks, if you fit in either of these categories, we got to get with it and step up as soldiers of the cross! Satan loves this mess, and it is helping him hang on that much longer. God is using this level of spiritual warfare, to winnow out His true church and test our metal as followers of Jesus or simply people who go to a church somewhere.

When asked if there were any issues that came up during their daily routine, I could not possibly remember how many said that daily frustrations and scheduling nightmares were causing them to, as one guy put it "just lose my religion!" I heard that well, because I too came from a very secular, pseudo-Christian background with no church relationship until I was nearly fifteen. Even then, I was on my own about going to church, with no family encouragement. To be honest, as a new believer, it was all very confusing, Temptations like anger, pride, jealousy, greed and yes, lust were all items that many of my new church friends reported as ways that evil would rear its ugly head in their cluttered minds. Yet no one knew what to do about it. Older Christians advised me to just keep on going to church and stay involved in the work of the church, and I would be fine. If they weren't fine, how was I going to be fine? That one kept me on my knees for a long time, even after I became a pastor and later, a missionary.

So if you are like me, this issue of spiritual health is at the top of the list for many of the sweepings that you will present to the Lord, even though the sweepings may be interrelated with emotional or physical issues. Don't be tempted to be legalistic or rigid with how you categorize evil. Just jot it down after this section as a potential you are seeing, and move on. You can come back later to pray over the highest priority sweepings and begin to work the formula through with Bible in hand, your prayer closet in sight! Use the following section to list those spiritual health sweepings.

FIRST: What needs to be swept?

SECOND: How is Satan using circumstances to fortify his attack?

THIRD: Have I gone to the Lord with this sweeping, and asked for His guidance in genuine repentance? Have I asked friends, family and prayer warriors to pray with me in this sweeping? Have I gone into His Word to seek biblical counsel?

FOURTH: What spiritual fruit will I employ upon this sweeping in order to fill the void left by my genuine repentance?

FIFTH: Have I gone into His Word to seek biblical counsel?

SIXTH: What spiritual fruit will I employ upon my sweeping in order to fill the void left by your genuine repentance?

B. **EMOTIONAL HEALTH –** Many people feel the need for some immediate sweepings from this grouping. Some speak of depression, anxiety, panic attacks, chronic worry, stress related illnesses and substance abuse or addictions as high priority strongholds for Satan. The people that I talked to had many addictions that were hurting them emotionally and physically, like prescription drugs, recreational drugs (alcohol in most cases), while a lot more cited food addictions, dieting, weight loss and all that junk Satan tries to drag along with that trail of tears.

For me it is snacking late at night, which makes it pretty hard to maintain steady numbers in blood sugar. But still others cited relationship problems as a way they felt Satan was attacking them, by inciting conflicts with spouses, siblings or children. Issues of unresolved anger seemed to be a prominent sweeping in the making for many. Unforgiveness, bitterness and unresolved conflict seemed to be the richest soil for the Devil to attack many (and remember, I was talking to people in traditional churches). A long-standing grudge or protracted arguments yet to be reconciled seem to have some devastating affects upon some of our brothers and sisters in Christ. Satan can use these emotional battles to bring those brothers and sisters in Christ to the point of abandoning church and putting their spiritual health on the back burner. You guessed it—many of those folks have found their emotional health to get worse in proportion to their spiritual health. Sadly, that chalks up temporary kudos for the Devil.

Satan uses stress and anxiety as prime targets for the weapons in his arsenal, to discourage folks from sweeping out those emotional health issues. In examining the situations of many, it seems to me that Satan dovetails stress and anxiety with relational health. He can rattle many cages with a little anxiety based anger or impatience. Kindness, gentleness and goodness seem to fly out my window when I am stressed! So sweepings in this realm can be chronic; that is, *tough!* The "demons" in our sense of the word may try to reoccupy your house more than once if you don't fill this void with some practical applications of all nine of the fruit of the Spirit.

Depression caused by anxiety, panic or chronic worrying can cause all sorts of physical ailments to develop, making it extremely difficult to deal with the actual sweeping. Most say that they are just too focused on the down side of these satanic tools to have any energy to deal with depression triggers like diet, marital problems. Satan influences people to do a self-styled makeover for the use of the *Three T's* of **T**ime, **T**alent and **T**reasure.

Satan desires you to overreact or react negatively to life's most stressful situations concerning the clock, the activities of the day and the checkbook. It does not matter whether the stressor rises from being rushed, overworked, under-appreciated, or just emotionally under-allocated (like finding the money run out before the month did). People speak of being so preoccupied and distracted by the emotional and physical pain of depression and anxiety disorders that they cannot even begin to concentrate on the normal focuses of life, let alone personal devotions.

As for the real purpose and focus for why we are on this planet: to honor and to glorify God...well, these folks can't get past their emotional pain to focus on glorifying God. That group includes about seventy-five percent of the local church. So Satan sits back pretty well satisfied with himself with those poor souls (of whom I am numbered during a couple of periods of my life). These emotional temptations and attacks are what many would aptly describe as joy *robbers!* They are at the crux of how Satan battles us...with our minds. Many authors write about the various aspects of this arena as a kind of battlefield for your mind. How spot on correct that analogy is! Satan wants to control your mind in order to control your emotions so that he can attack your emotional well-being in order to attack your physical health. But the worse part of this assault is that he practically takes your spiritual health right off the battlefield! You just can't be spiritually healthy if the Devil is messing with your emotional well-being.

The more extreme cases of the emotional genre lead to thoughts and attempts of suicide. Hardly anyone reading this book has not either known of or known personally someone who either attempted or committed this horrible defeat by Satan. While psychiatry and psychology will not even touch the spiritual dimension of behavioral nightmares like suicide, anorexia, bulimia, cutting, or other similar disorders, Satan does. He attacks the person who is going through this mind trauma, and he attacks the caregivers who are trying to cope with those loved ones without losing their own minds in the process.

Satan does not care if the condition is physical, emotional or spiritual. He just wants to destroy any possibility of that person coming to a relationship with God. He torments the victim, he torments the family and I am sure he frustrates the fine medical professionals and pastors who try responsibly to treat these conditions. Where medication is indicated, he will tempt the person to stop taking the medicine or to refuse to cooperate with caregivers. He will seek to depress the person through difficulties with relationships or bad experiences with people who mean well but really don't understand what that person is going through. Or he will just torment the tormented, with suggestions and discouraging thoughts.

We must sweep emotional health battles! Their deception creeps into every area of life. Despite being related to simple problems at first, they seem to grow with each stressful, nerve wracking circumstance. But be not fooled—they are easily defeated through the right filling by the Holy Spirit. Prayer will uncover them as very artificial. *Satan is not creative because he is not the Creator*! Therefore, he has to build upon what is already there with half-truths or outright lies. To this end, he seeks to bring a person to complete breakdown of all resistance to the depression or anxiety by removing all hopeful thoughts. King Saul would easily fall into this category if he were around today (1 Samuel 18, 19 and 20). He eventually allowed Satan to drive him to a self-styled, self-destructive suicidal behavior.

What about the most radical of all sweepings?

I truly believe that at that point there are the radical situations when a person either cries out for help of rescue by attempts to hurt himself/herself, the person is successful in hurting himself/herself either by accident or on purpose, or the person tries to hurt others. Suicidal tendencies have nothing to do with whether a person is saved or unsaved, because the issues range far outside the spiritual realm. Maybe you are thinking right now of one you lost to suicide and just how special, creative, smart and giving that dear soul was. Yet unexplainable psychiatric and psychological conditions, terminal diseases like cancer and excruciating chronic pain, both physical and mental—these are just a few of the physiological causes for persons to consider suicide. While the medical professionals work toward healing with the these precious ones, the powers of darkness often seize this pain to invade their thinking to convince them that there is no way out and only one way to relief. It can go far beyond what the medications can relieve or control. At that point that special creation of God is deceived into considering the worst and most damaging solution to life's most painful crises. The ones left behind are left to question why, how, and what if...

Some who are reading this are confronting either a seemingly insurmountable physical or mental illness in your life or alongside the life of a beloved family member or friend. Especially at risk are our veterans of military campaigns, teens who are finding it difficult to find their way in relationships and both young and old who are grieving losses of soul mates, careers or seemingly insurmountable consequences of past decisions. Substance abuse is another point of entry for evil to confuse and deceive the mind to consider ending what God so desires to heal and rescue.

These are radical sweepings. Each one requires the person with the problem to pray, to understand about the fruit of the Spirit, and most of all (and most lacking), to seek what is now called Biblical Counseling, so that he/she knows of the redemptive and healing power of the Holy Spirit, before it is too late. In concert with any medical care indicated, a time with a Biblical Counselor will help the person reflect on a much-neglected area, the person's spiritual health. If anyone is reading about this sweeping and senses this situation in your own life or the life of someone you know, pray now that the Holy Spirit will be permitted to intervene in the life of this person so that he/she will call out to the Lord and to a pastor, counselor or physician.

This step in this sweeping will be the greatest defeat of Satan apart from the decision to receive Christ as Savior. Follow the six-step process after you have confessed this need to someone you know and trust. You will not regret participating in this miraculous deliverance of your life or that of someone you know. Suicide falls into the strongest satanic category. The person who entertains suicide is agreeing with evil to take control of the life decision, which is only to be decided by Almighty God. Satan causes a person to become weak from physical or emotional pain, listen to negative voices both real and exaggerated vestiges of the imagination and develops a thought pattern that by design offers the individual no solution to whatever provoked the suicidal desperation.

This lie becomes an embedded obsession, leading to all sorts of distorted messages, all lies and all designed to remove the positive solutions of hope. The greatest lie the Devil will deliver to a person contemplating suicide is that it will relieve suffering. It only worsens the suffering of the one who submits to the evil deception, and hurts every single person who cares about the person, leaving them confused, angry and even a sense of false guilt. Suicide is a moment when the most special of souls suddenly are deceived into a state of fear and desperation that no one can explain.

Those left behind a victim of suicide's deception are often left feeling abandoned, hurt and even angered that he/she was not given just one more chance to help, hug, love and listen. Our God surely is saddened when one of His children steps ahead of His opportunity to use that life for some purpose unbeknownst to mere mortals. Many who have lost loved ones to suicide ponder how God might have even used that life in that state of mental or physical pain to bless or even rescue another of His troubled children. God loves us so very much that we must remember His purpose for our lives no matter how hopeless or helpless we become. We are created to honor and to glorify our Creator, for all eternity—on this side in earthly existence and beyond. For some that means bravely resisting the pain, loneliness or despair a bit longer, most likely for a far higher purpose than any of us can fathom.

The comfort that can come from prayer, reading the Bible and talking to someone about your spiritual condition can make a huge difference in actually experiencing healing again. Most of all the Biblical Counselor can put the person in touch with friends, family and persons who are going through the same torment, so that the feeling of being alone and abandoned can be dealt with.

Confronting Satan's Masterpiece:
Sweeping Chronic Depression...

Finally, in a very personal sidebar to all that we have discussed, many reading this book may have fallen prey to a very spiritually, emotionally and physically debilitating attack by Satan. Chronic to severe depression is an experience that no one can describe adequately. It is like an endless, hopeless hole into which you have fallen. Troublesome thoughts and worries become so dominant that the person cannot even carry on a conversation with complete attention. The object of your depression is vague and often generalized. Associated circumstances to what brought you down in the first place can make you very nervous and contribute to anxiety and panic moments. Nothing is fun anymore. Fear sweeps over the depressed person over doing the most routine things.

I am not a doctor, not even close. But I have experienced this kind of depression and I can say at least from my experience that I know Satan was attacking me and rendering me helpless to overcome the depression. Only intense prayer and Bible saturation can help you out, along with a trusted friend and prayer partner with whom you can pour your heart out. The sweeping includes gaining the victory over silence in order to attempt to share what is going on with that special person of trust (in my case my precious wife). The Great Physician healed me, and He led me to a doctor who understood how diabetes actually triggered my depression. This encouraged me out of the hole and back into joyful service. Do not let Satan rob you of complete healing. God heals us spiritually and He heals physically, and yes, he uses doctors to bring miraculous healing as well. Fill the void with both and soon you will be claiming Philippians 4:4 again!

FIRST: What do you need God to sweep?

SECOND: How is Satan using the circumstances to fortify his attack?

THIRD: Have I gone to the Lord with this sweeping, and asked for His guidance in genuine repentance?

FOURTH: Have I asked friends, family and prayer warriors to pray with me in this sweeping?

FIFTH: Have I gone into His Word to seek biblical counsel?

SIXTH: What spiritual fruit will I employ upon my sweeping in order to fill the void left by your genuine repentance?

C. **PHYSICAL HEALTH** – People are just too busy with what is cluttering up their lives spiritually and emotionally to deal with physical health these days, despite their preoccupation with all of their chronic ailments like arthritis, migraines, fibromyalgia, allergies, sleep deprivation, indigestion/reflux and other digestive issues (from constipation to diarrhea). Medical coverage is at the tip of everyone's tongues and fear of not having it is causing many a sleep-disturbed night for many. Satan is probably having a little fun with this trend in America. The whole time this dialogue is going on, with all the commercials and meds being touted on TV and the Internet, that same audience (you and me), are abusing our bodies with overeating, poor dietary habits, overdoing everything from beverages to snacks. We are taking in too much salt, sugar, fat, transfat (not even in the dictionary, by the way), and getting far too little exercise for caloric intake.

I do not know much about the chemicals that they use to preserve our food, but I do know that the natural or organic stuff costs so much that many of us can't afford them. So Satan is probably just laughing his evil head off at how we have been duped into focusing upon the symptoms instead of the solutions.

So, exercise, a healthy diet and enough sleep fall prey to many unnecessary thoughts about maintaining our unhealthy lifestyles by over medicating ourselves with over the counter analgesics, antacids, laxatives and anti-diarrhea medications, not to mention the allergy relief stuff. Our schedules dictate a lot of this...just too busy to take care of what really matters. As though our jobs were not enough to overfill the day, we add on a score of activities that leave us tired, stressed and frustrated. Saying no to anything has become almost profane, while saying yes to eating right, exercising and going to bed has become almost impossible, in the face of so many nonessential items in the day's agenda.

Satan can and does use busyness. He adds to the day-to-day stuff gradually, to guide you away from the best that God has to offer you through His Word and time alone with Him in effectual, fervent conversation, and time for fellowship with loved ones. Person after person with whom I talk speak of every kind of activity being placed ahead of time alone with God. Andy Stanley has some great help with this overscheduled and cluttered lifestyle, at the expense of what is *really* important. If you go to this link, I believe his messages on ***Breathing Room*** could help you in this sweeping and filling. He refers to breathing room as the space in your schedule, budget and lifestyle at your current pace and according to your spiritual, emotional and physical limits. I could not urge you enough to go to this link and listen to those inspired messages!

**http://northpoint.org/adults/short-term-groups/
breathing-room/**

So Satan is doing a number on us in our physical health,
because if you are not healthy, you cannot be at 100% in any
other area of your life. Your body *is* the building or temple
of the New Testament church (1 Corinthians 3:16, 17; 6:19).
Many sweepings need your immediate attention in order even to
feel like spiritual warfare with many other important sweepings.
Genuine repentance in how you eat, drink, exercise, sleep and
the medicines you take (your doctor may even remove some
of the medicines you take after taking care of body business!).
Physical health can enable you or render you helpless to improve
relationships with God, others and even your own self-esteem.
Get alone for some effectual, fervent prayer about the sweepings
related to physical health. Let go and let God if you feel convicted
that God's Temple needs some attention.

Josiah rent his clothes and humbled himself to the point
of total reform when He discovered that the Temple had been
neglected for so long that the Scriptures had been lost somewhere
inside (2 Kings 22, 23). Hezekiah was so moved by the neglect
of God's Temple and the proper worship and sacrifice that he did
everything in his power to open the doors again and resume real
worship, after years of his father Ahaz doing everything possible
to prohibit God's house from bringing the people closer to Him
(2 Chronicles 28-31).

That was the Temple made with block and mortar, wood and
stone, furnished with precious stones and metals. You have been
designated that temple since Christ arose and ascended! What
is the condition of that temple as of today? Is it in need of self-
examination and needed repairs? Has the Word of God been lost
somewhere inside? Have you brought the Scriptures out from a
hidden or neglected place, so that once again it can be returned

to the most holy place of your heart? This is the sweeping that without exception, all of us need to focus. So I am giving some specifics for you prior to going through the six steps, since this is where you need to begin in this phase of spiritual warfare. Like Elijah in 1 Kings, chapters 17–19, your spiritual and emotional health will improve as you allow God to guide you in the care and discipline of your physical health.

FIRST – What needs to be swept? My physical health and each of the deficiencies that I discover in my Temple (diet, exercise, sleep all need to be separate sweepings).

SECOND – How is Satan using the circumstances to fortify his attack? What issues in your physical health and daily habits is Satan able to use to render you "unhealthy" or an "unfit Temple"? What spiritual and emotional health issues are contributing to the bad conditions in your Temple of the Holy Spirit? (Each of the issues you might reveal needs to be a separate sweeping).

THIRD – Have I gone to the Lord with this sweeping, and asked for His guidance in genuine repentance?

Have I asked friends, family and prayer warriors to pray with me in this sweeping?

Have I gone into His Word to seek biblical counsel? This sweeping will overlap into many other sweepings, so it should be a very high priority sweeping at this point, possibly even the first one you focus upon.

FOURTH – What spiritual fruit will you employ upon your sweeping in order to fill the void left by your genuine

repentance? As in my example a few pages back, prayerfully work through each of the nine fruit, looking at practical ways to apply them as you give God permission to appropriate them freely in this sweeping. In Day 9 you can find more specific definitions for each fruit attribute, which will help you all along in pinpointing ways that the fruit of the Spirit can forcefully be applied to the place where repentance has begun victory over those habits, attitudes or behaviors that Satan is using to interfere with your overall Spiritual, Emotional and Physical health.

FIFTH - Have I gone into His Word to seek biblical counsel?

SIXTH - What spiritual fruit will you employ upon your sweeping in order to fill the void left by your genuine repentance?

Now that you have learned more about filling in the voids left by genuine repentance, remember as you pray to ask the right questions about your sweepings. Through these times of effectual, fervent time with God, really, really listen to Him and be ready to be an obedient soldier. Remember a verse to memorize and claim as yours as you begin sweeping in any of these categories. As you commit to genuine repentance and allow the Lord to sweep out anything that does not need to be there, you are reconfirming yourself as a new creature in Christ Jesus. The newness may feel like it has worn off a bit after years of Satan making assaults at your Spiritual, Emotional and Physical resources, but you don't have to stay where you are...you can show Him once and for all that God's in charge of your life again!

Therefore if any man be in Christ, he is a new creature: old things are passed away; behold, all things are become new. (2 Corinthians 5:17 KJV)

In Christ, we learn of the perfect tool for maintaining our filling to win permanently, that battle against the world and the flesh, at the hand of the Devil. Our Lord Jesus taught us the best response to every situation, and to every temptation. Jesus filled every temptation from Satan with intimate and intensive prayer, along with the application of the Word of God. He exemplified prayer in times of testing. He even taught the disciples how to pray. This method for keeping out evil is principle three, we use this powerful dual weapon for keeping out evil—effectual, fervent prayer and a loving dependence upon God's Word.

Sweeping Moments for Today...

1) In order to sweep, fill and keep out evil, it is first necessary to know intimately the One who will be on the front lines of your heart and life, enabling you to fight the good fight.

Are you certain that you know Jesus in your heart as your personal Lord and Savior? If you died today, do you know where you would spend all eternity? To follow is a brief summary of the plan of salvation from God's Word. If you are already saved and certain, you might want to copy this block off on some pages and share it with friends for whom you are not certain of their salvation. Talk about spiritual warfare! Paramount is a precious soul coming to faith in Jesus. Almost as threatening to Satan are your efforts to share Christ. Fear and intimidation over personal evangelism is a major sweeping, by the way. There are so many that are committed to Christ, yet unable or unwilling to share Him with others. Satan's attacks include excuses, interruptions and fear of failure or embarrassment. Along with your own personal story of how you came to Christ, this little block, left with a friend to think about because you think so much of him/her, may be the seed necessary to unlock that heart!

Now is the perfect time to talk to Him and receive Jesus as your Lord and your Savior.

First - Recognize your separation by sin from perfect God.

Next - Recognize that there are no good works, reform or religious practices that can remove this separation.

Next - Recognize His provision for your salvation. Only the perfect sacrifice of God could do this. His only Son, dying on the cross is that provision. Recognize that this provision was done so that all who believe would have everlasting life. Moreover, recognize that in this provision He not only died for you but also He rose from the dead on the third day, revealing Himself to many.

Next - Ask His forgiveness for your sin, and accept that He died for you to cancel your eternal separation from God. Even more amazing, He did this so that your life in this world would have the fullness and meaning that God desires for everyone!

Finally - Receive Him as your Lord (master boss chief) and as your Savior (redeemer, rescuer and sacrifice in your place). Invite Him to live in your heart forever. Confess your faith in Him aloud right now, believing in your heart that He lived as the Bible says, that He died for your sins and that God raised Him from the dead.

Now, go and tell someone what has happened in your heart and in your life...tell that person, "I am Saved!" Welcome to the family of God! At this very moment, the Holy Spirit entered your life to indwell or to lead, guide

and direct just as much or as little as you permit. Begin visiting churches this week to find God's place for you!

2) So far, we have engaged in a lot of discussion about the Holy Spirit. Share with your group or record in your journal the state of your relationship with God's indwelling Spirit. How would you describe that relationship?

   a. My relationship with the Spirit is vague and poorly defined.

   b. My relationship with the Spirit is real but not as intimate as I would like

   c. My relationship with the Spirit is growing and powerful... God in me.

3) For a long time now, Christians have had many differing viewpoints about what it means to be "filled with the Holy Spirit". How about you?

   a. What are some of the ways you have heard others use this term as you talk with friends from various segments of the Christian faith?

   b. Now, let's examine what the Bible says about being filled with the Holy Spirit. After various members of your group share their findings about the following verses, discuss what it really means to be spirit filled. If studying individually, jot your findings down as you search these Scriptures.

Ezekiel 36:27; Zechariah 4:6; Matthew 3:11 and 12:28; Luke 11:13 and 12:12; John 14:17, 26; 15:26; 16:8, 13; Acts 1:8; 2:3, 38; 8:17, 39; 10:19, 20, and 44; 13:2; 16:6; 19:6; Romans 8:9–16; 1 Corinthians 3:16; 2 Corinthians 3:6, 16; 1 Thessalonians 5:19; 1 Peter 3:18.

4) Go back to Graphics 1, 2 and 3 located back in Day 2. Examine them again and see if the formula for sweeping makes more sense to you now than when you first saw the graphics. Take this hypothetical sweeping and walk through the graphics with it. If in a group, have different group members participate in this walk-thru.

FIRST - What needs to be swept? "I have an addiction, and it is a habit I have been trying to kick for years. I would like to pray and truly, genuinely repent of this. Lord, please help me to deal with the why and the how of this sweeping, and please sweep it from my life once and for all!

SECOND - How is Satan using the circumstances to fortify his attack? Every time I try to make headway with quitting, circumstances just seem to crop up that make it very convenient for me to stop trying and go back to the addiction. My self-esteem has been pretty well crushed by all these failed attempts, and it is as though the Devil is whispering to me that I am a failure, so I might as well give up on quitting this, and accept that I am a weak person. Sometimes it just has to be evil when I think, hey, I deserve to do this...I am an adult and besides, what business is it of anyone what I do, and really, what harm is it doing to anyone else? I just don't want to go to church, let alone read the Bible—you know what I mean?

THIRD - Have I gone to the Lord with this sweeping, and asked for His guidance in genuine repentance? Yeah, I pray, who doesn't? But it doesn't seem to be doing any good. I feel like praying is just a ritual anyway, and it doesn't seem to be getting me anywhere...I just don't feel close to God when I pray.
Have I asked friends, family and prayer warriors to pray with me in this sweeping? Are you kidding? They would

laugh their heads off! They don't pray all that much, I don't think. I did think about asking someone I know at church to pray for me, and they have a prayer list at church...I could put my name on that list, but what would people think if I tell them I have this addiction?

Have I gone into His Word to seek biblical counsel? I honestly don't know where to go in the Bible to work out this problem. Maybe I could ask a preacher or go on the Internet...or maybe that woman that teaches Sunday School might know some places in the Bible.

FOURTH - What spiritual fruit will you employ upon your sweeping in order to fill the void left by your genuine repentance? I know from a sermon awhile back I heard on TV that the fruit of the Spirit are located in Galatians 5:22, 23...man you ought to see that list in verses 19-21! My addiction and the related problems with it are there in several of those...how you say it, "works of the flesh"!

FIFTH: Have I gone into His Word to seek biblical counsel?

SIXTH: What spiritual fruit will I employ upon my sweeping in order to fill the void left by your genuine repentance?

Now here are a few others that you might want to use as a walk thru:

    a. "I have a terrible time with profanity and off color jokes...I just can't seem to stop letting them fly!"

    b. "I have gained like 30 pounds this past year, and would really like to not only lose the weight, but to stop all of this gaining and losing. I get started off right, but then something always derails my best plans...*I don't know... go figure...whadayado?"*

    c. "Over the past few years I have developed this really negative attitude about most everything. I am always seeing the worst in everyone and worse, I have to comment about it to them before I know what I have said with all this discouraging stuff blurting out of my big mouth all this cynical, pessimistic junk."

    d. "My spouse and I just can't seem to get along anymore. We still love each other, but our communication just isn't what it used to be and we both seem to feel so distant from one another. Just about every discussion ends up in an argument."

5) Take a few moments to see if you can recite in your own words the following key points to our Basic Training, thus far:

    a. Matthew 12:43–45...

    b. The three main principles of Sweeping Out the Demons...

    c. My description of our Enemy...

    d. The difference between a Joseph type lesson and a Jonah type lesson...

    e. The six steps in Day 8 for working through a sweeping to arrive at the filling of the void...

    f. A simple and natural way for me to share my faith with someone else...

DAY 9

Understanding the Weaponry
for the Battle Within You...

This I say then, Walk in the Spirit, and ye shall not fulfill the lust of the flesh. For the flesh lusteth against the Spirit, and the Spirit against the flesh: and these are contrary the one to the other: so that ye cannot do the things that ye would. But if ye be led of the Spirit, ye are not under the law. Now the works of the flesh are manifest, which are these; Adultery, fornication, uncleanness, lasciviousness, Idolatry, witchcraft, hatred, variance, emulations, wrath, strife, seditions, heresies, Envyings, murders, drunkenness, revellings, and such like: of the which I tell you before, as I have also told you in time past, that they which do such things shall not inherit the kingdom of God. But the fruit of the Spirit is love, joy, peace, longsuffering, gentleness, goodness, faith, Meekness, temperance: against such there is no law. (Galatians 5:16–23 KJV)

In Galatians 5:16–21 Paul speaks of the battle within you, between self or the flesh and the Spirit. He explains that the works of the flesh or self and the fruit of the Spirit are contrary to each other, direct opposites. If you live controlled by self or by the flesh, God and the qualities with which He desires to fill you cannot control you. This is why the fruit of the Spirit are presented by Paul in direct contrast to the works of the flesh—each is the result of either the Holy Spirit having control of what you think, say and do or the sinful nature having that control. This is spiritual warfare. In Day 7 and Day 8, you looked at the nuts and bolts of filling. Today we are going to deal with the challenges involved and how God has *already* equipped His soldiers to overcome them.

We have just discussed in Days 7 and 8 about the "good stuff"—the fruit of the Holy Spirit. When you were saved through Christ, God began fighting for you in this spiritual warfare, whether you knew it or not. The indwelling of the Holy Spirit in your life was the way Jesus kept His promise to the Apostles and the earliest disciples, right down to you and me! (Acts 1:8) When we talk about being "filled with the Spirit" that means that you have received God in you. That's kind of weird sounding I know, but that is exactly what happened. He lives within my heart and yours, to give us the guidance, instruction, conviction, encouragement and courage to live a life that shows the world how to fulfill our purpose for being created: to honor and to glorify the Lord in everything we think, say and do. Now if you are like me the first time someone tried to explain this, you would be thinking, I don't think, say and do everything that honors or glorifies God—far from it! That is so true, but you have been forgiven for your Adam nature or sin nature through accepting what Jesus did for you on the cross. So we are still sinners, yet sinners saved, rescued and reconciled by the substitution of our lives on the cross for that of God's only son, Jesus Christ. At the moment you accepted what Jesus came to do; that is, *"to seek and to save that which was lost". (Luke 19:10b)*, you received what Jesus described as His Spirit, entering your heart, mind, and soul to dwell invisibly. He explained that the purpose for sending His Spirit was to give us His *empowerment.* That endowment, dispensation, distribution of power is described in various places in the Bible, whenever the Spirit is mentioned. However, just before He ascended to heaven He mentioned that we are to be His witnesses in all the world.

In John, chapters fourteen through seventeen He explained just how His spirit would operate as our comforter, counselor, teacher and guide through spiritual battles. Jesus went to great detail to reassure the disciples both then and now, that in the absence of the crucified, risen Lord would be this invisible, transcending presence of the Father and the Son in the form of the Spirit of God. To explain fully the Holy Spirit would be like trying to explain electricity or atomic energy, like trying to describe air or any other invisible substance. Just as each of these are undeniably present by virtue of their resultant power, God's Spirit is ever present, made real and mighty and personal through His influence upon the believer.

When you give that Holy Spirit the acknowledgement of His position and the reality of His presence in your life, the Spirit will bring your life into agreement with its purpose, enabling you to realize that reason for why we "live and move and have our being". At the moment you recognize and commission the Holy Spirit's constant presence, you give the magnificent offering to the Godhead—**glory, honor and praise!** You open up your life to being a vessel or jar of clay, a designated love offering of blessing and honor to God. Like opening a long anticipated gift at Christmas or on your birthday, you are unwrapping unspeakable potential for great joy in your life.

We have discussed at length how this acknowledgement can be demonstrated to God: by giving Him *permission* to operate in your life. To give validation to the filling and indwelling of God's Spirit means that you are relinquishing your carnal or fleshly spaces in your "house". God is given room in your physical, emotional and spiritual desires to appropriate what for lack of a better word we call *power*. That power or spiritual synergy is fleshed out through God-qualities called the fruit of the Spirit.

This is why we have given so much attention to these attributes of the very character of our Lord, now awaiting activation in your life. He will use these attributes or fruit to *empower* you to live on a *supernatural dimension*! Besides developing your life into the witness that He commissioned you to be, (see Matthew 28:18–20), he will use them to deepen your relationship with Him and the world (see Mark 12:29–31). The work of the Holy Spirit is to vacate, evict, deport or simply crowd out the works of the flesh that we just read about in Galatians 5:16–21. Another way of describing this occupation by the Spirit is to say that the world's moral, ethical and volitional waste has been thrown out like garbage in order to reallocate that space for the presence of the Lord. This vacancy sign goes up in your life every time you allow God to bring you to the point of genuine repentance over a work of the flesh. Like the fruit of the Spirit, the works of the flesh not only describe specific evil, but also represent categories for more general works of the flesh. They can serve as examples for those broad sweepings like pride, anger or fear. For example, "being jealous, angry or selfish can conjure up many specific ways that you could act out or express jealousy, anger or selfishness, such as biting words, road rage, or not sharing what you have with others.

Remember, the Holy Spirit living in you will only deal with these sin problems when you permit the supernatural power of God to apply the specific fruit into the way you think, act, speak or relate to others. That happens when you pray in a real and intense manner, honestly and sincerely. We have come to refer this kind of praying as the kind in James 5:13–16. In verse sixteen, that kind of praying is described as ***effectual and fervent***. That's really the only kind of praying that really is praying!

That kind of praying will make God's Word more readable and clear to you. God can give you special interpretation of your reading, regardless of your reading comprehension level. He will slow you down and show you word by word what key passages mean...just ask Him, be patient, get all the tools out like the concordance or references in the back of your Bible, or go online to free Bible study places like biblegateway.com, etc.. There are even places where you can hear the Bible read instead of just reading them to yourself! But effectual (purposeful, serious), fervent (intimate, personal, intense) prayer will show you how the Word can speak to your heart, and how the Word can counsel and teach you as you pray (Psalm 32:8).

Think of the fruit of the Spirit like an athletic team or a surgical team. Each fruit serves to enhance and make possible the results of the other fruit, as team members serve in their specific roles in order to accomplish the overall objective of that team. Like each player or medical personnel, the fruit of the Spirit are actually dependent upon one another to perform their specific functions...and to help you have some awesome fillings or sowings!

The playing field or operating room for this team effort of spiritual fruit is where you have previously allowed Him to sweep clean any work of the flesh, through genuine repentance. So when permitted, just like a great athletic or surgical team, one fruit of the Spirit builds upon the others so that each finds strength in the way you permit God to sow the others into your life. You will have no problem knowing where to sow the fruit, because what has been swept was the result of your intensive prayer for repentance, forgiveness and restoration. The fruit are kind of like Lego blocks. The fruit interlock with one another in the way you act, react, think and speak. Just as interlocking many Lego blocks makes the project stronger, each fruit of the Spirit enables you to apply the others more firmly and permanently into the repented area of your life!

You will be stronger spiritually, emotionally and physically, every time you permit the fruit of the Spirit to make a practical application in the way you act, think, or speak. When applied to a repented area of your life, that area becomes more and more solidly, firmly and permanently *filled* with the fruit, leaving no more room for what was swept out by your repentance.

Each fruit has the purpose of allowing us to be more like Jesus. Each one has specific distinctions, so that you can prayerfully allow God to "fit" them into your life where you have need, and particularly where God has swept clean. This is the way a Christian grows spiritually, by permitting the fruit to replace the works of the flesh. Is there any area of your life where you know that significant spiritual warfare is necessary? To answer that question you must ask another more basic question. Is there any area where your life appears to be in direct conflict with your close and personal relationship with Jesus Christ?

As promised in Day 7, to follow is a more in depth examination of the fruit of the Spirit. Examine these Scripture references, which accompany each fruit. Use the leading question as you read, "How does this fruit "fit" into how I think, act, react, speak and relate to God, others and myself? Begin some role-play with the fruit to imagine how that fruit of the Spirit could be applied practically in a sweeping that you are anticipating or currently battling.

Love - Filling # 1 For Any Sweeping:

(John 3:16 and 11:33–36; 1 Corinthians 13:1–10; Luke 7:36–50; 23:34; Ephesians 5:1,2; 1 John 4:7–12; Romans 5:5; Mark 10:21 and 12:30,31).

This type of love was known as *agape* (ah-GAH-pay) in the original language of the New Testament. The closest synonym in English would be charity. It is the highest form of love, best described through the love of God as distinguished from all other types of love, in the gift of His Son Jesus to the world. Jesus exemplified agape as He delivered Himself to the cross for our pardon and forgiveness from sin. Think of the cross and you have the love idea down! Adjectives to describe this fruit are sacrificial, unconditional, complete and genuine, to name just a few—what are some others that come to mind?

It is the basis for the perfect relationship between you and the Lord. It has a focus on God, then others and only then upon your own needs and desires. It is not selfish or self-centered. It always compels us to ask the question, "How would Jesus love in this situation?" The fruit of love enables us to love even the unlovely or that which rejects or contradicts our best efforts to apply the fruit. Love enables all of the other fruit to operate freely and complement in a loving, Christ like manner.

This fruit implies a sense of self-sacrifice and a placing aside of self-interests and desires in favor of what will please God and give honor to Him (look at John 15:13 and Galatians 2:20 as possible memory verses). That means that the fruit of love operating in your life enables you to be both empathetic and sympathetic to the needs of others. For example, even if I have not yet experienced what you have, I am to love you as though I *have* experienced it, so that my love for you is willing to hurt with you, cry for you and suffer with you in your pain or problem (check out John 11:33–36).

To fill a void with any of the fruit, you must first go to the Lord in effectual, fervent prayer, giving the Holy Spirit the permission and room to love through you like Jesus loves us. Wrestle in prayer with this kind of love! Consider how much God loves you and to what extent that love will take you, in order for God to fill up the swept area for which you have prayed. This kind of love includes an important Spiritual/Emotional element. It includes loving *yourself* enough to know how much God values you, instead of allowing Satan to bring you down to his level by stressing out on your faults, mistakes, sins, errors of judgment and faulty decision making, both past and present. God's loving fruit enables you to stop beating up yourself with Satan's tools of false humility, fear of failure and that low self-esteem that he so wants you to endure. You are a child of the King! You are loved with an everlasting love, that has forgiven your iniquities and remembers your sins no more (Jeremiah 31:3, 34) He has great plans for those He loves, plans for good and not disaster, plans for a future and a hope like no other (Jeremiah 29:11)!

Once the fruit of love is engrained in your heart, *agape* will show you how to be confident in your love for others, because of the intensity that God's Holy Spirit has expressed that fruit of perfect love in your life. When you pray, ask God to grow the fruit of love in your heart more and more. Ask Him to show you practical ways to express agape to family, friends, coworkers and strangers. Finally, remember that agape or God's kind of love is what has enabled you to allow God to sweep anything that is contrary to God's desires for your heart—anything! His forgiveness at Calvary paid for your privilege to be called a child, even a friend of God! How big or expansive is the love that is appropriated for sweeping?

The LORD is merciful and gracious, slow to anger, and plenteous in mercy. He will not always chide: neither will he keep his anger forever. He hath not dealt with us after our sins; nor rewarded us according to our iniquities. For as the heaven is high above the earth, so great is his mercy toward them that fear him. As far as the east is from the west, so far hath he removed our transgressions from us. Like as a father pitieth his children, so the LORD pitieth them that fear him. (PSALM 103:8–13 KJV)

As you dedicate yourself to bold spiritual warfare, a very worthy and significant sweeping would be to ask the Lord about sweeping out any hate or resentment, anger, jealousy or selfish desire that might be getting in the way of your relationship with Him, with anyone you know, or especially with yourself.

Another very strong sweeping might be asking God to sweep out any kind of love that you have been substituting for agape in relationships. Impure love can contaminate this fruit and hinder it from operating freely once you have asked for its appropriation in a sweeping.

Right now, pray: *Lord, I thank you for the fruit of the Spirit known as agape love. Now that I understand more about love, I ask that your Holy Spirit appropriate that fruit in every area of my life: my thinking, my actions and reactions, my speech and my attitudes. I humbly ask that this love would have unfettered access to every area of my life in order to rebuke and denounce anything that Satan might have placed on my spiritual battlefield to discourage, distract or defeat me from your kind of love. For it is in Jesus' lovely and loving name I pray, Amen.*

Joy—profound happiness, no matter what!

(John 15:11 and 16:22; Romans 12:9–12; Philippians 4:4; Psalm 30:5 and 37:4, 5).

Once that love has permeated the way that you think, act and respond to life in general, the Holy Spirit can enable you to experience a type of happiness that is not dependent upon circumstances. Does this sound impossible? Well, in human terms and with our own resources, yes, it is impossible. Oh, you can make the best of bad situations or endure painful experiences for a time, but only through the *power* of the Holy Spirit can you have what could be described as *joy*.

Joy allows you to know that regardless of what today slings at you, good or bad, happy or sad, there will be this unshakable, indescribable inner happiness that senses God is in control so everything is in the hands of God the Father, God the Son and God the Holy Spirit. He IS in control, guiding, guarding, protecting you, so that no matter what the circumstances, you can know that *"the joy of the Lord is my strength,"* so that you can confidently say, *"Rejoice in the Lord always, and again I say rejoice!"* This joy is consistent, constant and maintains a feeling that the God who saved you, sanctified you and who resides in you will get you through anything and everything!

In contrast to joy, most of what the world experiences is happiness rather than true joy. Happiness is dependent on circumstances that bring us pleasure, convenience, comfort, security, positive reinforcement and an overall sense of gratification. Joy is a kind of bulletproof form of happiness! Holy Spirit endowed joy enables us to experience a sense of peace and contentment even in times of displeasure, pain, inconvenience, discomfort, insecurity, negative reinforcement or an overall sense of unmet need. It's contrary to human logic and reason—it just does not make sense! However, it is what Paul described in Romans 8:35 (KJV):

Who shall separate us from the love of Christ? shall tribulation, or distress, or persecution, or famine, or nakedness, or peril, or sword?

Paul had endured all sorts of suffering, but he maintained a joyful heart during those difficulties, because he *knew* without any doubt that God's constant presence in his life would give him the peace of mind and strength to see God smiling at him. That degree of joy is almost as if God was telling Paul (and you), "I'm right here, so don't be afraid. Be happy because when this is finished, I have better moments for you than you can possibly imagine, and I will give you a feeling in your heart that will make you happier than if you were in the most festive and happy celebration ever!"

That joy is internal, moving outward into your emotions and relationships. On the inside, it will refine your thoughts and your attitudes to react in harmony with how Jesus endured the pain of the Passion. Just as Jesus suffered for you, He is suffering with you or crying with you in the same way He suffered with His friends Mary and Martha when their brother and His good friend Lazarus died. Joy kept Jesus from rushing over to their town right after the death. The wisdom of God gave Jesus the joy to wait until the Heavenly Father could be further glorified by the miracle of raising Lazarus long after he his body should have been in a state of decay.

Joy gives us that kind of wisdom because joy limits worry and **anxiety**. Joy reduces crises down to their lowest common denominators and calms during the suffering and pain that goes on almost daily. Perhaps even more amazing, joy not only brings supernatural endurance, but it causes happy moments to be even more awesome, by reminded you where and with whom they originated. Joy enhances happiness while neutralizing the evil effects of sadness, suffering or pain. I cannot fully explain joy, even though I have experienced it during both the darkest and brightest moments of my life. Like the love that makes joy possible, joy can serve intensify love as well as all the other accompanying fruit of the Spirit, as they are practically incorporated into fillings or sowings in your life.

Joy is essential to most fillings, because Satan desires to bring us to the point of hopelessness and helplessness as we react to difficulties or temptations. A joyful person is *God-confident*—it's difficult to convince that joyful one that God does not have this one in His everlasting arms! Do you remember the poem Footprints in the Sand, by that most quoted writer and poet, *Anonymous?* Like that poem, the Holy Spirit will somehow just make you happy, contented and joyful in your heart that you are not alone—ever! Your strength for those difficult moments is not a singular strength based upon your own physical and emotional resources. It's a supernatural vitality made possible through a supernatural connection.

Joy frees the mind to develop wisdom and faith, so that no one can explain it away or discourage you from experiencing joy. I have had a very frustrating emotional problem all of my life, even as a child. I hid it from nearly everyone, while it tormented me whenever I was alone, at night, during the day or anytime I was about to confront a difficult situation. It could be the classic definition for a "joy robber". Nowadays they have names for such panic and anxiety, but back then, it was just a highly nervous kid being tortured by worry, dread and fear of failure. I used obsessive/compulsive behaviors, self-designed in my superstitious imagination, to calm down.

When I was fifteen, I gave my heart to Jesus. As my girl friend (now my best friend of nearly fifty years) reminded me the morning she led me to the Lord, I now had the joy of knowing that I am never alone. At times, Satan still uses this as a sort of thorn in the flesh in his spiritual warfare against my spiritual growth. Many years ago, I was reading in Acts and it suddenly occurred to me that even Paul had a doctor with him—Luke! That helped me to see how God heals miraculously in an instant. However he also heals through His "Luke's" out there. Phyllis shared that joy with me one Sunday morning during a telephone call before she headed out to her church. Having shared joyfully time and again about the joy of her salvation, her joy finally healed my despair. That morning, the Holy Spirit appropriated her practical application of the joy in her testimony to draw me to God. Over the phone, I joyfully prayed with her to receive Christ! Joy is a marvelous weapon against Satan, because it negates all of his negatives and pessimisms that serve as joy robbers. So an appropriate sweeping could be formulated in your prayer as "Lord, what have become the joy robbers in my life?"

Right now, pray: Lord, I thank you for the fruit of the Spirit known as joy. Now that I understand more about joy, I ask that your Holy Spirit appropriate that fruit in every area of my life: my thinking, my actions and reactions, my speech and my attitudes. I humbly ask that this joy would have unfettered access to every area of my life in order to rebuke and denounce anything that Satan might have placed on my spiritual battlefield to discourage, distract or defeat me from your kind of joy. For it is in Jesus' joyful and joyous name I pray, Amen.

Peace - loving right and receiving the joy that carries you through the best and the worst...peace will result in a peace that surpasses all understanding!

(John 14:27 and 16:33; Philippians 4:6, 7; Psalm 119:165 and 34:14).

Peace, brother! Along with the index and middle fingers upraised in a "V", my generation propagated peace. But the fruit of the Spirit kind of peace is unique and only available through the power of the indwelling Holy Spirit. Again, like joy, the fruit of peace makes no sense by the world's standards. When you permit or open your heart for the Holy Spirit to appropriate this peace, it can keep you tranquil and calm, totally at rest no matter what is going on around you or inside of you. Satan desires confusion and chaos to rule your day. He works best when you are distracted. The peace of God focuses on God and places all the chaos and crisis in the background. Though fictional, these examples really do describe what many have testified about true peace ruling their hearts in a tense moment.

In one baseball movie, the star is an aging pitcher who is in his last days as a player. In his best moment, he has this experience of total and complete concentration where the crowd noise and all distractions seem to disappear or go deathly silent. His concentration is absolute at that moment. In another movie about a famous amateur golfer, scenes would focus upon his concentration becoming a state of aloneness. All of a sudden, there was silence and the entire gallery standing on either side of the fairway mysteriously disappears from his sight. At that moment, his concentration and focus are in a state of perfect peace.

Now friend, I testify to you of experiences that I have had and that many other believers (including you) will readily report. For me, God appropriates that kind of peace every time I get up to preach. It is as though all other thoughts have disappeared from my mind and all that God has shown me in the study from His Word comes out in a manner that I cannot describe. In preaching in Portuguese during our many years in Brazil, I would experience this kind of peace "that surpasses all understanding", and I would begin using vocabulary that I could not ever remember even learning! I would use sentence constructions that sounded like I was a Brazilian! Now after thirty years I can communicate well in Portuguese, but those moments were clearly over the top and beyond my abilities. I was at such perfect peace, in the center of God's will for those moments, that He was able to have my undivided attention—the fruit of peace brings "Wow" moments when the fruit of peace is unleashed from any restrictions that my fleshly nature could stop.

One night Satan was attacking Phyllis and me in a very intense manner. On the way to church, we turned a corner from our house and a person was exposing himself to us! Shocked and shaken we drove on. The traffic was horrendous, even more so than normal for a city of three and a half million people in an area about the size of a U. S. city of fifty thousand. Finally arriving at church, I went to the stage area and prepared to bring the message while Phyllis sat in our usual place. During the service, this guy sat down beside her and began asking her all sorts of questions about a form of sexual immorality that he obviously was a part of in a big way. She was given words to say and Scripture to share (in Portuguese), that to this day she doesn't know how or where she was able to assemble those verses and that much technical construction in Portuguese. She too testifies of having such a peace and focus at that moment that as she said, "it just rolled out". The guy left near the end of the service and no one had ever seen him before. Some friends in another part of the sanctuary said that they did not even see anyone sitting beside her. So I commend to you, permit God to appropriate peace in your life. Your focus will be intensely personal with the Lord, and you can handle situations of tremendous pressure and stress as though God is handling them for you—which by the way, He really is doing just that!

He wants to pour it into you...a peace that is some kind of wonderful! It is serenity in the face of danger. It is calmness in the midst of tension. It is strength and focus in the heat of a battle at work, at home or a battle in your mind. It is an inner quietness reigning in a very noisy and chaotic world. Fill any void with this peace and you will be able to see the light at the end of the pain, pressure, suffering, sickness, frustration or any other "tunnel" that Satan might use as a challenge to your peace of mind and sense of stability.

It is so different from the peace of mind that comes when you are relieved about something being over or when you are at peace with a decision you made. This fruit of peace goes beyond all of the situations when God just lets you know, "It is absolutely all right and perfectly in my hands, regardless of the outcome." No matter what, the fruit of peace builds upon agape love and inner joy to melt worry into a calming confidence in the God of peace. The fruit of peace is the result of perfect confidence in God. Consider the person in your life with whom you have the most confidence and trust, that you know loves you no matter what. Now consider a love and confidence and a trust that is a thousand times stronger. Only God can go to battle for you every time Satan strikes. No loved one can be with you *"24/7/365"*, but our Lord is with you! The peace that the Holy Spirit wants to give you for your sweepings is sufficient to fill your void with the confident promise that He is with you in all situations, so that you will have supernatural coolness in the heat of the battle. This peace will make mental, emotional and even physical space for wisdom, knowledge and discernment to take over where panic and confusion reigned just seconds before.

The fruit of peace is also restorative. If by chance you do lose that sense of inner peace in the heat of battle, as we all do, the fruit of love and the fruit of joy will have a divine compensation or dispensation of *power* as long as you permit the Spirit to operate freely. In Psalm 23 we are reminded, "He restoreth my soul." Restoration is available while you are repenting and during the sweeping, so that you will have a peace that God will see you through even though you are sensing a weakness in your own strength to continue. The fruit of peace has carried many a believer to sweep out permanently a bad habit, bad attitude or destructive behavior, even after feeling shaky about going on, because undergirding the soldier is the **Leader of Leaders**, who is perfectly capable of carrying you when wounded or too tired to sweep any further. A peace that surpasses all understanding can give you a "second wind", knowing that God has got this one!

Right now, pray: Lord, I thank you for the fruit of the Spirit known as peace. Now that I understand more about peace, I ask that your Holy Spirit appropriate that fruit in every area of my life: my thinking, my actions and reactions, my speech and my attitudes. I humbly ask that this peace would have unfettered access to every area of my life in order to rebuke and denounce anything that Satan might have placed on my spiritual battlefield to discourage, distract or defeat me from your kind of peace that truly does surpass all of my understanding. Please build upon the other fruit this peace, for it is in Jesus, the prince of peace's name I pray, Amen.

Longsuffering—that is patience on steroids! Patience is the awesome capacity to wait upon God to speak, act and intercede.

(See Matthew 15:15–20; Luke 9:51–55; Romans 12:12; Proverbs 16:12; Ephesians 4:2; Colossians 3:12).

Job knew about patience long before the first century Christians, because he saw God bear with him through the most intense and terrible testing that Satan was permitted to submit. Patience even when being provoked, tested, aggravated, frustrated or misunderstood is best termed *longsuffering*. This fruit is so much more complete than mere strength or willpower, because it is supplied divinely and supernaturally by the Holy Spirit to serve as your most potent support weapon for the fruits of love, joy and peace to be unleashed and function at full strength. It is likened to the artillery on the ship that is miles to the rear of the front lines. Though unseen by the Enemy, when given the order to fire with the correct coordinates...watch out Devil! Godly patience can be just the ingredient for perfect timing of your counterattacks or sweepings. The fruit of patience is the proving ground for the Holy Spirit to confirm that you are still open in heart, mind, soul and strength to His outpouring and His timing. The fruit of patience refines your use of time in terms of quality rather than quantity. There are two kinds of timing spoken of in the Bible. In the biblical Greek, they are the words *kairos and kronos (also chairos or chronos)*. Kairos is the quality of time...how it is used and to what extent time is used toward the greatest benefit. Kronos is time as we measure it, seconds, minutes, hours, etc. We all have the same capacity for using the same amount of kronos in a given day or week, but the **way** that you patiently use those precious ticks of the clock determines the **kairos of the kronos** that God has entrusted to you as His steward.

Patience is waiting with confident peace in who is in control of the clock and the calendar. Longsuffering best fits as the type of patience that develops endurance, stamina and the ability to see beyond the apparent outcome during a time of pain or stress. The fruit of patience serves as a powerful tool in sweeping out many works of the flesh, because inherent in those sweepings is Satan's best attempts to reintroduce the evil to you in various disguises, many of which call upon you to make snap decisions and eat it, drink it, share it, take it or spend it right now. The fruit of patience will invoke the obedience amendment...no, not now.

The fruit of patience is especially effectual with regard to sweepings that involve your tongue, mouth, vocal chords...you know, your pie trap! Man, does mine ever get me in hot water! You could spend the rest of your life on sweepings that are related to your talk, your conversation, your monologues and your dialogues, not to mention your monotones of gossip, lies and most recently, what politicians have come to call "misspeaks". Huh? Why not just admit it was a lie or that I put my foot in my mouth, saying too much or too little at the wrong moment, with the wrong intent, inaccurately, mean-spirited or expressed in a thoughtless manner.

Nuff said...the fruit of patience can be your best defense against "foot in mouth disease". Patience can serve as the antidote for the poison tongue by fortifying another fruit. The fruit known as self-control is extremely dependent upon the fruit of patience, as are all the other fruit attributes. Patience is a big deal! It might be thought of as the accelerator, breaks and transmission of the fruit of the Spirit.

When the fruit of patience is permitted to complete its good work, that fruit emerges out of a cocoon into a beautiful character

Rob Hefner

quality best known as perseverance. Look at how the fruit of patience, if permitted, emerges in godly character.

Knowing this, that the trying of your faith worketh patience. And let patience have its perfect work, that ye may be perfect and entire, lacking in nothing. (James 1:3, 4 KJV)

And not only so, but we glory in tribulations also: knowing that tribulation worketh patience; And patience, experience; and experience, hope: And hope maketh not ashamed; because the love of God is shed abroad in our hearts by the Holy Ghost which is given unto us. For when we were yet without strength, in due time Christ died for the ungodly. (Romans 5:3-6 KJV)

There is an old saying, "Lord, give me patience and give it to me **right now**!" It is a tongue and cheek expression of how misunderstood the fruit of patience is. What is the potential of a sweeping that confirms genuine repentance, then replaced by fruit that includes patience? Isaiah said it far better than I could possibly express this kind of patience:

But they that wait upon the LORD shall renew their strength; they shall mount up with wings as eagles; they shall run, and not be weary; and they shall walk, and not faint. (Isaiah 40:31 KJV)

Right now, pray: Lord, I thank you for the fruit of the Spirit known as patience or longsuffering. Now that I understand more about patience, I ask that your Holy Spirit appropriate that fruit in every area of my life: my thinking, my actions and reactions, my speech and my attitudes. I humbly ask that this patience would have unfettered access to every area of my life in order to rebuke and denounce anything that Satan might have placed on my spiritual battlefield to discourage, distract or defeat me from your kind of patience that will lead me into godly perseverance. Please build upon the other fruit this patience, for it is in the name of Jesus, the one that will lift me up on his eagle's wings that I patiently pray, Amen.

Gentleness—this is the translation of Jesus' love that brings you inner joy and peace, to respond patiently, with the attitude of the Holy Spirit!

(Proverbs 15:1; Matthew 5:52 and 11:28–30; 1 Corinthians 4:21; 2 Corinthians 10:1; Psalm 103:17; Ephesians 4:2; Philippians 4:4–5; Titus 3:2; 2 Timothy 2:24; James 3:13; 1 Peter, 3:4, 15).

Remember the Golden Rule (Matthew 7:12 and Luke 6:31)? It says, "Do unto others as you would have them do unto you". That rule *rules* when it comes to the next three fruit that I like to call the *relationship fruit of the Spirit*. Gentleness and meekness come out of the original Greek New Testament vocabulary as synonymous. Gentleness, meekness, kindness and goodness are so close that they definitely cannot be applied separately from one another in your practical applications of the fruit. They are an unbreakable chain designed to pull you out of any sweeping that is relationship based. They are keys for the fruit of self-control to do its job.

Jesus loves you with a love that will treat all persons with the same mercy and compassion that He desires for them to treat you, only with more intimacy and intensity. Jesus' love went far beyond mere Golden Rule love...He gave Himself for us. Gentleness and meekness are the soil from which sacrificial agape love springs from the garden of relationships. Meekness is not weakness...it is born out of a gentle heart for the feelings and needs of those who cannot fend for themselves or do not yet understand fully what is going on around them or within them. Meekness or gentleness is the best way I know to move people forward in their understanding of any issue. People respond to gentleness better because if you think about it, how many ways can you react to someone gently explaining something or showing you something out of loving patience? Even when people overreact and things get out of control, as Solomon reminds us, "a gentle answer turns away wrath."

Gentleness strives to make others feel loved as Jesus loves you. Think about how you feel when someone treats you with gentleness or meekness. That attitude and demeanor seem to diffuse any growing resentment or frustration with a challenge or a difficult to accept decision. The fruit of gentleness goes beyond mere gentleness to incorporate patient love, so if the other person still reacts with persistent anger, frustration or resistance, your gentle spirit will continue to patiently tolerate and love right on through the dislike. Marriages just cannot survive the long haul without gentleness! Parenting a teenager absolutely will drive you crazy without appropriating the fruit of gentleness. Your job is maddening without it. Gentleness seeks to love in the way that Jesus loves us, despite our often-unlovely actions and attitudes.

The fruit of gentleness gets angry for all the righteous reasons and remains calm in the face of the wrong ones; therefore, you cannot be a wimp and exercise the fruit of gentleness. That would be hypocrisy and double mindedness, not meekness like Jesus demonstrated. God is gentle, because God loves you unconditionally but hates the Adam nature in you...not **you**! Have you ever seen Satan help an argument along until the main issue disappears and the two personalities are being insulted and defamed? Sweepings involving conflict resolution demand gentleness, because if you step back with patience, you will conclude that you don't hate the person with whom you are arguing—you hate the position that he/she is taking on an issue.

Gentleness appropriates the nature of God, which reacts with perfection. We are not to hate anyone, but rather hate anything that is contrary to what God would desire for that person to think, do or say. Keep conflict on the level of the meekness of Jesus and you will see a lot more reconciliation and diffusion than ever before. Even when an issue does not get resolved, gentleness will employ the fruit of loving patience so that you can just walk away and try again later, when minds and hearts are calmer and more reasonable.

Right now, pray: Lord, I thank you for the fruit of the Spirit known as gentleness or meekness. Now that I understand more about gentleness, I ask that your holy spirit appropriate that fruit in every area of my life: my thinking, my actions and reactions, my speech and my attitudes. I humbly ask that this gentleness would have unfettered access to every area of my life in order to rebuke and denounce anything that Satan might have placed on my spiritual battlefield to discourage, distract or defeat me from your kind of gentleness, that truly does turn away wrath. Please build upon the other fruit this gentleness, for it is in the name of the one who taught that the meek shall inherit the earth that I pray, Amen.

Kindness—this is generosity in action, in order to bless others the same way that you have experienced blessings.

(Luke 6:35; Acts 10:38; Psalm 25:6 Proverbs 11:17, 31:26 and 21:21; 2 Corinthians 6:6; Ephesians 2:6–7 and 4:32; Colossians 3:12; Titus 3:4; 2 Peter 1:7).

Kindness is very much akin to grace. This fruit expresses your patient love for others in a gentle manner, regardless of whether the person is deserving or worthy of that expression. If grace is God's unmerited favor, impossible to earn, then kindness is the acting out of that grace for others through your generous attitude. The spiritual fruit of kindness is sometimes expressed in the Bible as "lovingkindness". Referring to God's lovingkindness, the term is used twenty-nine times in the Old Testament, principally in the Psalms, Jeremiah and Hosea (see reference tool on Bible Gateway. com). We should take note that this older "KJV" term describes God's kindness toward man. Here is an example:

*The Lord hath appeared of old unto me, saying, Yea, I have loved thee with an everlasting love: therefore with **lovingkindness** have I drawn thee. (Jeremiah 31:3 KJV)*

God offers us the best example of this fruit, in the way that He relates to us daily. Sometimes examples of this fruit can tutor us on the fine art of kindness. Take Joseph in Genesis 50:21: after all the water under the bridge between Joseph and his brothers, they figured that when Jacob died that Joseph would exact revenge on them for selling him as a slave to the Midianites so many years before. But the fruit of kindness influenced him to calm their fears, assuring them that he would continue to take care of them and their children. Maybe a light is going on for you right now from previous chapters and you are saying, "Here's a Joseph type lesson!" Yep, you're right. Thinking about the character of Joseph, we see that kindness tempered his emotions, caused him to be patient and forgiving, even to persons that had done him a great wrong. Kindness helps you to intensify the other fruit by the way you react to people. I sometimes think that Joseph always had the perfect right to let his brothers have it with all kinds of vengeance. But the fruit of the Spirit were already evident in this context as well as in the context with other Old Testament heroes. Joseph desired to be just like God in the way he demonstrated kindness, just as God demonstrated His lovingkindness to them.

One more of many examples will drive home kindness better for you. In Acts 16:33, focus on a Philippian jailer who experienced kindness. When God's Spirit opened the prison gates and unshackled the prisoners (including Paul and Silas), the jailer was panic stricken, only to discover that no prisoners were escaping. This kindness by the prisoners saved this man from death at the hand of Caesar, but more immediately from himself as he prepared to kill himself rather than face the music with the emperor. The prisoners exercised a forgiving and compassionate thoughtfulness in not just running out of jail, shouting for joy over their freedom. Instead, they looked around for the one who might be suffering most, the jailer, and delayed their freedom in order to see this man saved. The jailer learned the ultimate lesson in forgiveness, and it caused him to reciprocate kindness by acknowledging their faith in Christ. That kindness also caused conviction in his heart, causing him to ask how he too might be saved. Paul and Silas had won him to Christ, so in loving compassion he dressed their wounds from the whipping that they had endured hours earlier. So another distinctive of this fruit is the capacity to recognize kindness and to feel compelled to return kindness with kindness. As you have probably surmised, kindness had made apparent the spiritual gift of mercy or helps. The fruit will serve as catalysts for all of the gifts of the Spirit when given permission to operate freely in your heart, mind, soul and strength. The spiritual fruit of kindness also carries with it the capacity for an attitude of gratitude. A truly thankful person readily recognized kindness and feels humbled by it.

David exhibited this fruit many times with the way he treated King Saul during his many jealous rages. Despite such treatment by Saul, David treated Saul and Jonathan's family with great kindness during the years after Saul's and Jonathan's deaths.

And David said, Is there yet any that is left of the house of Saul, that I may shew him kindness for Jonathan's sake? (2 Samuel 9:1 KJV)

The fruit of the Spirit known as kindness is best used in sweepings related to interpersonal conflicts. Kindness can also be useful in gaining respect in relationship building, in the workplace, and in your OIKOS in general (OIKOS is the Greek term for your circles of relationships in general). Kindness can kindle the fires for potential friendships or extinguish the sparks that ignite potential conflicts.

Right now, pray: Lord, I thank you for the fruit of the Spirit known as kindness. Now that I understand more about kindness, I ask that your holy spirit appropriate that fruit in every area of my life: my thinking, my actions and reactions, my speech and my attitudes. I humbly ask that this kindness would have unfettered access to every area of my life in order to rebuke and denounce anything that Satan might have placed on my spiritual battlefield to discourage, distract or defeat me from your special fruit of kindness, that so mirrors our Jesus. Please build upon the other fruit this kindness, for it is in the name of the one who embodies lovingkindness that I pray, Amen.

Goodness—this is the qualitative identifier of gentleness and kindness, a god quality that serves as the benchmark for gentleness and kindness.

(Psalm 23:6; Matthew 19:17; Romans 2:4; Galatians 6:9, 10; Ephesians 5:8–10.)

Goodness is a fruit that combines and complements gentleness and kindness. In Scripture, goodness is equated with God. Only God is good in His nature and activity. For you and me, possessing the image of the creator while also possessing the Adam nature resulted in our dual nature as a sinner. The goodness of God's love then revealed how to be saved by God's grace from that original sin nature, through the only good (worthy) provision for your salvation—God's Son. So being created in the image and likeness of God, and being redeemed or rescued through the sin sacrifice of Jesus, you have the potential for goodness, through that perfect image once again being unleashed in you through God's Holy Spirit. However, that complete power of God's Spirit can only be unleashed in proportion to how much you permit God's goodness to access your mind and your will. The Holy Spirit endows and appropriates this goodness in full supply so that you might know God more intimately and make Him known more clearly to others. Like all fruit of the Spirit, goodness must be given access to your time, your talents and your treasure—that pretty well sums up all facets of who you are. Since the purpose for your creation is to honor and glorify God, spiritual warfare is about to become hand-to-hand combat with a jealous and threatening Evil One, who desires above all for you not to become good.

Why is that so pivotal to spiritual warfare? The reason is simple: because after the first tier of character and personality shaping fruit (love, joy, peace, patience), this second tier is designed to sharpen those character and personality shaping fruit to produce the kind of fruit that will honor and glorify God. The more of God's goodness you permit to flow into the way you think, act and react to life, the more the fruit of gentleness and kindness will be appropriated into your character and personality. The newness in Christ (see 2 Corinthians 5:17) is only possible through your appropriation of that goodness.

Goodness serves as a kind of catalyst for the fruit of gentleness and kindness, to generate and appropriate them in full measure into how you respond to life. People who don't know God through Christ can act in gentleness and kindness, to be sure, but they cannot act in those qualities in full measure because they lack the reconciled and atoned relationship with the only one that is good...God. When anyone uses the word *good* in general conversation, even about something said or done by another, the word *good* is incomplete or inadequate goodness. Originally, of course, this was a different story. In Genesis, chapter one, we see that every part of creation was described as *good*. That is, until God created man in His own image and likeness (Imago Dei). In Genesis 1:31, God described this phase of creation, man, as *very good!* You were originally planned as being good like God's dimension of goodness. The goodness was marred by sin. Perfect goodness could not have complete honor and glory apart from our fulfillment of His perfect objective for humanity. Therefore, any use of the word *good* is incomplete goodness until that image of God is restored in a person to original condition. That was promised in the Old Testament and fulfilled in the perfect moment of history when God chose to send the only perfect substitutionary sacrifice to pay for sin, remove its blemish and restore the complete reflection of the Imago Dei (image and likeness, personality and character). With God, no other goodness than God Himself was necessary, coming in the person and nature of His Son, Jesus Christ.

So goodness is a *big* deal. Any time you speak of gentleness or kindness, you are speaking about having already permitted the room in your heart and life for goodness the only one that is good. (I help myself to remember this by seeking God-likeness in repentance and sweeping). Certain religious sects presume to say that man can become God, where real Christianity declares that God came in the form of a man to reconcile us unto Himself. So that vestige of the image of God already present in the created has the potential to come shining through in you and me.

This takes place through the only one who is *good* operating goodness through His power being released from a repentant heart. That repentant heart says, "Come Lord Jesus, I want to let go and let you have the space, time and access to my mind, my heart, my soul and my strength, so that *your* goodness might influence all that I say and do". Wow! God loves you that much, so that regardless of the junk you may have piled up in your life along the way, if you will but genuinely repent of it, giving it over to the Goodness who died for your badness or darkness or sinfulness. Then repentance will clear the way for a void or empty space where sin once lived. That space can be filled by practical application of whatever fruit seems necessary for the filling. So ask for God's goodness and mercy to have free access to your emptied, repented "space". Then you will finally understand fully what the Psalmist was talking about when he said,

"Surely goodness and mercy shall follow me, all the days of my life, and I will dwell in the house of the Lord forever." (Psalm 23:6 KJV)

Just ask God to fill you with goodness when you repent of something. As soon as God has swept that from your life, allow Him to fill that space with the character and personality builder fruits (love, joy, peace patience). Make *sure* that you ask Him to make an appropriation of goodness as well, so that all of the fruit will be tempered by the very image of God in you through Christ, Goodness Incarnate. Then the catalyst of goodness, like a chain reaction, will accelerate love, joy, peace and patience. This in turn, will miraculously release the complementary fruits of kindness and gentleness. The love will be more lovely, the joy more joyful, the peace more peaceful and the patience more longsuffering.

What you actually are doing is allowing God to give you a spiritual warfare makeover! The result is a soldier ready to march in step with the Master General! In addition, as you might have guessed by now, the practical applications will just come so much more readily to your mind. Your putting the fruit of the

Spirit into practice in ordinary, daily situations will come more naturally from the Spirit's goodness being permitted to flow through you like a mighty river. When permitted to take control, God desires to do great things with your same ole, same ole. You give Him glory and honor by submitting and permitting! Go to your Bible right now and check out Ephesians 3:20–21. Use these verses as a mighty weapon against the forces that would minimize or even deny God's powerful nature of goodness to take you farther, deeper and higher than you ever imagined!

Another way to remember how goodness operates in you is to think of building a motor, without any purpose whatsoever for running that motor. The motor is completed and beautifully manufactured, yet until it is placed into a machine like a car, truck, tractor or whatever, the result will be just something beautiful to look at, a conversation piece, where you can only talk about or imagine its potential. That pretty well describes you standing before a loving God who created you. The Psalmist declared:

I will praise thee; for I am fearfully and wonderfully made: marvelous are thy works; and that my soul knoweth right well. (Psalm 139:14 KJV)

Goodness is that vehicle that frames your potential to reflect all of that perfection that God has built into the uniqueness of **you**. The fuel for all of this is the Holy Spirit fire, motivation and inspiration, giving you the spark to fight spiritual warfare and win! The starter could be thought of as your effectual, fervent conversations with God, praising, confessing, thanking and interceding. Have you ever heard the expression, "Why, he is as good as can be!" My friend, that saying can only be accurately applied when the whole armor of God (Ephesians 6:11-17) has been put on. When you wear the armor, the fruit can become the weapons that destroy the Destroyer, and free you to be the soldier of the cross through whom God is honored and glorified.

Because you placed on that helmet of salvation, all the other armor becomes official! That helmet shows the world that God's image of goodness has been restored, so that He has the free reign over your will, your mind and all that you God's fearfully and marvelously made crowning creation.

Right now, pray: Lord, I thank you for the catalytic fruit of the Spirit known as goodness. Now that I understand more about real goodness, I ask that your Holy Spirit appropriate that fruit in every area of my life—my thinking, my actions and reactions, my speech and my attitudes. I humbly ask that this goodness would have unfettered access to every area of my life in order to rebuke and denounce anything that Satan might have placed on my spiritual battlefield to discourage, distract or defeat me from your special fruit of goodness. I pray that because of giving you free reign to appropriate this goodness, that my life will be closer to your image and more ready for your direction. Please build the other fruit all around this goodness, for it is in the name of the one who **is** goodness that I pray, Amen.

Faithfulness – is the confidence in God being in control while living a life that recognizes that I'm not. This spiritual fruit grows in direct proportion to how completely I trust God to fill me with his goodness, so that he can appropriate all of his fruit in every area of my life.

(Psalm 119:90; Matthew 25:23 and 26:52–54; Luke 16:10 and 22:42; John 9:4; 1 Corinthians 4:2; Hebrews 11)

The collective fruit of the Spirit are enabled by faithfulness. The fruit of faithfulness when permitted to operate in your life, results in a filling/attitude adjustment that becomes increasingly loyal to God and His Word. God's promises and His faithfulness continually affirm and reinforce an attitude that agrees with 2 Timothy 1:12 and Jude 1:24:

For the which cause I also suffer these things: nevertheless I am not ashamed: for I know whom I have believed, and am persuaded that he is able to keep that which I have committed unto him against that day.

*"He has been faithful in my life in every single situation, and the more I allow Him to take me to tests of going beyond my limits to trust His limitless ones, the more I know that He is **faithful**, to keep that which I've committed against that glorious day!"*

In stewardship sweepings, the fruit of faithfulness again holds great importance. In the Parable of the Talents, Jesus taught:

*His lord said unto him, Well done, thou good and faithful servant: thou hast been **faithful** over a few things, I will make thee ruler over many things: enter thou into the joy of thy lord. (Matthew 25:21 KJV)*

Then on another occasion, His teaching on the relationship between stewardship and faithfulness went like this:

*He that is **faithful** in that which is least is **faithful** also in much: and he that is unjust in the least is unjust also in much. (Luke 16:10 KJV)*

Faithfulness as a fruit of the Spirit is like all the other fruit, derived from the example of the Almighty...only He is truly faithful in all and through all:

*I will sing of the mercies of the LORD for ever: with my mouth will I make known thy **faithfulness** to all generations. (Psalm 89:1). But the Lord is faithful, who will establish you and guard you from the evil one. (2 Thessalonians 3:3 KJV)*

Because God is faithful, He has extended that potential to you through the power of the Holy Spirit. The fruit of faithfulness can give you the God-confidence and courage to persevere long after your willpower or inner strength has been expended. This fruit can cause you to fill the void left by repentance from such demonic tools as pessimism, cynicism, skepticism and negativity, all of which can turn the primary action verb in your life into discourage and the expected outcome of all you attempt into despair. This is a vital weapon in spiritual warfare, and will turn the tide of battle your way every time!

Faithfulness generates hope, the great killer of Satan's attempts to take you down, so that you cannot move toward any positive, hopeful or visionary thinking. Your revitalized faithfulness is a threat to the Devil, since God might be seeking to interject other spiritual fruit into your attitudes and actions. Hebrews 11:1 suddenly becomes your mission statement instead of an unrealistic suggestion. Filling the voids with the fruit of faithfulness can be the most powerful tool for repentance. This fruit will give you the doubt cancelling hope as you return God to the powerful place in the center of your life. Faithfulness will equip you to be decisive in your repentance. Satan so wants you to lack conviction and to be somewhat casual about sin. God has *so* covered that through His faithfulness to us, which serves as both inspiration and as our example.

The God who was faithful to the pinnacle of faithfulness, offered Himself as the sacrificial blood atonement. He came in confirmation and affirmation of His promises as the Incarnate Immanuel. Timeless, limitless and boundless in His faithfulness, our God was faithful, is faithful and will be faithful! The fruit of faithfulness, when permitted to flow, will take you beyond the limits that Satan can attempt to place in your path, right up to the one that holds so many of us back, enslaved...the fear of death.

Forasmuch then as the children are partakers of flesh and blood, he also himself likewise took part of the same; that through death he might destroy him that had the power of death, that is, the devil; And deliver them who through fear of death were all their lifetime subject to bondage. (Hebrews 2:14, 15 KJV)

God's Spirit has endowed you with all of the spiritual fruit. The fact that He has given them to be at your disposal anytime and anywhere is no small indication of His love and faithfulness! Things can move forward in your spiritual warfare because you just know that you know because of being known by the One who created all knowledge. By faith you will be able to permit God to present you to the world from a completely new perspective—the new creature in you begins to record over the junk, essentially erasing it from the way you relate and respond to all of the *whatever's* that life has indiscriminately delivered your way. If goodness is seen as the catalyst for the fruit of the Spirit, we can agree that faithfulness is the fuel for the other fruit to accelerate and advance your warfare all the way to permanent and ultimate victory over evil and its inevitable fallout or consequences.

Giving permission for the maximum release of the fruit of faithfulness in your life is a huge step in spiritual warfare, one of those game changers that turn you into the soldier God so desires you to become! As you will study in Day 9, maintenance or the keeping out of the demons from a **reoccupation or re-infestation** of your "house" has everything to do with this fruit of faithfulness. An essential stewardship principle is best known as *the Luke 6:38 Reciprocity Principle*, first coined by Pat Robertson in his excellent book **The Laws of Stewardship**. The more you give over your life to a faithful trust in God's decisions and to His will for your life, the more He will bless you with all of these answers to life's questions. Things just begin to add up on dreary and frustrating days...God has not fully unfolded all of the details, but as the old hymn writer Daniel Whittle put it so beautifully,

> "But I know Whom I have believed,
> And am persuaded that He is able
> To keep that which I've committed
> Unto Him against that day."
> (*pub.*1883, Copyright: Public Domain).

Right now, pray: Lord, I thank you for the fuel of the fruit of the Spirit known as faithfulness. Now that I understand more about real faithfulness, I ask that your Holy Spirit appropriate that fruit in every area of my life: my thinking, my actions and reactions, my speech and my attitudes. I humbly ask that this faithfulness would have unfettered access to every area of my life, in order to rebuke and denounce anything that Satan might have placed on my spiritual battlefield to discourage, distract or defeat me from your special fruit of faithfulness, so that my life will be closer to your image. Please build the other fruit all around this faithfulness. I pray in the name of Jesus, the one who **is** faithful and just to forgive my sins and purify me from all unrighteousness, Amen.

Self-control: This is the version of self-control or self-discipline that is in endless supply through the Holy Spirit. This can be thought of as the throttle or carburetor for spiritual warfare. Self-control is really God control over Satan's attempts to regain the control of your self-control. It is never to be confused with willpower or intestinal fortitude, a.k.a., guts. Quite to the contrary, the fruit of self-control is the method whereby God's Spirit releases all the power of all the fruit into every area of your life that you so desire.

(Psalm 1:1–3; Proverbs 25:28 and 29:11; Matthew 26:63–68; Luke 22:41,42 and 23:6–11; Philippians 4:5; 1 Timothy 6:6–10; Titus 2:6; 2:11–12; Hebrews 2:1; James 4:7; 1 Peter 2:23; 2 Peter 1:5,6)

The spiritual fruit version of self-control is like the final delicate brush strokes on a beautiful work of art. Filling with permanence must allow the Holy Spirit to have unlimited access so that the fruit of the Spirit type of self-control is not supplanted by your proud efforts to do it yourself in your own willpower and fortitude. God gave you (and all humanity) a certain measure of self-control. It's kind of part of the self-preservation kit from the Creator. But He desires for each person to have so much more than mere basic, worldly levels of self-control, which vary, according to the personality and orientation or worldview.

God desires to give a person who has come into a faith and love relationship with Jesus Christ a dimension of self-control that is top-drawer, top-notch and beyond any level of self-control that is a natural part of your personality. What is the purpose of such a special endowment of self-control? Well, it was not so you can sweep out the demons on your own! Likewise, it was not so that you would not have to wait on God! Moreover, it *sure* wasn't so that you would not have to bother Him with such trivial matters! That whole reasoning of "Don't worry God, I've got this one!" is like walking into a minefield even though you know it has not been swept.

The spiritual fruit of self-control utilizes the level of personal fortitude that you have been gifted, be it great or small, and takes it to the unlimited next level of the supernatural. From the moment that you ask God to give you His self-control, your self-control is put on reserve like a car moving up into fifth gear or overdrive. Your involvement is critical and words like self-discipline, training, life application and reaching for your best are still very much in the game. Nevertheless, the Holy Spirit fruit of self-control assumes the coordination and harmony of all your best alongside God's power in order to form one very reliable set of disciplines. All the prayer, Bible study, training in discipleship and past promises fulfilled all come together to make your self-control work beyond that breaking point, where it has faltered or fallen short in the past. Your own self-control is reconnected and recharged to be channeled to the max with God-control to give you access to all the other fruit of the Spirit in full measure. This is the essence of filling or sowing for spiritual warfare in the first century and the twenty-first century.

All of the fruit of the Spirit are placed into the equation of self-control and God-control in order to give you all the resources you need for the moments when temptation is about to make an evil sniper assault. Through effectual and fervent prayer, God's supernatural self-control, is permitted to be released in your mind and body, becoming like a powerful dam to resist what isn't needed, while permitting your resources to flow through floodgates of release in order to advance your spiritual warfare beyond Satan's evil limits. This is the point at which believers testify of being Spirit-filled or Spirit-controlled. At this point, God is permitted to pour out the desires of His heart upon the believer. So whether a person is mainline Protestant or Pentecostal in theology, biblical agreement for the true definition of being filled with the Spirit emerges here. Emotion or reverence or piety aside, this process is the real deal, so deal with it joyfully and embrace it completely!

Consider for a moment, all those verses that you have read and memorized. Now think about all those messages and Sunday School lessons that you have hidden in your heart. How about all those promises God has kept for you in the days gone by? If you will permit such ammunition to be appropriated, it will just flow through the gates of self-control to make you stronger and more able to hang on far longer than you possibly could have persevered through your own natural levels of self-control. These kinds of ammo will cause you to fight with over-preparedness, with an overflowing of potential for both offensive and defensive battle plans. This is the process we have been pointing toward throughout *Sweeping Out the Demons,* best described as "letting go and letting God".

What about people you know who have stopped drinking or smoking or overeating or taking drugs or cursing or gossiping or...whatever? What about those who *claim* to accomplish this on their own? What about those who say they stopped without asking the Holy Spirit or anyone else to sweep or to fill with the fruit of self-control? They claim their own willpower and inner strength for the deliverance. Please pay attention here, because this is so cool to see what has actually happened. Yet at the same time, consider how so not spiritually cool and how very dangerous for those blessed but arrogant souls who arrogantly claim that God didn't have a thing to do with their victory over a vice.

Take this to the bank. Someone was praying for those persons somewhere, either by name or without ever even knowing them! Otherwise, this quitting of the habit is just a temporary resolution and is only a will weakening temptation away from the "demon" and worse consequences just watching and waiting to reoccupy the swept clean yet still empty "house".

Therefore, it was not the self-control alone but rather the divine intervention of God that enabled this victory as a measure of His grace and redemptive love. Now the cool part: God gave these people a great level of self-control in the first place in order to draw them to Him. Now the dangerous part: if you or someone you know has had this kind of victory and is not closer to God as a result, watch out! If that person has not given the glory and honor to the Sovereign for this healing or deliverance, then that person or persons better beware, because they are in direct conflict with a sweeping and filling principle, as stated in 1 Corinthians 10:13 (KJV):

There hath no temptation taken you but such as is common to man: but God is faithful, who will not suffer you to be tempted above that ye are able; but will with the temptation also make a way to escape, that ye may be able to bear it.

God's level of self-control has been granted and in the case of an unsaved or backslidden person, this has been granted as a work of grace in that person's life by God's Spirit, in order to draw that person to Jesus Christ. He seeks to save those that are lost (my version of Luke 19:10). It is a selective, special rescue operation. It is reserved for a person like you or me that God has chosen for something important and special.

These supernatural defenses in spiritual warfare happen far more often than we could possibly count. They happen in the lives of people all over this planet. As Jesus told John in the Revelation, "He who has ears, let him hear..." Help those unbelievers and those Satan has in a web of self-love and pride to see God's hand in their victories before it is too late!

So as you can surmise, the spiritual fruit of self-control is very complex, because it is woven into what God has already given you to handle sickness, pain and abuses to your mind and body. Self-control was available to all humankind, from Adam and Eve, right on up to (your name here). Like the original Jonah lesson, long before Jonah, that Adam and Eve taught us, many persons throughout history have chosen not to recognize the limitations of self-control apart from God. In so choosing, they did not allow God to magnify to the fruit level this self-control... but right now you can choose to make the paradigm shift and follow God, not man!

All the Jonah-type lessons in the Word could have been reversed by asking God to magnify and extend physical, emotional and spiritual resources. In so doing permission would have been submitted for God's Spirit to activate self-control only as God can! Appetites, impulses, urges, desires, emotions and instincts would have come seamlessly under the dominion or control of the Holy Spirit. The word for this kind of self-control in the original Greek language of New Testament times is *enkrateia*. The prefix en means something like in, and the noun *kratos* means vigor with some kind of dominion or power. This invigoration gives strength that is throttled or governed like a gasoline motor on your kid's cycle or ATV! The power and the strength to motor are there, but it is under the dominion of a governor on the carburetor. The Holy Spirit is the throttle and the governor on your personality and your emotions, but only when permitted to flow by getting out of the way and allowing Him to appropriate power and strength under His self-control.

Right now, pray: Lord, I thank you for the "throttle, automatic choke and governor" of the fruit of the Spirit known as self-control. Now that I understand more about your version of self-control, I ask that your Holy Spirit appropriate that fruit in every area of my life: my thinking, my actions and reactions, my speech and my attitudes. I humbly ask that this spirit-filled level of self-control would have unfettered access to every area of my life, in order to rebuke and denounce anything that Satan might have placed on my spiritual battlefield to discourage, distract or defeat me from your special fruit of self-control, so that my life will be closer to your image. Please build the other fruit all around this self-control, for it is in the name of the one who **is** in control of all things that I pray, Amen.

Filling is a result of permitting the Holy Spirit to release the fruit of the Spirit in a life of a soldier that has chosen to let God outfit him/her with the whole armor of God, as Paul described in Ephesians 6:11-18 (see Day 6). In Day 10 we will tie all of this together for you as you put into practice the filling of the voids left by your victories through genuine repentance, so that you can consistently let go and let God win the battle within, filling for keeps, for perpetuity, from now on, forever. Let's bring it to the barn, see some powerful results and truly reflect Christ in daily living!

Sweeping Moments for today...

1) What do you see as the "Battle Within You"?
2) Which fruit of the Spirit is easiest for you to relate and to apply in your life? In your opinion, why is that? Which one is the most difficult for you to relate and to apply? In your opinion, why is that?
3) Is there any area of your life where one or more of the fruit is lacking most or even non-existent? Have you seen this as a hindrance to finding victory over attitudes, actions, habits or destructive behaviors? What will be necessary for this fruit(s) to be returned to its rightful place in your arsenal?
4) Do any of the works of the flesh as described in Galatians 5:16-21 form the basis for some immediate sweeping, filling and keeping out in your life?

Take time right now to consider some sweeping that is desperately needed in your life, and apply the prayer time after each fruit during your next time alone with God. Take your time with this over a few days or more, and when ready, allow God to have the permission to appropriate that fruit in your sweeping. As you begin to see God working through your permission to appropriate the fruit, discuss the experience with your small group (or with a friend if studying individually).

5) We have discussed how essential it is to make practical application of each fruit of the Spirit in your filling. Jot down a few of your ideas for practical applications of each fruit as you work through these with the Lord in prayer and Bible study. Share your ideas with your group or with a friend if studying alone. Brainstorm other ideas for applications of each fruit in the following types of sweepings:

   a) Trying to beat a destructive habit like gossiping...
   b) Seeking to have God sweep a bad attitude about someone...
   c) Rethinking a sweeping that has been swept and returned time and again like profanity/foul talk or negative talk...

6) Try to retell by memory Matthew 12:43–45. Explain how this is a Jonah type lesson as it applies to the Pharisees and Jesus.

DAY 10

Sweeping And Filling For Keeps... Sealing the Deal...

Is any among you afflicted? let him pray. Is any merry? let him sing psalms. Is any sick among you? Let him call for the elders of the church; and let them pray over him, anointing him with oil in the name of the Lord: And the prayer of faith shall save the sick, and the Lord shall raise him up; and if he have committed sins, they shall be forgiven him. Confess your faults one to another, and pray one for another, that ye may be healed. The effectual fervent prayer of a righteous man availeth much. (James 5:13–16 KJV)

When God placed this material upon my heart, I was overwhelmed by the complexity of writing it all down, after having lived it all out in some of the most intense tests of my life. Therefore, having tried my best to set forth spiritual warfare, as it must be fought in the new millennium, I want us to finish strong. I have had this fear that you might end up closing the book after the last page, yet unsure about how to fight evil and win every day. Day 10 will be about making sure this does not happen. Before you close this book for the last time, please go through this next paragraph. If there is but one of these questions that you are unsure of, go back now and look over those areas of *Sweeping Out the Demons* one more time. This is life changing information for which you will forever be changed for the better. Satan would most assuredly be grateful to you and me if you just brush this aside as another study course completed, to be given casual consideration sometime in the future.

No! This life-changing Christian principle was given to me by God to share so that you can bring your spiritual warfare to the convergence of total victory. God desires for you to finish strong! It is the most important information you will ever incorporate into your life since you gave your heart to Jesus. This is like being given the secret to a cure for a fatal disease, or the inside information for striking it rich!

In order to honor and glorify God, He wants you to have the best in your life, spiritually, emotionally, physically and even in some cases, materially. So are you ready and willing to let God do the filling? Have you understood how Matthew 12:43–45 holds the key to being an excellent soldier? Do you understand without a shadow of a doubt that spiritual warfare is impossible apart from genuine repentance? Do you now realize how futile your battle plan is without filling the empty place left by real repentance with something far more substantive? Have you realized just how evil that *evil* is, and that God has permitted the Evil One to escalate his useless attempts for survival in order for the church to emerge as radiant, holy and blameless, without spot, wrinkle or any other blemish (Ephesians 5:27, 28)? Now, do you think of Satan, a.k.a., the Devil, as the defeated foe who is more desperate than the worst criminal in history? At this point, are you ready to admit that you need to shore up your defense for an enemy that is doing all that is possible to enter the back door of your "house", in order to hold you hostage and beat you up, in order to remain free to roam just awhile longer?

OK...now that you have read and responded to what could be the thesis paragraph for the entire study, let's seal the deal!

You now know the Enemy, his strategies and the intensity of his desires to have dominion over you. You now know what it truly means to repent of some evil influence in your life. You now know that only divine intervention can truly sweep out that evil influence. You now know that the repentance, while essential, is not complete until you fill up the void with practical applications of the fruit of the Spirit. Let's say that you have already tried this to the point of spiritual victory. What is next? Satan and his demons will be roaming and seeking to reoccupy your "house" where the repentance has left things all tidied up, swept clean and filled with spiritual fruit. Because Satan is *that* desperate to sustain yet more time on this earth to reign as the Prince of Darkness, he will inevitably try to bring the sweeping and filling to an abrupt halt by attempting counterattacks. You must follow through now, with the sealing of the deal, or in Paul's words:

For the perfecting of the saints, for the work of the ministry, for the edifying of the body of Christ: (Ephesians 4:12 KJV)

Peter expressed the result of a life controlled by the Holy Spirit. He shows us the fruit of the Spirit in another form, that demonstrates the building and cumulative qualities of spiritual fruit. As you read Scripture and pray effectually and fervently, other attributes of the fruit of the Spirit will emerge in proportion to how you give permission for the Spirit to operate in your walk, your talk, and your "thoughts".

And beside this, giving all diligence, add to your faith virtue; and to virtue knowledge; And to knowledge temperance; and to temperance patience; and to patience godliness; And to godliness brotherly kindness; and to brotherly kindness charity. For if these things be in you, and abound, they make you that ye shall neither be barren nor unfruitful in the knowledge of our Lord Jesus Christ. (2 Peter 1:5–8 KJV)

You can accomplish this sealing or keeping out evil from ever again showing its ugly face around your "house" by taking the measures that God has provided for you in order to withstand the fiery darts of Satan. After truly repenting of some action, attitude, habit or destructive behavior, would it not be the best feeling ever to know that this can never get back into your life? Let's finish our journey together with that in mind.

Athletes do not gain a sense of true victory until the game is over and they can see that their efforts have paid off in a win. How would you (or your boss) feel if you had worked on a project but never quite finished it—or as folks say a lot these days, never *sealed the deal?* It would make you and your not so happy boss feel that all that effort was in vain...a waste of time, right?

Today let's see how to seal the deal in your spiritual warfare, completing even the most challenging attacks by the Devil. Let's shore up our defense and sharpen our offensive so that even if Satan makes some further counteroffensives, you are ready, willing and able to defend and repel whatever this defeated foe might attempt to sling your way! And I think we have surmised in these days together that he will try repeatedly, but you do not have to let him back in—*Ever*! And if you *do* crack the window a bit or allow him an inadvertent foot in the door of your "house", let's make sure that you know how to smash his fingers and crush his foot in the door of your "house". This third part of the formula for sweeping out the demons will equip you to keep evil out and to keep being filled with the Holy Spirit, maintaining those practical applications of the fruit!

Keeping your filling that resulted from your sweeping demands our oft-repeated egalitarian dynamic duo. These two most essential spiritual weapons must be continually at the base of all your daily skirmishes in spiritual warfare. Total, lasting victory depends upon *effectual, fervent prayer* and the powerful impact of *a love for God's word.* In order to keep Satan and his demons repelled and retreating in their counterattacks upon your mind, you must allow God to have time with you in real prayer that is focused upon Him. That focus must be allowed to develop into an intensely intimate encounter with the Father. This kind of contact with the Lord will reveal all manner of insights as you open His Word. His Word will reveal numerous insights as you talk with Him in prayer. Then, as the compilation of crises and complications converge on an average day, these weapons of effective, purposeful praying, coupled with a deep saturation in God's Word will be the turning points for victory every single time.

I know that these two weapons might seem so simple and basic, but if you fire away with these at the onslaught of the enemy, on a daily basis, any attempts for evil by Evil will be quelled. Your effectual and fervent moments with the Master will grow into powerful events that you will look forward to. Any efforts by the Father of Lies to confuse you, or any of his subtle suggestions designed to manipulate you will be crowded out. You will shake your head and smile to yourself at how empowered you have become as a result of effectual, fervent prayer and a loving dedication to Scripture as your rule for faith and practice. You might even be amazed at your responses to evil at how sharp and quickened your spiritual warfare has become, every time you receive the alerts in order to avert those surprise or sneak attacks by Satan! You will definitely be blessed as you realize how many times you are resisting inappropriate reactions to life's daily dilemmas.

What seemed to be the norm for falling prey to temptation will become foreign behavior for you, even when he attacks through junk he might whisper in your mind's ear to cancel out good or to discourage you. Finally, you will have confident responses when he attempts to use a circumstance to make you angry, suspicious, greedy or otherwise tempted. When the Devil

Rob Hefner

tries to entice you toward any of the works of the flesh, you will be "prayed up" and your mind tuned to the Word. Your defense will be that effectual and fervent prayer that invites the Holy Spirit to accompany you. Coupled with a deep entrenchment in the Word of God, the Spirit will be permitted to call to mind Scripture. These weapons will sound the alarm of discernment. You must remember daily that this powerful reconnaissance is only possible via a loud sounding from God's Word and your special times at the feet of Jesus on a regular and frequent basis. God will fight for you but you must open your eyes, ears and heart to let Him speak to you, comfort you, encourage you and prepare you for spiritual warfare in the twenty-first century. You are assured as never before, that Satan is more desperate, vicious and needy than at any point in human history. Effectual fervent prayer and an passionate encampment around the Word of God will make you ready!

Let's get specific. Suppose that you have just decided to eliminate a bad habit from your lifestyle, like overeating. Where do you begin? The starting point for repenting of overeating is to *take a stand on your knees*! You absolutely have to enter into times of effectual (real, specific and honest), fervent (serious, intense, urgent times in which you truly want to talk to and listen to God) ***prayer***. This is the bugle blast for beginning your spiritual warfare battle of the day. Sweeping has begun at this point. This point in the when the intensity and intimacy of your prayer leads you to the point where repentance gets real. Repentance is the change of your heart's desire about overeating. It is a turning over to God the very way you think about overeating. Repentance means that you are willing to relinquish all of your rights and privileges for overeating to God. It means an about face in your battle march, transforming the way you think of food or any contributing factor from the way the world has programmed you to think about overeating (or any sweeping you are doing). To state it as strongly

260

as possible, you must come to the point of mourning or hating that evil influence and what it is doing to your relationship to God, to others and to your own health and well-being. Sweeping has to be specific, real, honest and sincere. Listen to God as you meditate over the sweeping so that He can have your attitude, your schedule for overeating and any contributing factors. You may want to journal with God as you pray, jotting down what you are feeling as you open your heart to him.

This kind of praying is intense and can get messy, in the sense that you might be uncomfortable laying bare all of your feelings before the Lord about the issues behind this sweeping. Even so, go for it, because He even can help you truly to mean it this time. You even can come to the point in which you will confess to Him your true feelings about the sweeping, why you desire it and what it is doing to your level of honesty and openness with Him. This may guide you to understand your relational problems with others, leading to some major conflict resolution. God will bring you to a new and deeper understanding of yourself—with how you are dealing or not dealing with your situation. This keeping out principle will build a soldier's kind of perseverance, guiding you to a new level of waiting on the Lord. He will use the fruit of the Spirit to enable you to wait on God's timing—as long as it takes you to see it His way, especially if you are dealing with a secret sin that you have never divulged to anyone else.

But hey, He already knows about it anyway, so God is glorified and honored in your confession and outpouring to Him—which is a vital result of this crowing principle to Sweeping and filling. He loves you so much...He is just waiting for you to come clean and come to Him in contrition, sorrow and mourning over the seemingly unforgiveable stuff. Once again, grace will become real and precious—that Jesus died for that kind of dirty laundry in your heart! He not only paid the debt with His own lifeblood, but even better, He wants to restore you to spiritual health through the power of His Holy Spirit. Worry, worldly fears based on guilt and regrets, bitterness, unresolved anger, self-abusive habits and ethical or moral train wrecks...God has heard them all and knows about your mess even before He is permitted to apply His **best** to heal your mind, renew your mind and energize it to reroute your walk and talk. These moments will overtake who you were before, and take prisoner what is robbing you of who you can be from this point forward. Honesty with the Lord is an amazing weapon in spiritual warfare. This open intimacy will lead you to tell God why you want this or that swept from your lifestyle. The open forum with the Father will let God's Holy Spirit move you from a selfish desire to change, reform or make some lame resolution, to honestly transferring your desire to God's desire for your heart (Psalm 37:4,5). In this manner of repentance, you are actually invading and attacking Satan and his army of demons way behind enemy lines. Armed with God's armor and His weapons of spiritual fruit, your depth of prayer and saturation in Scripture eventually will run so deep than the Devil will have to flee frequently from God's presence into which you have entered.

What are the implications for permanent influence upon chronic sweepings for which you have battled repeatedly and? In my own life, I have continually battled with some of what Hebrews 12:1 labels "the sin that has so easily beset us". One prime example is the battle against procrastination as I complete this manuscript. Another would be the generalized anxiety that I mentioned earlier in this book. Even after what I considered a victorious sweeping, every so often, it can still be a tool of threatening for the Evil one, even after being healed and restored. How? When I am involved in any ministry or opportunity that God is clearly leading me into, the Devil will attempt to interfere with my weaknesses and vulnerabilities. So the pattern for keeping out evil will assure you that you are free of the likes of fear of failure, worry over trivialities. Real prayer and a passion to remain in the Word can deal you out of more specific sweepings, like late night temptations to stay up, overwork, eating too many snacks or just allowing the mind to mull over the day's activities and tomorrow's negative possibilities...in short, borrowing trouble and cheating the body from Psalm 4:7, 8:

Thou hast put gladness in my heart, more than in the time that their corn and their wine increased. I will both lay me down in peace, and sleep: for thou, LORD, only makest me dwell in safety. (KJV)

It is for this reason that we must seal the deal, or close the ranks in on Satan's attempts for reentry to your clean, spirit filled "house". So the reality that the Devil will still try to mess with you beyond victory should not be a surprise. However, the new reality that He has no chance to do so might be a bit of a shocker! If your past spiritual warfare included some incidences of evil kicking your tail after some spiritual victories. Endearing moments with God will lead you to meditation and reflection, allowing you to retrace your steps after the victory gaining assurance. A certainty will guide you to sealing adjustments so that you will not fail! God will prevail! No matter how fierce the Enemy assails, God will maintain your sweeping and filling and you will move consistently forward, instead of a few steps forward followed by a couple of devil tripping steps backward.

Sealing the deal...

1) **Pray effectually and fervently!** Pray with purpose, talk and listen to God as your best friend, your closest relative, and your most trusted counselor or advisor. Make that conversation often, special, honest and with the intensity and intimacy that you talk to your spouse, parent or best friend—only more so! Intimacy with God does not happen

by accident any more than intimacy with another person does. It takes time, sacrifice, willing dedication and yes, the fruit of the Spirit type of self-control. At first, it may not seem natural or may seem awkward or even tiresome. That is, until you start praising Him and thanking Him and worshipping Him as you spend time with Him. Listen for His voice! Don't be deterred if your mind wanders... just say what you would say to a friend if you did that: "Sorry, Lord, but my wandered off...I must have dozed off or something...I'm still pretty new at this, but wanting time with you so much! Now, where were we, Lord?" Because of many Jonah-type *pray-ers* throughout Scripture, we can be sure that He's cool with that, because of your desire to be with Him is growing.

Sing with God or play your favorite Christian music with Him. Another way to get close to God would be to read your favorite verses to Him, or better still, try to share with the Lord those verses you have recently memorized. Read a Christian book or devotional guide with the Lord, including Him in the reading, asking for His counsel as you read. Keep a journal and write as you talk to Him, talking through your pen and pad or tablet and keystrokes!

Make the time special—after all, we do not have a bit of trouble making special time with a spouse, a family member or best friend Ask yourself, why is prayer such a chore? What is it about this time that makes me put it off or rush it up? How important is it, really, for me to be with God? Why don't I pray without ceasing, long after those times alone with Him (1 Thessalonians 5:17)? Why am I not calling upon Him all through the day, chatting and consulting with Him as I daydream, as I wait in line or as I drive or walk? Have you never silently talked to yourself? Then why is it so strange to go about the day talking to the Living God? Set aside a time each day to be with Him. It is okay to put a time limit on it. It is okay to have interruptions and to come back later to where you left off. And it's okay with God for you to pray different ways. God is good with your most sincere communication with Him. As we can ascertain through dialogues of Bible personalities with the Lord, He must love to hear our laughter, share in our tears and serve as the Divine Sounding Board for griping or complaining about whatever. Just as long as you are truly dialoguing with Him, God hears and feels and responds. Listen carefully for His voice through quiet moments of meditation, through His Word, through circumstances, through experiences or through the Jonah or Joseph types of counsel from friends or family. God is your filter for wisdom, knowledge and discernment, and He has your back if you will just talk to Him and hear Him out, heart-to-heart!

Discuss sweeping with Him, and discuss the three principles. Ask God where you are at this point in a current sweeping, filling or keeping out of an attitude, action, habit or pattern of behavior. I used to ask my seminary students in Brazil, concerning church planting, "Now what is the first step in planting a church?" They would reply, "Pray!" Then I would ask them what the second, and the third and the fourth steps were, upon which they would reply with grins, "Pray!" And so it is with any endeavor in life. Resolve right now that all we think say or do must involve being with God. Effectual, fervent prayer is the essential first step in order to seal the deal with any sweeping, whether an automatic sweeping, a simple no-brainer one, or one of those chronic, stubborn, "Hebrews 12:1" sweepings, born out of a complicated web of other problems and temptations.

Pray as you fill the void left by the repentance, asking God to keep your mind on track to allow the Holy Spirit permission to take control. Pray as you seek to keep out evil. Pray that God will guide you to stay close to Him and find precious promises and other experiential gems for counsel in His Holy Word. Pray in the imperative, giving God permission for release of His spiritual warfare offensive, and for appropriation of His fruit in order to fill up the space left when He swept the lie, the lust, the disobedience, the rebellion, the willfulness, the anger, the bitterness or the temptation to (you name it) in excess or to the point of abuse. After specific and honest sharing, ask God to show you specific practical applications to each fruit of the Spirit as it relates to your sweeping.

These practical applications are ways to cancel out the works of the flesh, or to have an opposite or even retaliatory result upon what has been swept. Pose questions to the Lord like "How can I show your love in this situation? Am I allowing you to make me more joyful as you sweep this from my life? How can I change to reflect your peace in this? With these questions, you can place any of the nine fruit of the Spirit in the place of the ones I have just used. Then wait for God to show you, and be ready to do what He asks or requires.

What we are discussing here can be more extensive and complicated than anything you have ever experienced, so if you get into the confession and restoration mode and find it too heavy to handle emotionally, you may want to talk to a trained pastor, a Christ-centered Biblical counselor or even a very trusted Christian friend. The goal is to honor and glorify God, so get ready to be blessed as you sort out all the "if only's, what if's and what now's?" to your talks with Jesus. Sweeping, Filling and Keeping out evil are incomplete until you can read with a smile and an affirmative nod Paul's feelings about restoration in his letter to the Philippians:

Rejoice in the Lord always: and again I say, Rejoice. Let your moderation be known unto all men. The Lord is at hand. Be careful for nothing;

but in everything by prayer and supplication with thanksgiving let your requests be made known unto God. And the peace of God, which passeth all understanding, shall keep your hearts and minds through Christ Jesus. Finally, brethren, whatsoever things are true, whatsoever things are honest, whatsoever things are just, whatsoever things are pure, whatsoever things are lovely, whatsoever things are of good report; if there be any virtue, and if there be any praise, think on these things. Those things, ye have both learned, and received, and heard, and seen in me, do: and the God of peace shall be with you. (Philippians 4:4–9KJV)

Now a final and very important orientation needs to be given concerning prayer that is effectual and fervent. In our much-repeated passage on spiritual fruit and the works of the flesh, Paul alerted the Galatians about the works of the flesh in Galatians 5:19–21. This list reflects weapons of evil designed to cancel out the fruit of the Spirit, if left unchecked...

1) Sexual immorality.
2) Impurity.
3) Lustful pleasures.
4) Idolatry.
5) Sorcery.
6) Hostility.
7) Quarreling.
8) Jealousy.
9) Outbursts of anger.
10) Selfish ambition.
11) Dissension.
12) Division.
13) Envy.
14) Drunkenness.
15) Wild parties.
16) All other sins that have these kinds of evil influences.

As you engage in the powerful weapon of effectual, fervent prayer, with regard to these temptations and their offspring, you should consider adding to your spiritual warfare arsenal the anti-aircraft of prayer assault: *fasting!* Such self-sacrifice and self-denial, coupled with the real kind of conversation with God declares in a very loud voice that your devotion to the sweeping and filling is total, complete and prepared for a stunning victory in Jesus!

Fasting is denying one's self of food, drink or any other necessity or creature comfort for a determined period. The fasting is a turning away from the world and toward a reflection of how deeply you desire your focus to be upon worshiping God and God alone. In the Old Testament, these periods of fasting were solemn offerings before God, to reflect a deep yearning for the hand of God in battles against foes of Israel, but ultimately they reflected the desire for repentance and a turning back to the Lord of Hosts. Joel 2:12 sums the feeling that you must adopt in order to couple prayer with fasting:

Therefore also now, saith the LORD, turn ye even to me with all your heart, and with fasting, and with weeping, and with mourning: (KJV)

Entire studies are devoted to discovering the spiritual strength to be gained through the spiritual discipline of fasting, but as a soldier of God's army, you need but the basics. During a time of great spiritual testing or need, you go to the Lord in prayer. Declare in humility to Him that you will fast and pray at this time about your burden and in submission to His will for your life to approach a deeper level of devotion for Him. Abstain from food or **any** substance, attitude or activity that you hold in high esteem or affection. Jesus warned about making a big deal out of fasting in Matthew 6:17, 18:

But thou, when thou fastest, anoint thine head, and wash thy face; That thou appear not unto men to fast, but unto thy Father which is in secret: and thy Father, which seeth in secret, shall reward thee openly. (KJV)

Actual situations given to fasting in the New Testament include Jesus informing His disciples as to why they could not rebuke the devil from a possessed son of a follower. After He rebuked the devil from the child, the disciples asked why they could not drive the demon from the boy. Jesus replied that their faith was not strong enough for this kind of deliverance without the intensity of prayer and fasting (Matthew 17:20, 21).

God is honored and glorified when we spend time with Him on a regular, even constant basis. The most prolific prayer warriors that I have had the privilege of knowing were those who prayed all day long as they went through the day. They truly exemplified Paul's admonition to the Thessalonians: "Pray without ceasing". (1 Thessalonians 5:17). That should be your goal, to begin the day with prayer and continue it until you lay your head on the pillow at night. This kind of prayer will seal the deal!

2) **Stay in the Word of God!** As we mentioned earlier, prayer and a love for Scripture are an inseparable pair of weapons. One can precede the other at any given God-moment. They are cooperatives with a design toward the same objective: honoring and glorifying God.

Hebrews 4:12 describes just how powerful the Word of God is. If it is able to penetrate any surface problem or deep situational crisis, then God's Word can show you how to escape evil and return to God. In the earlier chapters, we walked through time alone with God. In order to seal the deal and make *Sweeping Out the Demons* permanent, you must do more than merely read the Bible, or study it, or meditate over it or memorize it or even apply it to your life situations. Those will mean zilch if you do not first pray effectually and fervently for this humongous desire to grow in your heart as never before:

You must fall in love with Scripture!

The Bible can be a challenging book to understand in the beginning of your quest to have a spiritual love celebration with the sixty-six books of life and light. At the outset of this romantic quest with the love letter from God's own voice, inspiration and revelation, it is a good idea to "road test" various translations and paraphrases of the Scriptures. Find one, oral or written, that is easy for you to understand...that you "get"! Along with this version of God's Word, look online for some study notes, or use a study Bible to help you with areas that you find difficult to understand. How will you know which one is right for you? Read a section of Scripture where you are familiar with the basic story or context. Then see if you can explain to yourself or someone else what that section means to you.

Return to the Sweeping Moments of Day 2 to guide your study of the Word to become pure joy. Set aside time for the Bible, and enter into each time with—you guessed it, *effectual, fervent prayer*! In the final analysis, only the Holy Spirit will truly guide you to understand what God wants you to receive from His Word. But don't let Satan block this appropriation from the Lord by not employing every Bible study help available to help you achieve two goals in your reading:

First - to get a full understanding and joy in the reading of the <u>Word of God.</u>

Second - to develop a deep loving relationship like never before with the <u>God of the Word.</u>

Hiding the Word of God in my heart is the way that I fell in love again with Scripture. As I began to memorize again after years of neglect in that discipline, I realized that Satan had tricked me for so long into busy-ness in lesser pursuits designed to detour me from the Word and its awesome power. I rediscovered how amazing it is to go through the day with special passages coming to mind. My attention on memorized verses during empty or idle moments of the day has caused me to be more focused upon the application of Scripture to specific sweepings and fillings. I also discovered what lies Satan is capable of concerning my ability to memorize Scripture. He must hate it terribly to attempt to block our efforts.

Then it came to me, how did I memorize the last joke I heard or the plot to a favorite book or TV show? I do not know about you, but honestly, I didn't even try to memorize those books, TV shows, internet blogs or YouTube films. Those thoughts about each of those mediums of communication just naturally filled my mind with the memories based on what the story had meant to me at the time. A basic sweeping and filling for me emerged as very essential to all other sweepings. I had to repent of a disdain or neglect of Scripture memory, because there was/is no reason why God's Word should not be even more compelling than any other story I have ever seen or heard.

You need to engage in this sweeping as well! You can read the Bible with that same mindset! Get hungry and thirsty for it as your next piece of literature in the mornings, or before you go to bed, or at your lunch hour. Matthew 5:6 shows what Jesus thought about the first disciples' attitudes about righteousness and the quest for it. There is no greater fountain or buffet than the Bible for satisfying the thirsting and hunger of your soul for counsel, comfort, inspiration, correction and encouragement!

Hunger and thirst for the Word like you do the next episode of your favorite TV show. Do not treat Bible study as a chore or a task, but as an act of love to the Heavenly Father. Memorize Scripture by your own version of the actual meaning. Say it in your own words in a way that you will remember the lesson behind that passage. Suddenly as you pray effectually and fervently, you will see God speaking through the verses or chapters you are reading as highly practical and contemporary for your context in life. Ask God to make one of the desires of your heart a deep love for His Word. Ask Him to help you to visualize the Bible stories and teachings like you mentally picture the characters and situations in your favorite novels. Imagine how it was in the real life Bible times and how that context will reflect in your life.

Record the rescues! Reflect on the lessons learned! Talk to God as you read! Enjoy the reading as never before by inviting the Lord to go along with you as you read. The Holy Spirit will show you deep truths that possibly no other believer has ever seen about a passage as it relates to your life situation.

Effectual, fervent prayer and truly falling in love with the Bible will jump start you into being able to get past years of trying on your own to fill up areas of your life where bad stuff could have been swept clean and filled with spiritual fruit. The Master of Deception has tried to deceive you and me for years with lies like:

The Bible is too antiquated and difficult to read. This is the infamous generalization dodge...most who use it have never read very much of the Bible. Satan expands it by using liberal Bible scholars that come up with all these contradictions and questions about veracity that are especially appealing to Millennials and many other post modern and post Christian thinkers.

I can't read that well anyway, let alone understand a complicated book like the Bible...who do they think I am, a preacher or something? This is the self-abasement dodge. I excuse myself by saying I don't have the skill or ability when I have tried and failed or when I don't want to try at all. As we mentioned earlier, there are many versions of the Word that are designed to help us understand the Bible, no matter what level of reading comprehension. It is a soldier's act of faith to trust God to give understanding to the reading or hearing of His Word. There is absolutely no excuse for someone not to love how God has given us access to His Word while millions would give up eating to have an entire copy of Scripture.

I have neither time nor interest in reading the Bible. It is for church reading by the preacher, not for me to pick up and just...read. This is the time dodge. Everyone has time to do what he or she wants at some point in a busy day. If I wait for only the preacher to share and read the Word, I will have deprived myself of as much as if I were to wait for food or water to come up and jump in my mouth instead of picking up the knife and fork!

I start reading the Bible and no sooner than I get started, I come to something I do not understand—then what do I do? What am I to do about those genealogies and all those places where they count people in the Bible...*boring*! This is the ignorance dodge. You will never appreciate anything if you don't at least try it. The wrong attitude will make you hate doing anything, from vacations to ice cream! And so what if you don't understand it all? Ask someone or look it up in a reference Bible. If you were working on the motor in your car or cooking a new culinary delight, you wouldn't mind picking up a copy of a mechanics repair manual or a cookbook, now would you. It wouldn't be that complicated to ask a fellow mechanic or another cook, now would it? I don't know a mechanic that doesn't consult the repair manuals or advice from friends. And I don't know of a kitchen in America that does not have at least one cookbook nearby. So please don't dodge God's Word with lame excuses! Pray, ask God for understanding, put together the right study tools, and hook up with a Bible study group or a good Sunday School class. If those are not viable, get online and do a search with Bible study tools. It won't come back empty, I promise!

Getting back to the fruit of the Spirit, you will find hundreds of practical lessons about how to put into practice the fruit of the Spirit right there in the Bible itself. Reading intentionally and reading expectantly will help God to see you through to complete passion for His Word. He will be glorified and honored by the time you spend with Him in prayer and in His Word.

I don't read much beyond the newspaper and my Facebook. I was never much of a student. In fact, I hated school, so what makes you think I could get into Bible reading? This is the oldest dodge in the book. It is the academic dodge. You automatically assume that reading the Bible will be like schoolwork. Way to go Satan! He duped you or a friend into forgetting that the Bible is not just another book...it is God's inspired written revelation to mankind. It was written so that He might draw us back into a personal relationship with Him. After reading a comic book or a novel, or even watching a show on the tube, don't you have some kind of emotional response (laughter, sadness, frustration, warmth, confusion or just a feeling of wanting to react to the story)? Treat Bible study for what it is: time alone with God in His message to fallen man. It has healing power for the mind and heart, but only if picked up with the right attitude and interest.

So, are any of these so-called "dodges" keeping you from releasing yourself to a genuine love of Scripture? Instead of these excuse dodges, become a soldier trained in the elite force called the Devil Dodgers! Be constantly astute, discerning, vigilant and watchful for what Satan might have up his sleeve to tempt, trick, test, discourage or defeat you from sweeping, filling and keeping out of evil desires and actions. This is only possible through God's greatest weapons, effectual, fervent prayer and a true love for

Scripture. Intensive prayer and Bible saturation will enable you to be ready for any dart the Evil One fires your way.

Go back to Day 4 and look at how we have described our defeated enemy called Satan. Do a battle review of those distinctive facts about him so that you can sharpen your warfare to both defend and attack before he can tempt, test or otherwise thwart your walk.

In the Word, you will discover a wealth of reconnaissance information for a most excellent battle strategy for sealing the deal on sweeping, filling and keeping evil at bay! So just what is Satan getting ready to fire at you as you seek God's sweeping miracles of repentance? As you fill, what will you confront from the Enemy as you seek to let go and let God? What is going to keep you from keeping on in spiritual warfare? What are the barriers and blockades, the roadblocks and the impediments to walking with Jesus consistently and steadily forward to the day of His glorious appearing?

There are key areas in God's Word where Satan is interested in either opposing your application of fruit or distorting and diluting this absolute truth as it applies to your life. For our starting point, we focus upon these. Go through each with the sweeping questions from Day 8 with each of these key areas in Scripture.

A) The Ten Commandments (Exodus 20:1–7): Moses was given this framework for sweeping through genuine repentance. Deal with these biblical mandates and your sweepings and fillings will be impermeable to Satan's fiery darts! Evaluate where you are with each of this Decalogue with an attitude of effectual (purposeful, specific), fervent (intensely personal, intimate and painfully honest) pray

B) The Great Commandment of Our Lord Jesus (Mark 12:28–31): Jesus condensed the general application of the Ten Commandments in His Great Commandment. In that profound declaration, we see the purposes for the soldier's warfare as well as the purposes for the entire church. Loving the Lord with all your heart soul, mind and strength brings to mind worship of the Living God, discipleship and evangelism. Loving your neighbor as yourself brings to mind fellowship, ministry, service and missions.

Both the Ten Commandments and the so-called Great Commandment of Jesus frame for us the defense fortresses that God has established. The Pharisees, the Sadducees and the Scribes listened critically to Jesus' teachings. The Decalogue, as viewed from their perspective, formed a legalistic pattern of do's and don'ts. For you, the soldier of spiritual warfare in the twenty-first century, they serve as road signs of warning on the highways of life. When the Devil seeks like a roaring lion to find the right weapon to fit the weakness and subsequent temptation to attack that weakness, he will seek to usurp these important guidelines with half-truths and ways to sidestep them. Satan is in fact doing this in America today as each of the Ten Commandments are distorted and watered down to become words that contain truth rather than absolute God-truth. Remember: you don't have to allow Satan to do any of that because now you are a child of the King, no longer a child of Adam. Permitting the fruit of the Spirit will make his demons flee (James 4:7–8). As you fall in love with Scripture, make sure that your study begins with prayer for understanding in relation to your new role as a soldier of the cross.

C) In Proverbs 6:16–19, we find a negative list of attacks designed to cancel out the commandments and teachings of God. While Satan seems to apply these broadly in the secular worldview, he will specifically fashion temptations to adapt any or all of these to spiritual counterattacks upon you. Be ready! Pray through each one when they become potential stumbling blocks. Evaluate using the questions from Day 8 to insure that no potential sweepings have been devised by Satan in these broad stroke sweeping areas:

1) A proud look.
2) A lying tongue.
3) Hands that shed innocent blood.
4) A heart that devises wicked plots.
5) Feet that are swift to run into mischief.
6) A deceitful witness that uttereth lies.
7) Him that soweth discord among brethren.

D) There is another perspective on the biblical arena for spiritual warfare. Old Testament examples show Satan wants to entrap you with the misuse of Scripture in order to make his point. Earlier in our discussions, we talked about so-called "Jonah type lessons". Instead of doing the opposite of the negative or rebellious "Jonah type response", Satan would have you to rationalize and go along with the wrong way, in order to get you farther and farther off the track of following Jesus. In a day when Satan has reduced absolute truth to being relative to the situation, he can easily tell you that everyone else is doing it that way now, so why don't you? Like Jonah's rebellious disobedience in the face of God's clear direction, Satan would cheer you on in this kind of thinking. So Jonah got deeper and deeper into hiding his sin and deceiving both himself and the others on the boat. He knew the real problem was resentment and rejection of God's plan for Nineveh.

You may have some "Nineveh" in your life that needs to be addressed. Do you resent God's plan for sweeping, filling and keeping out evil when it does not match up with your personal plans? In this case, the Jonah lesson was a result of taking life into his own hands instead of leaving himself in God's hands. Self-rule instead of God's rule always gets you in trouble. The best response to a Jonah type lesson is to do the opposite from the way Jonah responded. Many sweepings and fillings can be achieved in God's power if you respond correctly to the Jonah type lessons in your life. They usually have a "Nineveh" or point of conflict between your desires and God's desires attached. Pride, fear or anger can most often be the reason behind your following Jonah instead of God.

A love for Scripture will make you have a discerning eye for both Jonah and Joseph type lessons. The Jonah lessons should help you to know how not to respond or react. The Joseph lessons, or those positive examples, will help you to know how to respond or react. Either you see negative or "how not to do it" lessons, or positive "how to do it" situations in Scripture. This fine-tuning of how you evaluate Scripture will help you to fight the good fight and prayerfully apply the Bible to your life in order to resist temptation and emerge appropriating the fruit of the Spirit every single time! Just always remember that Satan works best through the Jonah type lessons, but will fight tooth and nail to make you skip over the positive lessons in the Joseph examples of God's Word. You've got this one, if you *pray like you mean it, and read the Word like you love it.*

Besides the Joseph model in Genesis, there are many, many other positive examples in Scripture for you to emulate as you battle to win over life's frustrations. However, beyond Joseph and ultimately our Lord Jesus, there are fewer Joseph type examples than Jonah lessons. For example, Moses has so many Joseph type lessons built into his life, yet Moses struck the rock for water as instructed by God in Exodus 17, but in a prideful type of Jonah move, he struck the rock instead of speaking to it as instructed by God in Numbers 20. The first was a Joseph type lesson demonstrating his dependence upon God and his obedience to God's commands. The second one was a Jonah type lesson, and resulted in his being prohibited from entering the Promised Land. So as you can surmise as you look at the likes of Samson, Gideon and most of the kings of Israel and Judah, the pure Joseph type lessons are much fewer that Jonah variety lessons.

David is considered as "a man after God's own heart"(Acts 13:22). His Joseph type lessons are many, but among the Jonah ones is his affair with Bathsheba and his mishandling of the situation with his son Absalom. Likewise, Solomon asked for wisdom instead of great wealth, and God granted him both in legendary measure. Near the end of Solomon's reign, he exhibited greed and married in a manner that caused other religions to mix into Jewish culture.

So you see, as you fall in love with Scripture, there are adventures like discovering all of the Joseph and Jonah lessons, as well as how they can be used as mighty weapons in your sweeping, filling and keeping out evil. Word studies will also cause you to escape into the world of the Word and search for the deepest meanings and applications of the fruit of the Spirit, as well as discovery of your gifts of the Spirit and how many of the New Testament heroes applied the fruit and their specific gifts. You can fall in love with reading, studying, meditating over, memorizing and applying the Bible in every area of your life! The illustration of the five fingers as reminders of what to do with the Word might be a great place to go right now, committing yourself to allowing God to lead you into all these five areas (see the Sweeping Moments for Day 2).

As for the Jonah lessons, they need special attention. Let's close out our work on *Sweeping Out the Demons* with a look at the potential threat posed by Jonah lessons to your defenses as a soldier of spiritual warfare in the twenty-first century! The Jonah lessons are the most basic of all. You can create an arsenal of defense by reacting to their variety of pride, arrogance and the desire to take matters out of God's control and into their own hands.

GENESIS 3 – Adam and Eve: We inherited the Adam nature from this original sin. We became sons of Adam and slaves to sin. This slavery is over! You are freed from that bondage forever as a child of the King (Hebrews 2:14–15)! A joyful reading of Romans, chapters six through eight will reinforce this sense of victory over sin and motivate you to live out your inheritance... to fight like the winner you are!

GENESIS 4 – Cain: The Jonah type lessons we learn from Cain are jealousy, anger and resentment. The cause and effect of Cain's lesson rose from not giving his best to the Master. From this Jonah type lesson, we see how Satan can encourage laziness and blaming others for your mistakes and your lack of effort. Passive aggression is one of the major causes of many Jonah lessons related to the Cain factor. When you claim to be the victim and can never assume responsibility for your actions, the Cain factor is the tool of choice for the Devil.

GENESIS 9 – Noah: The greatness of Noah would be difficult to debate. However, even a Noah can be brought down by strong drink. You just have to know that Satan will try to use the trip wire of drunkenness or excessive use of any substance to draw your attention away from God. Watch out for habits or any activity that has the potential for either mental or physical dependence. The dependencies go from drugs to video games. They are as diverse as to involve anything from sex to sports. One of the most common traps for so many people is not that diverse. It leads one from food to...more food, and to all kinds of problems with overeating to binge eating to anorexic starvation.

You get the point. It does not have to be something inherently bad for Satan to tempt you to become obsessed with the pleasure, convenience, comfort or security that it derives for you.

GENESIS 12 - Abram: He left all he had and went toward a land that he knew nothing about, just because God told him to. Even a man with such faith can be tempted to this Jonah zinger...*lying*. Out of fear for his life and in an effort to quick fix matters without consulting God, Abram figured that he could save his neck by telling the Egyptian king that Sarai was his sister, not his wife. The self-made solution almost caused a far more fearful situation than Abram could possibly have imagined, and all because of Satan's astute use of fear leading to dishonesty and half-truths in order to perpetrate a scheme. Satan's schemes are intricate and often you won't see them unfold until it is almost too late, unless you stay in the Word and keep the conversation alive and vibrant with your Lord.

GENESIS 25 - Esau: He was the oldest of the twins born to Isaac and Rebekah, very different from his twin Jacob. He was given to impulsiveness in weak moments, like selling his birthright to brother Jacob for a bowl of soup. This Jonah lesson teaches us not to make any monumental decisions when hunger, anger, sadness, loneliness or fatigue might influence the choice. *Sweeping out the demons* is all about eliminating the causes for the leading battle injury: guilt that results in regret. There are some decisions that when made, are irreversible. It is better to stay in the Word and keep in touch with the Master so that you will have His input 24/7/365!

GENESIS 45:24 - To Joseph's brothers we are indebted for a very significant weapon for sweeping and filling. Don't get sidetracked along the pathway of your spiritual warfare! The scene is when the brothers were returning to Canaan to fulfill a promise made to that Egyptian governor (unbeknownst to them their younger brother Joseph). They were to bring (his) brother

Benjamin back with them. Joseph warned them not to quarrel on the way back as he knew they were prone to do. His warning becomes an important Jonah lesson for you: "See that ye fall not out by the way..." is how the King James puts it. In the New King James, the phrasing tells them not to "...become troubled along the way". Satan desires this for you more than just about any temptation he can muster. Dozens of times a day he will try to lead you to become "troubled along the way". Your reaction to life's interruptions is the difference between becoming sidetracked with works of the flesh, or continuing that sweeping and filling with consistency.

EXODUS 4 - Moses: He had seen the signs from God after seeing of all things, a burning bush! Yet he still made excuses for his ability to speak, despite God's confirmations for how He would faithfully guide Moses through it all. Instead of complete trust in God's already proven promises, Moses persisted in his fears, excuses and limitations. So, God allowed his brother Aaron to help. Of Aaron it is said, "He can speak well..." (4:14). Of Moses, we find that he regarded himself as "not eloquent...slow of speech and of a slow tongue" (4:10). Ironically, things would have gone *so* much better had Moses trusted God to give his slow tongue the inspiration and guidance of His Spirit. Instead, Aaron was enlisted as a mouthpiece for his brother. God allowed this, omnisciently knowing that Aaron would weaken long before Moses. Ergo, one golden calf later, we see how Satan can use weakness to impair from seeing God's strength and God's desire to make him/us stronger. You need to trust God in your weaknesses so that He can be permitted to empower you "from on high" to reach the point where His strength becomes sufficient for all your needs.

These examples are but a scratch at the surface of all the gems and treasures you will discover when you fall in love with God's inspired, inerrant, perfectly revealed and communicated **TRUTH** for life! When you finish this book, what will you do and where will you go with your spiritual warfare? Have the principles of Sweeping, Filling and Keeping Out evil become relevant and workable for you? Will the way that you view Matthew 12:43–45 change your life forever, after seeing the importance of filling where God has swept through your genuine repentance? Do you have a handle on genuine repentance now? Are the dynamic duo of effectual, fervent prayer and a love for God's Word going to be your primary weapons in the arsenal of spiritual warfare for the twenty-first century? Finally, and perhaps most important, can you take an attitude, habit, activity or destructive behavior in your life and wipe it out through the process you have learned in *Sweeping Out The Demons*?

If there is even the slightest doubt in your response to any of these questions, please, please, *please* go back and read again the "Days" where these questions were discussed. It has been my very blessed and joyful experience to begin with you the process of sweeping as you specify exactly what you desire to have swept. It has been a privilege to walk with you to the point when you will come to the process of praying through to genuine repentance in those areas of your life that need sweeping. This process is painful and agonizing at times, but finishes with such cleansing joy that I can't even describe the intensity that you are going to feel! I can only imagine how great it will be for you when repentance is complete and full of contrition, mourning and agreement with God. Man, the resolve you will be filling when you agree with the Lord that the area of your "house" to be swept cannot remain! What freedom is yours as you begin filling by looking at each fruit of the Spirit, to make a mental or written list of possible ways that God has shown you how to apply that fruit to the area that has been swept.

In most cases, this cancels out the fleshly/self motivated desires, exchanging them for God's desires for you heart. However, in the case of stubborn or difficult habits, attitudes or really destructive influences to your behavior, all of this may need to be repeated... repeatedly, until God has been given complete reign and control. This is another blessing as you do this with the weapons Satan so hates, effectual, fervent prayer, and a new found or rediscovered love for God's enduring Word. I wish I could be there when you testify to a pastor, a friend or a family member of nothing short of miraculous transformations on that battlefield for your life!

During all of this process of sweeping and filling, the weapons of war must be fired strategically with pinpoint accuracy. Real praying and real passion for God's living Word will *seal the deal*! I am confident, based on my experience in the very difficult sweepings with which I have wrestled, that if you commit yourself to effectual fervent prayer and continue searching the Scriptures daily, hourly and minute-by-minute, this work as a soldier will become more and more automatic. A peace will overwhelm you in the frustration of life's bumps and bruises that will help you to keep on keeping on, no matter what. Your testimony will grow as will your boldness for showing Jesus to others.

All of this will gradually make your faith stronger, causing you to have greater stamina when Satan tries to lure you back into the same traps. After awhile, you will imperceptibly notice that you are resisting a test, trial or attempt by the Devil to thwart your day into misery...without even thinking about it!!!!

When you do recognize that your self-control has become God-control in a very difficult sweeping, you will be eligible for what I call the Medal of Honor in Christ, for excellence in spiritual warfare! You won't need a ceremony with the President or even your pastor to present this medal. It will be awarded posthumously as someday you enter into glory with the words of Jesus, "Well done thou good and faithful servant". Prior to that day some days, years or decades from now, you will daily sense the jubilation that this inward reward will give you as you know a confidence in the Lord that can never be taken from you. Far greater than merely overcoming some bad habit or temptation, you will know that God alone has exerted His Sovereign power in an area of your life to fill an empty place where once stood a stronghold of Satan! You will suddenly realize what the abundance of the abundant life is all about, because for perhaps the first time, you have allowed the grace of God that saved you to free you from a satanic deception of the mastery and bondage of sin that was in fact long ago forgiven, the moment you received Christ.

So what are you waiting for? You are just a prayer and a love affair with the Book away from receiving your field promotion to full rank as soldier first class in God's Army—a former civilian child of Adam. Only the freedom that Christ promises to His followers can move your life beyond the roller coaster struggle with the ups and downs of sweeping out those so-called demons—or factors that Satan uses for his demons to distract, distort, discourage and deter you from absolute freedom from those evil influences.

What is the potential result of your sweeping, filling and keeping out evil? I close with my favorite illustration that has been used to change the very way I preached through the years. I learned it from a sermon seed I have used many times from the book **Expository Preaching Without Notes**. Countless young preachers are indebted to Charles Koller for this story. It describes perfectly what you will be confronting as a soldier of the cross, praying and digging into Scripture to help you ***Sweep, Fill and Keep Out evil.***

Many years ago, men and women went out west, deep into the Rocky Mountains in search of gold. Each group faced their own challenges, but one of the earliest groups faced a rather insurmountable one. They were dying! After reaching an area where gold was discovered, they were inundated by all these snakes...poisonous rattlers and coral snakes by the hundreds, hiding everywhere as they dug and panned. The leader got very discouraged over the sicknesses and deaths of many of those he had talked into coming with him in search of this fortune. Finally, ready to give up, he informed all that on the next day they would have to break camp and go home, leaving all that gold behind. It was just too dangerous and the challenges of finding and killing all those snakes seemed impossible. So he went for a walk to sooth his conscience and sadness over this monumental failure. Feeling he had let all down, he just walked and walked, farther and farther up the mountains, higher and higher, until exhausted; he just sat down beside a large tree and soon fell asleep.

When he awoke, he discovered that he had been asleep not for minutes but for the entire night! Stretching and yawning he came to his senses and to his surprise and joy looked down at his pants, looked down his arms and hands to find no snakebites whatsoever. No one had slept uncovered or out in the open during the entire ordeal, knowing the snakes were lurking everywhere. All alone up there, he cried out,

"Hallelujah! I have found the secret to staying to mine and get rich!"

So down the mountain he literally ran, until breathless. As he approached the camp, he just fell in front of his comrades, all frantic about his disappearance.

"We were worried sick about you!" one shouted out..."Where in the world were you?"

Catching his breath a bit, he exclaimed, "I have found the secret to our dilemma...We can continue to search for gold and get rich! You see, I slept all night under a tree, uncovered, unprotected and as you can see *no* snakebites! I slept like a baby, and do you know why?" All were hanging on his every word now. "Apparently the snakes cannot or will not reside or survive above this altitude where we are mining. All we have to do is go up a bit higher and we will be living and working and discovering all the gold above the snake line!"

My friend, this is my prayer for you as you begin *Sweeping out the Demons in your life!* The result will be that you have discovered the secret to supernatural living in Christ. Your life will move upward, above **THE** snake line. The disguise of the Devil as the serpent reminds us that he is in fact a slithery, sneaky and scandalously evil snake in the grass, just waiting to "bite" you with temptation, testing and fear. You don't have to live that way! You can move above the snake line, up to the level where conversations with God and deep explorations into His Word guide you farther and farther, higher and higher above the darkness and evil that seek to keep you from living in the blindingly bright illumination of the abundant life. May your victories be many and your advancements to gain ground in your spiritual walk be constant!

Sweeping Moments for today...

1) Let's do some true and false statements to reinforce your knowledge and training in Sweeping Out the Demons. Discuss with your group why each is True or False.

   A) The focal passage for this time together is Matthew 12:43–45.
   True or False

   B) The key to spiritual warfare in the twenty-first century is owning up to your problems, pulling yourself together and with your own willpower and discipline getting rid of what you don't like about your life.
   True or False

C) Sweeping means to truly repent of some attitude, action or destructive behavior, asking God to do this sweeping from your life as you commit and agree with Him. True or False

D) Filling means to do all you can to get rid of your desire or your bad feelings the best way you can, on your own, with courage and willpower and your own inner strength. You fill with these so that you won't have to depend upon God or anyone anymore because you have found the diet or exercise how to book or the right treatment for getting rid of this mess! True or False

E) Sin will no longer have dominion or power to manipulate you like it once did, because you are no longer are fighting the battle, but rather the Holy Spirit is being permitted to operate freely through your mind, heart and physical strength. True or False

F) Filling the swept and repented areas of my life with the fruit of the Spirit is vague and non-specific until I allow the Holy Spirit to guide me to make specific and practical applications to each of the fruit. True or False

G) The "house" spoken of by Jesus in our key passage is synonymous with your church and the things that go on around that special place for worship and fellowship. True or False?

H) A Joseph lesson is a positive example in Scripture, while a Jonah lesson is a negative example for which I should do the opposite.
True or False?

I) Once I allow God to sweep, fill the void with spiritual fruit, then I am done with this battle, right? I mean, the Devil will never mess with me again in that area ever again, will he? True or False?

J) God and Satan are equals, but on opposite sides on everything. God is the good guy and Satan is the villain, like in the movies or in mythology. Neither has a real advantage over the other in spiritual warfare, until I decide which side I will fight on. True or False?

2) Take a moment to write down what the first sweeping will be for you, and how you are going to go about being freed from this bondage.

3) Write down the name(s) of someone you know with whom you would like to share the principles of **Sweeping Out the Demons**. Pray right now for God to open doors to share with him/her the book and your time to help with a chronic sweeping in that person's life.

Appendix 1 –
Small Group Helps

Getting Ready to Sweep Out the Demons –
Small Group Helps...

Note: these small group helps are for you if you want a more structured group. You can just meet, pray, sing a little, share a lot and discuss what you have read that week. Or, you can read the book together in the meeting. Don't let the structure of your meetings interfere with the real purpose of *Sweeping Out The Demons*...feel free to have your meetings as simple and uncomplicated as possible! Let the Lord lead. Now here are some tips if you would like the group to continue into a more permanent basis, or even start a cell church or evangelistic fellowship group from these weeks together.

If utilizing *Sweeping Out the Demons* with a Small Group, use the following steps to guide the First Meeting.

Group Objectives for the First Meeting

Have a time of sharing and prayer in which some can share why he or she came today. Another question might be to share about what his or her expectations are for these times together. Distribute the books if participants haven't already obtained copies.

Read the key scripture passage for this study (Matthew 12:43–45) with your group. Explain why this is the key scripture passage for understanding Sweeping Out the Demons. Have different persons in the group express their thoughts about this passage. You should begin to use the three diagrams of the Sweeping Principles as soon as possible so that each group member can begin to understand how the principles of Sweeping, Filling and Keeping fit together (See graphics 1, 2, and 3 in Day 2).

Invite all to find Day 1, taking time to discuss questions about the logistics for your meeting as well as any other concerns. You are walking through what each person will be doing at home to complete the Introduction. Explain that each week the group will try to discuss a Day as the chapters are called. However, the group can take two or even three weeks if necessary for each Day. Explain that the group does not need to get in a hurry to finish each week, but rather allow God to speak to each heart at the pace of the group.

When Day 1 is completed, encourage each member to read and reflect upon Day 2 during the following week. Encourage them to follow the steps in the pathway for each day's devotional study.

Optional

If you prefer to use the indirect leadership approach, (participant based, including/equipping others to lead future small groups), explain that you will have a sign-up sheet next meeting for those who would like to convene one of the meetings. Explain that the person would take your place in that meeting, following the steps which you will model in the Second and subsequent meetings. Your sign-up sheet will have the week/date to convene, and the person will simply place their name for Convener. This is a great way to develop small group leaders, as well as to help potential leaders to develop their leadership abilities/gifts.

Close the time together with prayer

Group objectives for the second and all other meetings.

1) Begin with words of welcome and a time of prayer.
2) Open a time for group members to share any victories, challenges, problems, questions or other concerns.
3) Utilize a break time to greet one another and to sing a song or two if you like....
4) Take time now for various group members who would like to share about impressions about the *Day* being discussed. Ask the participants to discuss the "Sweeping Moments", working through the discussion questions for that week. Seek to engage various group members in the discussion if possible. You may need to take a turn if the group is a bit timid or uncertain, but jump in only if necessary.

(The Convener should ask someone to call time if the group has agreed upon a specific period for the group meetings. Be sensitive to time constraints of your group members, and try to honor any time limits that the group has set.

Use any or all of the following discussion starters to guide the time together:

a) What part of Day ( ) interested you the most?
b) Would someone like to help us to summarize what Day ( ) was all about?
c) Was there some point in Day ( ) that you did not fully understand or agree with?

5) Draw the meeting to a close with a Prayer Circle. Encourage group members to keep sweeping! A time of praise or worship

could complete your time together, culminating in a prayer circle, praying for strength, wisdom and direction during the week to come. Ask group members if any need prayer for a sweeping. Pray effectually and fervently to allow God to sweep out the demons and fill in the voids with God's best, and keep out the evil through effectual fervent prayer and a love for Scripture!

If your group is utilizing indirect leadership in order to help train small group conveners, remind the group that each is invited to serve as a Convener one evening, and that there is a sign-up sheet. Remind the group that this is an excellent way for them to work on or to try out their leadership skills for small groups. Be sure to mention that no one should feel compelled to be a convener, only those who feel that they would like to attempt this. You may want to repeat the sign-up at other meetings so that those who are not yet comfortable with convening will have an opportunity to try it!

Another option is to meet in the homes of different group members for some or all of the meeting times. Meeting at a restaurant that has a meeting room is another possibility. Meeting at the church is yet another venue. You might want to have two separate sign-up sheets, one for Conveners and one for Hosts. If you are using the group as an outreach tool, refreshments or casual fellowship time could follow your group study.

If you are studying individually, you might want to keep a journal of your "meetings" with this book, *the* **Book**, and with the Lord. Discussing what you are experiencing with a close friend or your pastor will further enhance your time as you openly reflect upon what you have read and discovered through your times with the Lord.

Now, Here Are Some Places To Go To Learn More About Spiritual Warfare....

The following sources were instrumental in this work, and I gratefully acknowledge each one. Direct quotes from Scripture come exclusively from the King James Version of the Bible: KJV. The Scriptures cited were accessed via personal copies of the King James Version and through the online Bible application BibleGateway.com. I am deeply grateful to Bible Gateway for this tremendous online tool for accessing and studying Scripture.

Though no direct quotations were used from any of the following sources, I am grateful for the excellent key background information derived, from which to express my original thoughts.

1) Frank Stagg's commentary on Matthew, in The Broadman Bible Commentary, Vol. 8, Broadman Press, Nashville, TN, 1969, p. 151.
2) Maturidade Cristâ, Junta de Missões Nacionais da Convenção Batista Brasileira, Rio de Janeiro, RJ, 2010. Pages 80, 83. (Used with full permission from the Home Mission Board of the Brazilian Baptist Convention) The section in Day 9 discussing each fruit of the spirit owes a great debt to this Portuguese language Bible and doctrine study.

3) House, H. Wayne,, The Dimensions of the Imago Dei, pg. 83, Charts of Christian Theology and Doctrine, Grand Rapids, MI, Zondervan Publishing House, 1992 .

4) Go to **findbreathingroom.com** for Andy Stanley's excellent messages on this important area for sweeping. You can gain many ideas about your sweeping from such examples as you study from the works of popular Bible teachers. Read their books and watch/listen to their studies with a discerning eye for ideas on sweeping, filling and keeping.

Printed in the United States
By Bookmasters